CONCEALED CARRY
AND HOME DEFENSE
FUNDAMENTALS

2nd EDITION

SECOND EDITION, 2017
COPYRIGHT MICHAEL MARTIN

Printed in the United States.

Library of Congress Control Number: 2008933390

ISBN 978-1-4675-6144-0

Concealed Carry and Home Defense Fundamentals.
Second Edition. First Printing.

Written by Michael Martin.

Design by Michael Martin, Ken Wangler and Dusty Reid.

Cover photo by Ken Wangler and Dusty Reid.

Cover design by Dusty Reid.

Technical advisers include Mike Brickner, Steve Fischer, Kevin
Michalowski and Rob Pincus.

All photos by Ken Wangler and Dusty Reid or are licensed for
use, used by permission, or are copyright© Michael Martin.

USCCA is a registered trademark of Delta Defense, LLC.

To purchase this book in bulk at an instructor discount,
call 877-677-1919. To learn more about the multi-media
classroom materials used by USCCA Certified Instructors to
teach the USCCA course, *Concealed Carry and Home Defense
Fundamentals,* visit www.USCCA.com.

FOREWORD

THERE IS NOTHING MORE SACRED THAN LIFE.

Our entire society is built upon the idea that life is precious and is worth experiencing to the fullest. Our laws, our traditions, and our everyday choices all speak to the importance of preserving the unalienable right to life, and if you follow this philosophy through to its end, it is easy to understand why this book is so important. Michael Martin's understanding of this philosophy was instrumental in my decision to make his book, *Concealed Carry and Home Defense Fundamentals*, the textbook standard for any concealed carry class taught by the thousands of certified USCCA instructors. Not only is Michael a trusted, respected, and accomplished leader in the personal defense and firearms community, he also understands the "*why*" behind the "*what*." The "*what*" is the importance of personal defense, but the "*why*" is where so many people get tripped up. The reason that the USCCA exists, and the reason that this excellent book exists, is simple and profound: *To save lives and bring security to our communities.*

This book is a must-read for anyone who believes in the sacredness of innocent life.

If you are an accomplished and seasoned student of personal defense, you'll appreciate Michael's explanations and illustrations of topics that can confuse even experts; and if this is your very first experience with personal defense instruction, you'll walk away understanding not only the fundamentals of concealed carry and home defense, you'll also understand topics that might take years to understand otherwise. Michael has done a truly extraordinary job of making expansive and complicated subjects accessible and easy to understand for even the newest beginner. It is for this reason that I recommend this book as the best resource for responsibly armed Americans who are serious about becoming the most prepared that they can be.

This book is a shining example of the cornerstone values of the USCCA.

My sincerest hope is that this book will be something that you treasure for years, and are able to share with the people you care about the most.

Take care and stay safe,

Tim Schmidt
President and Founder, USCCA

While the attacks of 9/11 certainly had a lasting impact on our nation's sense of safety and security, the events of August 2005 may have had an even greater impact on our personal sense of safety and security, as the world watched as New Orleans slipped into chaos in the aftermath of Hurricane Katrina. While some who watched (or lived through) the aftermath of Katrina wrung their hands and cursed a government that couldn't protect them from all dangers big and small, the lesson that most Americans took away from Katrina was that taking personal responsibility for our own safety and the safety of our families could have a more reliable outcome than simply counting on the cavalry to ride over the hill just in the nick of time.

INTRODUCTION

The past decade has seen both tragedy and triumph in the never ending battle for the rights of gun ownership in America. While most Americans would agree that the unalienable rights of life and liberty would include the right to be free from murder, rape, robbery, assault, and mass shootings, too many Americans still disagree on how to meet that goal. Thomas Jefferson believed that, "Laws that forbid the carrying of arms disarm only those who are neither inclined nor determined to commit crimes," but tragic events such as the school shooting in Newtown Connecticut and the theater shooting in Aurora Colorado, have once again led a segment of the nation to blame the *gun* as the cause, rather than blaming the hearts of the evil men that perpetuated those crimes, or blaming the utter defenselessness of so called "gun free zones."

But during that same decade, there has also been an awakening in America. Generations of Americans who had been indoctrinated into believing that guns were evil, were slowly giving way to a new generation who believed that not only was firearm ownership a *right*, but that taking personal responsibility for the safety of ourselves and our families was a *responsibility*. While the mass shootings in Newtown and Aurora served as a battle cry for anti-gun forces, those same events and others, led *more* Americans to believe that the conclusions of the anti-gun forces (and the mass media) were wrong, and that in fact, the only thing that stops a *bad* guy with a gun, is a *good* guy with a gun.

After 9/11, the U.S. met the threat by installing sophisticated body scanners at airports, hardening cockpit doors, arming pilots, and expanding the armed Air Marshal program. But after Newtown and Aurora, the anti-gun forces ignored the obvious failure of "gun free zones," and once again went after "those who are neither inclined nor determined to commit crimes," by proposing a host of anti-gun bills. But assuming that *any* limitation on gun type or magazine capacity would have limited the carnage caused by the Newtown or Aurora shooters, would be like assuming that the 9/11 attacks would have failed if box cutters had been banned before the attack. A 9/11 response was needed after Newtown and Aurora, but today, most of our schools remain as unprotected as they were the day before the Newtown tragedy, and too many public and private establishments remain undefended, even advertising that fact with "gun free zone" signs, letting potential criminals or mass murders know that *no one here will stop you*. We remain a nation where even members of the most virulent anti-gun groups have grown to not only accept, but *expect*, armed guards to protect our banks, our museums, our airports, our politicians and our celebrities, yet they somehow find the thought of armed guards protecting our schools and our children abhorrent. In the words of John Caile, contributing writer to *Concealed Carry Magazine*, "If that's not misplaced priorities, I don't know what is."

But rather than dampening the nation's belief in the Second Amendment, the anti-gun legislation proposed after Aurora and Newtown had the opposite effect, with concealed carry permit applications and NICS checks (the national background check required for firearm purchases) reaching never before seen levels. But that upward trend actually began a number of years earlier, soon after the world watched

Whether a family survives or perishes in a residential fire is usually more dependent upon what the family does within the first few minutes of the fire, rather than what the professionals do within their first few minutes on scene. The same is true for violent crime. Despite their best efforts, the police simply cannot arrive in time to stop a violent crime in progress. If you are involved in a violent attack, the outcome will be determined by what you do within the first few minutes (or seconds), not what the police do when they arrive minutes later.

as New Orleans plunged into chaos in the aftermath of hurricane Katrina in August of 2005. While some who watched (or lived through) the aftermath of Katrina wrung their hands and cursed a government that couldn't protect them from all dangers big and small, the lesson that *most* Americans took away from Katrina was that taking personal responsibility for our own safety and the safety of our families could have a more reliable outcome than simply counting on the cavalry to ride over the hill just in the nick of time.

Today, the number of "right to carry" states stands at 42, and the number of permit holders has grown to more than 15 *million* nationwide, while the FBI's uniform crime report continues to show an overall drop in violent crime year-over-year, with a dramatic decrease in the number of deaths attributed to firearms, *including* a 125-year low in law enforcement officer deaths. Think about that for a moment—in 2016, more than 15 *million* permit holders were walking the streets, yet the last time police officers had been this safe was in 1887, when the Colt Single Action Army was still the height of firearms technology. If that doesn't prove that concealed carry permit holders are the good guys, then *nothing* will. Collectively, those facts fly in the face of anti-gun organizations' claims that more guns equals more crime, when in fact, the opposite seems to be true, with violent crime near a 39-year low, and gun ownership (and concealed carry permits) at an all time high. So that begs the question, "Is owning a firearm right for *you*?"

The decision to purchase a firearm for home defense, or a decision to apply for a permit and ultimately carry a handgun for personal protection, is a serious decision, but, it's no more serious than other decisions you've most likely made for the protection of yourself and your family, such as a decision to maintain smoke alarms and a fire extinguisher in your home, or a decision to learn CPR. Each of those decisions is nothing more than the recognition that your city's police, fire, and EMS services are not omnipresent, and will not suddenly materialize when you and your family are confronted by a fire, a heart attack, or a violent crime. When it comes to fires and heart attacks, we know that prevention matters, and the same is true for violent crime. To that end, Chapter One will kick the book off with a variety of topics focused *entirely* on prevention, avoidance, and awareness. Within this chapter, we'll discuss how to develop a "Personal & Home Protection Plan," which helps to ensure that we're *less* likely to find ourselves in a situation where we have no other option than to use a firearm, rather than *more* likely. Chapter Two will then introduce you

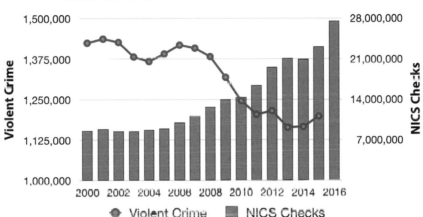

NICS Checks versus Violent Crime Trends

As the trend of firearm purchases and concealed carry permits has accelerated, violent crime has followed a downward trend.

to a wealth of information on different types of self-defense firearms including handguns, home defense shotguns, and the AR-15 platform, and we'll provide easy to understand explanations of the common terms used so frequently. The goal of this chapter is to de-mystify what can sometimes feel like a topic reserved for experts. Chapter Three will continue with the basics, including a very visual overview of what we call the "building blocks" or the fundamentals for accurate and safe shooting. Chapter Four covers important legal topics, including the laws governing the legal use of force inside and outside the home. In this chapter, you'll get a chance to test what you've learned, using several real world scenarios. Chapter Five covers the physiology of violent attacks, including a detailed section on the automated reactions that you should expect to experience if you're ever involved in what the police refer to as a critical incident. This section will take you on an amazing tour of the inner workings of the brain, which should convince you why we take the "simple versus complex" approach in our shooting fundamentals section in Chapter Three. This chapter goes on to explain what our options might be during a critical incident, and what we should know when dealing with the police after an incident has ended. Chapter Six will introduce you to the variety of gear and gadgets available for firearm owners, including holster options and other gear such as lights, lasers, and gun vaults. Chapter Seven summarizes the book with a number of basic and advanced drills designed to take your skill level beyond the building blocks introduced in Chapter Three, and dramatically elevate your speed, accuracy, and enjoyment at the range.

Before I kick off the book, I thought I'd help answer a question that you might be asked some day: "Why do you own a firearm?" Until recently, I'd answer that question by using the analogies mentioned earlier, and I'd compare owning and carrying a firearm to taking the time to learn CPR or taking the responsibility to keep fire extinguishers in my home. I'd also have thrown out a variety of statistics to prove my point (which are included in this book), or I'd have discussed the meaning of the Second Amendment. But my answer to that question got a whole lot easier after a long day shooting photos with photographer Oleg Volk. At the end of the day, we were heading back home with Oleg trailing behind, snapping a few last minute pictures. When I sat down to look at the results of the day, the photo on the opposite page caught my eye. Sam (then three years old) was about ready to fall asleep, and Jack (then six years old) was dragging his feet after the long day. A casual observer of this photo would tend to see nothing more than a protective father walking home with his sons, and it might take a closer look to realize that there's a firearm on my hip. That photo, above all others, reminds me why a firearm is included in my personal and home protection plans. Owning or carrying a firearm isn't about statistics or constitutional arguments, it's not about analogies or comparisons, it's not about the gear, and to be honest, it's not even about the gun. It's about taking a *small measure* of personal responsibility for our safety and the safety of our families. It's about making it home safe at night and being safe while in our homes. It's about recognizing that *we* are our families' first responder. And, it's about taking that responsibility seriously.

Michael Martin

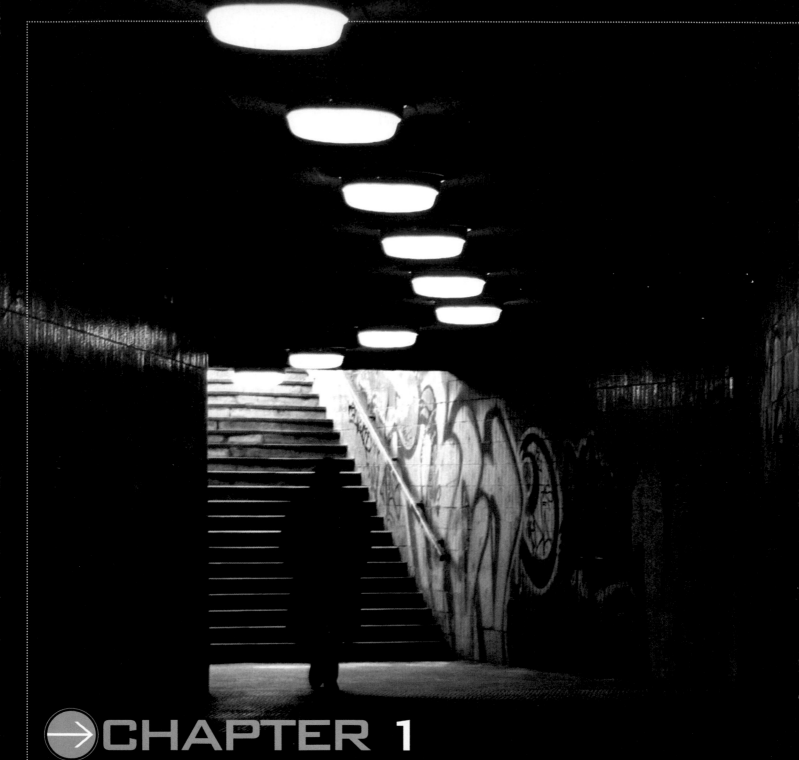

→CHAPTER 1

DEVELOPING A PERSONAL & HOME PROTECTION PLAN

Developing a personal & home protection plan is a key component of not only preparing for how we should (or might) react if confronted by a violent crime, but also how we might avoid violent crime in the first place. The first topic we'll cover in this chapter will take a look at violent crime itself in the United States, where we'll explain just how common it is compared to other risks we've already prepared for in our lives, such as the risk of injury or death due to a home fire. Within this chapter, you'll also discover that developing a protection plan is about much more than becoming proficient with a firearm or writing up a home invasion plan. It's a plan that must encompass awareness, avoidance, and preparation, so that we're *less* likely to find ourselves in a situation where we have no other option than to use our firearm, rather than *more* likely.

Think about it this way—if we only focused on becoming proficient with our firearm, but spent no time considering ways of avoiding violent crime, we'd be no different than a family who keeps fire extinguishers in strategic locations throughout their home and who runs annual fire drills, yet who fails to consider fire *prevention*, and continues with risky behavior such as leaving candles burning at night, or failing to monitor food cooking on the stove or in the oven. That family virtually guarantees that someday they'll have a chance to put their home escape plan to the test. We need to be better than that.

Topics in this chapter also include an overview of situational awareness and how we might take the idea of the President's protective bubble and apply it to our own lives. We'll expand on that topic by walking through the color codes of awareness, developed by a gentleman named Jeff Cooper, whom we've profiled in this chapter. These color codes are designed to make us more aware of our surroundings and to avoid what Cooper describes as the, "Oh my God, this can't be happening to me!" situation. The next topic will stress just how important situational awareness is, with a commentary on "Action versus Reaction."

We'll continue with a topic on "Observing Your Environment," which explains not only how to watch for and avoid areas that might be attractive to criminals, but to also look for objects in our environment that can work to our advantage. We'll also look at a number of home security ideas, and we'll have a discussion about how mental exercises can take us beyond the drills that we can run at the range. We'll wrap up the chapter with a discussion of exactly how a Concealed Carry Permit may fit into your overall plan.

How Does the Risk of Violent Crime Compare to Other Risks?

When contemplating whether or not to purchase a firearm for home defense or to obtain a concealed carry permit, many people ask the question, "Just how likely is it that I'll be a victim of violent crime?" While violent crime has been decreasing over the last three decades, it can occur anywhere, at any time. In the United States, there were nearly 1.2 million violent crimes in 2015, including 15 thousand murders, 90 thousand rapes, 327 thousand robberies, and 764 thousand assaults. Considering the importance that most families place on smoke detectors and fire escape plans, it's worth knowing that you are more than three times as likely to be the victim of a violent crime than you are to be the victim of a residential fire, and you are more than 70 times as likely to be assaulted than you are to be injured in a home fire. Purchasing a firearm for home defense, and getting a concealed carry permit are just two small steps in developing a personal and home protection plan. Situational awareness, mental preparation, planning, conflict avoidance, and ongoing training are all components of this lifestyle to ensure that we use force as a last resort; but if required, we're prepared to defend ourselves and our families.

Violent Crime   **Residential Fires**

1.2M

300,000

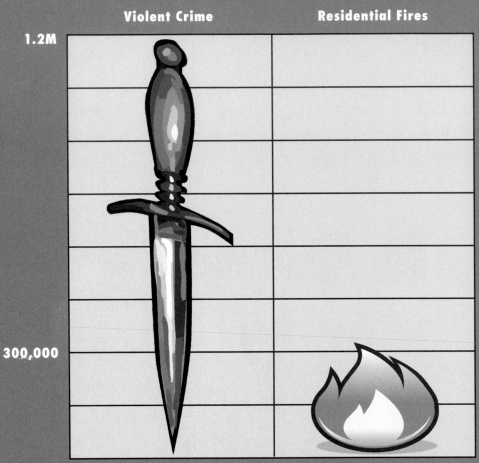

Sources: FBI Uniform Crime Report; and the U.S. Fire Administration.

DEVELOPING A PERSONAL PROTECTION PLAN

What exactly is the goal of a personal protection plan? At its most basic level, a personal protection plan is designed to help keep us physically, legally, financially, and morally safe. While our personal protection plans should include becoming proficient with a firearm or other defensive tool, our ultimate goal should be to *avoid* violent encounters in the first place by developing an acute awareness of our surroundings and by making intelligent decisions about our actions, behavior, and precautions. Three options typically exist when it comes to a violent encounter: avoid the situation entirely, escape from a situation that is already in progress, or defend ourselves from a situation that we weren't able to avoid and are unable to escape from. While the choice isn't always left up to us, the topics in this chapter help to increase the likelihood that we'll have an opportunity to avoid or escape from dangerous situations *before* a use of force is required.

Conflict Avoidance

So why is avoidance or escape so important, if legally, we have the right to defend ourselves from a violent attack? The answer is more than just the fact that the only guaranteed method of surviving a violent encounter is to avoid it in the first place. It's also because the law will place a special emphasis on our decisions and actions leading up to any incident where we were in possession of a firearm, and we'll be expected to have "known better" if we could have avoided a situation that turned violent. Prosecutors will want to know more than just, "Who was the assailant?" and, "Who was the victim?" They'll want to know *what did we do* to avoid or instigate the fight? In part, prosecutors will use what's known as the "reasonable person test." That means they'll weigh whether or not they believe a "reasonable person" would have believed the same things we believed to be true and would have reacted the same way we reacted. But here's the catch: "reasonable person" doesn't mean our friends, our family, the gang at the local shooting club, or other permit holders. It means 12 average jurors picked from the community. Because of that test, a use of force on our part must carry such seriousness attached to it that it's a fair question to ask, "Is this situation worth going to jail over?" or, "Is this situation worth dying over?" If the answer is "Yes," then we'll need to be prepared to live with the results. If the answer is "No," then we'll need to work hard to remove ourselves from the situation (quickly!) *before* the only option remaining is a use of force.

Said another way, a use of force on our part should only be done as a last resort, when we have no other choice, and when the risk of death or jail time is secondary in our minds compared to the necessity of defending ourselves from an unavoidable situation that we didn't start, and we couldn't escape from.

SECONDS COUNT

It's important to remember that a use of force is not the only possible outcome when it comes to a violent encounter. The *three* possible outcomes of avoidance, escape, or defense, share a key element, and that's that seconds count. If we go through life with a complete lack of awareness of our surroundings, the first two options are typically off the table, and our ability to defend ourselves is seriously limited. Think about the warning time that each of the outcomes might require. For us to *avoid* a dangerous situation in the first place, we might need anywhere from 60 seconds to five minutes to be somewhere else. For us to *escape* from a dangerous situation that's already in motion, we might require at least 30 seconds of prior warning. For us to *defend* ourselves from a dangerous situation when it's too late for avoidance or escape, we'll still require at *least* several seconds of warning to find cover and/or draw our firearm. You can see pretty quickly that being unaware of our surroundings doesn't leave us with too many options.

OUTCOME	WARNING TIME	POSSIBLE RESULTS
Avoid	1 – 5+ Minutes	• You'll never know for the rest of your life whether or not you just avoided a violent crime or whether you overreacted. Personally, we can live with that. • If you were right about the situation, you've just gotten a "Get out of jail for free" card and possibly a "Get out of the hospital for free" card. • Your blood remains in your body where it belongs; your money remains in your bank where it belongs; and you'll remain at home with your family, where you belong.
Escape	30+ Seconds	• You've identified a dangerous situation in time to "exit stage left" before your options are limited to defend, but you're still in the middle of a bad situation.
Defend	3 – 5+ Seconds	• While you still have plenty of options other than "shoot the bad guy," you've now crossed a *significant* line where every action you are about to take will be second-guessed by the police, the media, the prosecuting attorney, and quite possibly a grand jury and jury. On the other hand, if it was your *only* choice, you do have a good chance of surviving. • Think about it this way–if you *knew* that the use of your firearm in self-defense would result in your incarceration (that's not a true legal test, but it is a good litmus test) and would cost you tens of thousands of dollars in legal expenses, how would that knowledge affect your decisions leading up to your use of force?

■ Even with proper training and a highly developed sense of situational awareness, attacks almost always come as a surprise (in other words, if you saw an attack coming, you'd do everything you could do to avoid it). That's why it's critically important to train with your gun frequently, including knowing what to do when you must shift from focus level yellow to focus level red in an instant.

SITUATIONAL AWARENESS

So how do we gain those crucial seconds necessary to avoid or escape, or the few extra seconds that we'll need to find cover or draw our firearm if "defend" is the only option left to us?

A good start is to develop a keen sense of situational awareness. Like it sounds, situational awareness is an awareness of our immediate vicinity and of the people and objects within that environment. Being aware of our surroundings doesn't mean that we need to hire a reconnaissance team to scout out our shopping area in advance, but it *does* mean that we need to lift our heads up and observe more than just the cell phone in our hands while we text a message, or the few feet of sidewalk immediately in front of us.

Smartphones players can cause us to focus our entire attention on a small rectangle in front of us, making us oblivious to the rest of our environment.

Even without the distraction of an electronic device, too many people focus no farther than a circle of a few feet in front of them when they're in public.

Awareness Means 360°

When thinking about an awareness of our environment, we need to think about the 360 degree circle surrounding us, not just the individuals or objects to our front. When we move through public areas, we should think of a "bubble" surrounding us and our loved ones, and we need to be aware of everything and everyone inside of that bubble. Think about the way the secret service keeps a mobile bubble around the President of the United States. The secret service observes and categorizes everything within that bubble to identify any possible threat before it strikes. While we operate our own lives on a different scale, we can be no less vigilant—we are, in effect, our own bodyguards and first responders. Since we're lacking dozens of agents and overhead imagery, how do we go about monitoring that bubble around us? First off, it means that we need to lift our heads up from the sidewalk or our cell phones, and we need to watch where we're going. To get a 360 degree look at our surroundings, we'll need to use not only our peripheral vision (which provides about 180—200 degrees of visibility), but we'll also need to actually swivel our head to scan the area to our front, sides, and rear.

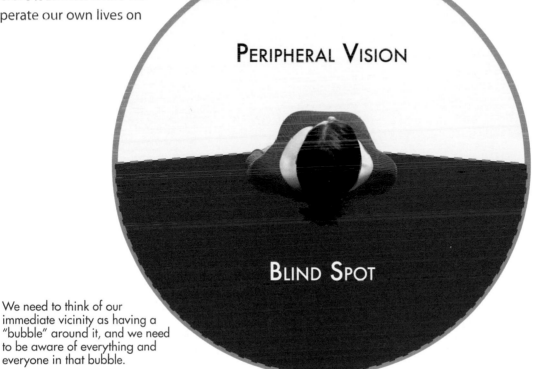

PERIPHERAL VISION

BLIND SPOT

We need to think of our immediate vicinity as having a "bubble" around it, and we need to be aware of everything and everyone in that bubble.

OUR PROTECTIVE "BUBBLE"

If you have a firearm and your attacker has a knife, you survive every time, right? Not necessarily. Lieutenant Dennis Tueller of the Salt Lake City Police Department demonstrated that simply having a firearm doesn't necessarily mean you could bring it into action in time to protect yourself, unless you closely observed threats (think situational awareness) within your protective bubble. Lieutenant Tueller observed that with practice, the average shooter could place two shots on target at a distance of 21 feet in about a second and a half. Tueller then ran another set of tests to determine exactly how quickly an "attacker" could cover that same distance, and discovered that it could be done in that same 1.5 seconds. Based on Tueller's experiment, most police departments in the U.S. now consider anything within 32–50 feet to be within the "danger zone," where an officer should be prepared to issue commands, increase distance, or gain access to a firearm.

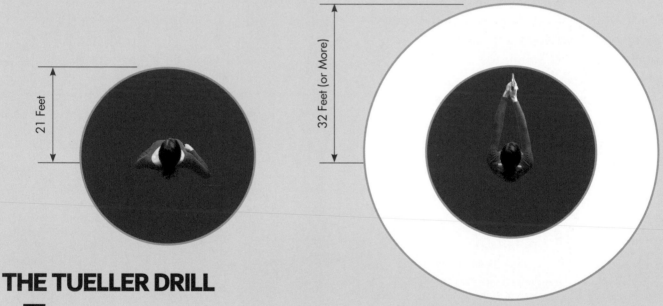

THE TUELLER DRILL

1 **Version One**. With the defender armed with a blue or red replica gun and the "attacker" armed with a blue or red replica knife, this drill begins with the defender's replica gun holstered and the attacker 21 feet away. Without warning, the attacker charges the defender. The defender is successful if she can clear her replica gun from the holster and get it on "target" prior to the attacker touching her with the replica knife. Most individuals CANNOT bring their firearm on target in time.

2 **Version Two**. With instructor supervision, an outdoor range version of the drill can be run with the "attacker" and shooter positioned back-to-back. At the signal, the "attacker" runs away from the firing line and the shooter unholsters her gun and fires down range at a target 21 feet in front of her. The "attacker" stops as soon as the shot is fired. This exercise can help each individual calculate his or her own "danger zone."

We also need to actually *look* at the individuals in our immediate vicinity (including those behind us) to do two things. First, we want to make a quick assessment of the threat level of the individual; and second, we want to send the simple message, "I see you." That doesn't mean that we need to "eyeball" potential threats, and our look shouldn't signal, "I'm tougher than you" or, "I'm carrying a firearm." It simply needs to imply, "I see you."

This individual turns her head to observe anyone in her immediate area, and quickly makes eye contact to inform the individual, "I see you."

If we see something or someone who sets off our warning bells, we need to move away from the potential threat by slowing down, speeding up, changing direction, or turning around. If someone is approaching us from the rear, the "polite" reaction is to not turn around. We're not worried with polite. If we *do* hear (or otherwise sense) an individual behind us, we should turn to observe, and if the individual causes us concern, we should take evasive action by changing direction and observing his reaction, if any.

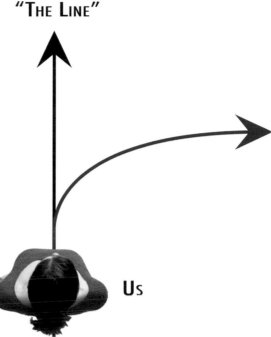

"THE LINE"

Us

To avoid a potential threat we may need to take evasive action, which might be as simple as "stepping off the line" by taking a right or left turn, then gauging your next move based upon the reaction. If the potential threat continues on "the line," then you can fall in step behind him. If he turns to follow you, then you need to increase your evasive action.

THE POTENTIAL THREAT

Regardless of how tough you might look on the outside, all a criminal will care about is whether you look like an easy victim. The truth is, an observant 110 pound woman is a less attractive victim than a 200 pound man who is entirely absorbed in his cell phone and is completely unaware of the attacker approaching from behind.

Not looking like a victim

When we observe our surroundings in this manner, it will be obvious to anyone watching us that we're being observant, and that fact alone will make us less attractive to potential assailants. We can increase that "unattractiveness" by walking with "purpose"—that is, we need to walk with our bodies erect and our heads up, and we should walk faster than the crowd, not slower. Imagine two individuals walking down the street—the first individual is walking with purpose, moving at a quick enough pace that she looks like she's going somewhere. That individual swivels her head to scan the area and she makes quick eye contact with any individual in her immediate area. The second individual is shuffling along at a slow pace, focused on a three-inch circle in front of him while he sends a text message on his cell phone. Which person do you think a criminal will want to target? When sizing up the first individual, the criminal will realize, "She's moving too fast and she saw me. She won't be easy to approach." On the other hand, he'll look at the second individual and think, "I can get right up on him,

and he'll never see me coming." Notice that we said nothing about the size or other characteristics of the potential "victims." The truth is, an observant 110 pound woman is a *less* attractive victim than a 200 pound man who is entirely absorbed in his cell phone and who is completely unaware of the attacker approaching from behind.

Finally, situational awareness shouldn't be thought of as something that needs to be "switched on," or as a chore. We personally make a game of it— when we're in public, we like to be people watchers, looking for a few different things. First, we like to challenge ourselves by trying to identify anyone else who might be carrying a firearm. It might be a slight bulge on the hip of another permit holder, or it might be the outline of a pistol grip under the shirt of a gang member, but that simple exercise ensures that we at least look at everyone around us. We watch hands, we watch eyes, and we pay extra close attention to people approaching or within our "danger zone." We also like to make a game of looking for individuals in focus level white (more on that in the next section). In other words, we

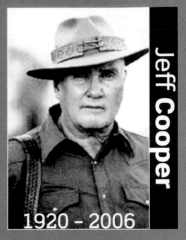

Jeff Cooper
1920 – 2006

Father of the "Modern Technique" of Pistolcraft

Jeff Cooper's accomplishments include author, columnist, professor, and WWII and Korean War veteran. Cooper is also widely recognized as the Father of the "Modern Technique" of Pistolcraft, including the development of the four universal safety rules; updates and refinements to Jack Weaver's classic "Weaver Stance;" and development of the four "color codes" of awareness. In 1976, Cooper founded the Gunsite Academy in Paulden Arizona, which is still in operation today. Although modern techniques and training methods have now moved beyond Cooper's early ideas, he will always be remembered as an early and influential pioneer.

like to look at things from the criminal's perspective. Next time you're in public, give it a try—look for individuals who are talking on their cell phones or texting and are completely absorbed by that task (and completely unaware of their surroundings). Watch for people who shuffle along slower than the crowd around them, looking as if they're going nowhere. One of our favorites (or biggest pet peeves) is observing people who walk down the middle of the driving lanes in parking lots or parking garages, and are completely unaware that a vehicle weighing several thousand pounds is bearing down on them. If they're not aware that a 5,000 pound truck is behind them, do you think they'll notice if a 170-pound rapist is sneaking up behind them? Finally, take the time to monitor yourself—how often do you find yourself out in public, immersed in a cell phone call and oblivious to your surroundings? How often do you discover that you're tailgating the only other vehicle on the freeway, when two or three other lanes are clear? To hone our situational awareness skills, we like to use the color codes of awareness developed by the late Jeff Cooper.

The "Color Codes"

Originally developed by the U.S. Marines in the Pacific during World War II to help mentally condition Marines to prepare for an attack, the Color Codes were later modified by Colonel Jeff Cooper and further modified by nationally known instructors such as Rob Pincus, for use in educating civilians to help us to become more aware of our surroundings, and to not only prepare for violent encounters, but if possible, to avoid them in the first place.

On the following pages, we've detailed what type of mental awareness we should have at each level, and what our actions might be. We've also included a quote from Jeff Cooper with his thoughts on each level of awareness.

"My advice isn't for everyone. It's primarily for legally armed citizens who refuse to be victims."
Colonel Jeff Cooper

The difference between a victim and a survivor isn't simply chance. It's very often the difference between someone who is willing to commit to an armed lifestyle, and someone who is not. It's the difference between someone who is unconsciously aware of everyone and everything in their immediate environment, and someone who is not. Or, it may boil down to the difference between someone who is willing to make a commitment to train frequently with their firearm, and someone who does not.

Unaware

In Focus Level White, you are unaware of what's going on around you.

■ You don't think anything bad will happen and may believe that violent crime happens to "other people."

■ Modern technologies such as smart phones create a perfect environment to lull individuals into focus level white, allowing criminals to approach within inches of their potential victim, making avoidance or escape nearly impossible.

■ Individuals in focus level white often fail to recognize emotions or aggressiveness in others and they might enter into arguments without realizing that they've moved beyond what's safe, or they might believe that they can talk their way out of trouble. They will also be unaware when they've strayed into unsafe areas such as poorly lit areas, areas with blind spots, or areas away from the crowds; or they might put themselves into unsafe situations by allowing their gas tank to go to "E" or forgetting where they parked their car.

■ It's the condition of most victims, and it's the condition that criminals look for.

■ You should never allow yourself to be in focus level white when armed, because your ability to avoid or escape a dangerous situation is compromised—that means that a defensive shooting might occur when it could have been avoided!

■ Although Cooper linked operating in this focus level to surprise attacks, we now understand that attacks almost always come as a surprise, otherwise they'd be avoided. The lesson learned since Cooper's early teaching is that through rigorous training, plenty of practice, and always operating in a level of focus higher than white, we do stand a very good chance of surviving surprise attacks, even if the attacker is *not* inept.

"If attacked in this state the only thing that may save you is the inadequacy and ineptitude of your attacker. When confronted by something nasty your reaction will probably be, 'Oh my God! This can't be happening to me.'"
Colonel Jeff Cooper

Unaware
This individual is preoccupied with her smartphone, and is *completely unaware* of her surroundings.

Aware

In Focus Level Yellow, you are aware of your surroundings.

■ This is the focus level you should be in any time you're in public.

■ You are aware of what's happening in the immediate vicinity, and you proceed with caution.

■ You are not paranoid or overreactive, but you keep an eye out for potential threats and their sources.

■ Your posture, eyes, and demeanor say, "I am alert" and you walk faster than the crowd.

■ You should become comfortable with simple habits such as scanning an area (rooms, street corners, etc.) before entering; and identifying exits and cover wherever you are.

■ You make brief eye contact with individuals in your immediate area, letting them know, "I see you."

■ Individuals in focus level yellow have developed safe habits such as avoiding arguments, identifying everyone and everything within their protective "bubble" (including objects that can work to their benefit such as cover, barriers, and exits), and following the conflict avoidance ideas outlined in this chapter.

■ Focus level yellow is a moderate level of focus. You aren't completely captivated by something, but you are paying attention to it. This level allows you to multi-task. An example would be when you are having a conversation with someone, but are still aware of the people standing around you. Most of us drive our cars with this level of focus as we pay attention to the road ahead, while holding a conversation at the same time.

"Relaxed alert. No specific threat situation. Your mindset is that 'today could be the day I may have to defend myself.' You are simply aware that the world is an unfriendly place and that you are prepared to do something if necessary. You use your eyes and ears."
Colonel Jeff Cooper

A Relaxed State of Awareness
This individual is consciously aware of her surroundings, and anyone within an imaginary bubble surrounding her and her vehicle. She makes eye contact with anyone approaching her to let him know, "I see you."

Focus Level Orange

Heightened Awareness

In Focus Level Orange, you have identified a possible threat or threats. This is a heightened state of awareness.

- You realize that something *may* be wrong.
- There *may* be a danger to yourself or others.
- You make a plan on how to react, including identifying cover, barriers, or an exit strategy.
- You may begin to take preemptive action such as turning around, stepping off "the line," increasing your distance, or making simple, direct verbal commands such as, "Stay back!" or, "Don't come any closer!"
- You decide on a mental "trigger" that will move you to take action, such as an individual refusing your verbal commands and moving closer into your "bubble."
- You mentally prepare yourself for a confrontation or a rapid escape.
- You may begin to feel the effects of adrenaline or other automated responses described in our physiological section in Chapter Five.
- Your pistol may remain holstered, but you should prepare to access it, such as brushing aside outer clothing; putting your hand in the pocket where you have your firearm in a pocket holster; or reaching into your purse and getting a tight grip on the pistol.

"Specific alert. Something is not quite right and has gotten your attention. Your radar has picked up a specific alert. You shift your primary focus to determine if there is a threat. In Condition Orange, you set a mental trigger."

Colonel Jeff Cooper

A Heightened State of Awareness
This individual is suddenly aware of a possible threat, and she uses both body language and verbal commands to tell the threat to "Stay back!"

Action

In Focus Level Red, action is immediate.

■ Your mental trigger has been tripped and you execute your plan, either to **escape**, **take cover**, or **engage the threat**.

■ Trust your instincts—it's better to run away from a situation that turned out *not* to be a threat than it is to get stuck in a mental block of, "This can't be what I think it is," and guessing wrong.

■ Instinct and adrenaline will cause involuntary reactions and *must* be calculated into your training program (See the section on the physiological reaction to stress in Chapter Five.) You should expect your hands to tremble and your fine motor skills to degrade.

■ At this level of focus, you are ignoring everything but the object of your focus, which has your complete attention. That level of focus may cause you to miss other things happening around you.

■ If engaging the threat, operate within the rules governing the use of force, including the obligation to retreat if possible, and the obligation to use something less than deadly force if it will suffice. See Chapter Four for a full definition of your obligations and rights when it comes to a use of force to defend yourself.

■ A use of force is *not* the required outcome. If you've closely observed the immediate area and have identified an escape route, retreat may be the most logical and prudent course of action.

"Condition Red is (action). Your mental trigger has been tripped (established back in Condition Orange). The mental trigger will differ depending upon the circumstances. Whatever trigger is selected, it is a button that once pushed, results in immediate action on your part."
Colonel Jeff Cooper

Action: Engage the threat
In this example, the individual points her firearm at the attacker and is ready to take whatever action is required to stop the threat.

IS ACTION FASTER THAN REACTION?

If an attacker unexpectedly lunges at you with a knife, can you draw your firearm in time to stop him? Can you "out draw" an attacker if he already has a firearm pointed at you? When the threat ends, how quickly can you stop shooting? Is there any plausible explanation for why an attacker might be shot in the back? These hypothetical situations all beg the question, "Is action faster than reaction?" or better yet, "Just how important is situational awareness, *really?*"

To help answer the questions posed above (and to help you understand the limits of human reaction time), we're going to take a look at two studies which analyzed reaction times to visual stimuli. The first study analyzed braking reaction time, while the second study analyzed the reaction time required for shooters to start shooting, and to stop shooting.

Braking: How Long Does it Take to Stop?

Before we delve into reaction times of responsibly armed citizens defending themselves from attack, let's take a look at a study analyzing the reaction times of drivers to a braking maneuver. In the article, *How Long Does It Take To Stop? Methodological Analysis of Driver Perception-Brake Times* published in 2000, researchers concluded that "reaction time" was actually a sequence of multiple stages. For our purposes, we'll group them into the following components:

■ *Perception/Cognitive Processing Time.* This is the time required for the individual to receive, recognize, and process the sensory signal (auditory, visual, etc.), and to formulate a response.

■ *Motor Reaction Time.* This is the time required for the individual to perform the required movement, such as lifting the foot off the accelerator and applying the brake.

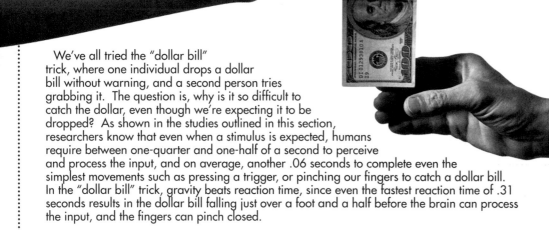

We've all tried the "dollar bill" trick, where one individual drops a dollar bill without warning, and a second person tries grabbing it. The question is, why is it so difficult to catch the dollar, even though we're expecting it to be dropped? As shown in the studies outlined in this section, researchers know that even when a stimulus is expected, humans require between one-quarter and one-half of a second to perceive and process the input, and on average, another .06 seconds to complete even the simplest movements such as pressing a trigger, or pinching our fingers to catch a dollar bill. In the "dollar bill" trick, gravity beats reaction time, since even the fastest reaction time of .31 seconds results in the dollar bill falling just over a foot and a half before the brain can process the input, and the fingers can pinch closed.

In this study, researchers tested braking reaction times under three different scenarios: when the braking maneuver was expected, when it was unexpected, and when it came as a complete surprise. The "expected" scenarios occurred when the test subjects knew that the test was to measure their braking reaction time, and they were prepared to brake as quickly as possible when signaled to do so. The "unexpected" scenarios occurred when the test subjects had to react to common, but unexpected signals, such as seeing the brake lights of the car in front of them. The "surprise" brake maneuvers occurred when something completely unexpected occurred during the scenario, such as an object suddenly moving into the driver's path. The results are summarized in the chart below.

As shown in the chart, when a braking maneuver was unexpected or came as a surprise, the perception/cognitive processing time that occurred before movement began ranged from just over one second to 1.2 seconds. Even when the maneuver was expected, the perception/cognitive processing time was one-half

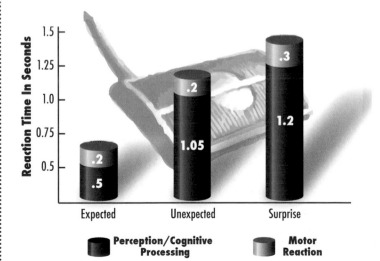

Perception/Cognitive Processing — Motor Reaction

second before movement began. Before analyzing these numbers further, let's take a look at the Tempe study, which analyzed police officer reaction times to start and stop shooting.

The Tempe Study

In 2003, 102 police officers from the Tempe, Arizona Police Department underwent a series of tests conducted by Dr. Bill Hudson and Dr. Bill Lewinski, to measure their reaction time to start and stop shooting based upon visual stimuli. In these experiments, the officers were expecting the stimuli; they knew they should start and stop shooting based upon the stimuli; and they began the experiment with their trigger finger already in the trigger guard (that is, perception/cognitive processing time, and motor reaction time were kept to an absolute minimum).

Experiment #1: Time to Press the Trigger

The first test was designed to determine the officers' average response time to press the trigger based upon the visual stimulus of a light. Results indicated that the officers, on average, took 25/100ths of a second to react to the light, and another 6/100ths of a second to press the trigger, for a total response time of 31/100ths of a second.

Experiment #2: Time to Stop Pressing the Trigger

In this experiment, the officers were intentionally misled as to the basis of the experiment. During the briefing, they were informed that the test was to measure how quickly they could press the trigger—the trigger press was to begin when the light went on, and end when the light went out. The officers were also

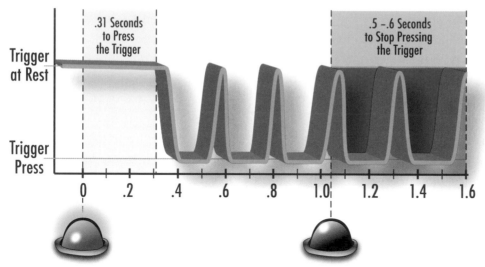

The chart to the left illustrates a "trigger pull plot" collected during the Tempe Study. The peaks and valleys indicate the actual trigger presses, with the upper boundary showing the trigger at rest, and the lower boundary showing the trigger fully pressed. The start of the plot shows the perception/cognitive processing time that occurred before the initial trigger press (the start of the first valley). The end of the plot shows two additional trigger presses after the light went out.

informed that they would lose points if they fired after the light went out—that is, they had extra motivation to react quickly, and to *not* fire the gun after the light went out. During this test, the researchers determined that the average officer required between 5/10ths and 6/10ths of a second to react to the light going out, and to stop pressing the trigger. Since the trigger could be pressed much faster (6/100ths of a second) than the officers could react to the changed conditions (at least 5/10ths of a second), each officer pressed the trigger at least twice, and sometimes *three times* after the light indicated they should stop shooting.

Multi-Tasking and its Effect on Reaction Time

In both studies, researchers concluded that the more an individual was multi-tasking or the more complex the required movement was, the longer the reaction times would be. That conclusion is echoed in a summary of multiple driving studies compiled by the National Safety Council, where the NSC concluded that driver multi-tasking added an average of .6 seconds to the response time required for braking. During the Tempe study, multi-tasking was limited (the officers were only focused on the light and trigger press), however the researchers pointed out that during critical incidents, officers were very likely "moving, pointing, ducking, seeking cover, shooting, processing, reacting emotionally, etc.," which would affect their overall ability to start and stop shooting.

Conclusion

Based upon the results of both studies, it's clear that "reaction time" is more than just the time required to draw a firearm, press a trigger, or press a brake—reaction time also includes at least one-quarter of a second, and as much as 1.2 seconds of perception/cognitive processing before *any* movement takes place (and that's in ideal, controlled conditions). Taking those numbers and placing them in the context of self-defense, let's try to answer the questions first posed in this section.

If an attacker lunges at you with a knife, can you draw your firearm in time to stop him? That depends on how close the attacker is. Since attacks are almost always a surprise, we should assume that we'd need at least one second to perceive and process the fact that we're under attack, plus the time required to draw our firearm and align it with the attacker. Let's assume the motor reaction time takes two seconds (the time to orient toward the attacker, and draw our firearm from concealment). That means that our full reaction might take three seconds or more, which is enough time for an attacker to cover more than 50 feet. So the answer to the question is, "Are you more than 50 feet away from the attacker?" or better yet, "How closely were you observing your surroundings?"

Can you "out draw" an attacker if he already has a firearm pointed at you? No. Based upon the results of the Tempe study, we can conclude that an attacker will require just 6/100ths of a second to press the trigger, while we'll need as much as 1.2 seconds of perception/cognitive processing time, before *any* movement can begin, including drawing our own firearm, or ducking behind cover. Our best bet in this situation is to count on Jeff Cooper's description of an inadequate or inept attacker.

When the threat ends, how quickly can you stop shooting? Based upon the Tempe study, the answer is at least 5/10ths of a second, and longer when engaged in multiple tasks simultaneously, such as moving, seeking cover, etc. Asked another way, "Once the trigger press has started, if the attacker throws down his weapon, can the defender stop himself in time?" The answer is no. The test indicated that the time required to react to the changed condition was more than *eight times* the time required to abort a trigger press—once the trigger press

began, it was simply impossible to stop it, even if the situation had changed.

Is there any plausible explanation for why an attacker might be shot in the back? Yes. An attacker, who has already made the decision to turn around, could complete that simple movement in as little as 2/10ths of a second, while the defender would require 5/10ths of a second or more to stop shooting. In the Tempe study, officers pressed the trigger twice, and sometimes three times after the conditions indicated they should stop shooting.

In summary, the short answer is that action *always* beats reaction. While automated responses (explained in Chapter Five) can be near instantaneous (such as ducking into a crouch when a loud noise occurs), the cognitive responses discussed here are not instantaneous. Because of that, we must compensate by:

■ Being hyper-aware of our surroundings and the individuals within our protective bubble.

■ Preparing for a possible attack *before* it occurs by increasing distance, orienting toward the possible threat, taking cover, and/or preparing to access our firearm.

■ Making intelligent decisions about our equipment and carry techniques—for example, too many holster retention devices, or too many layers of clothing, can slow a response.

■ Practice rapid, multiple shot strings of fire during our training sessions.

As you can see, "situational awareness" isn't just a fancy term that gets thrown out in self-defense classes, that can be discarded the moment you walk out the classroom door. It's a method of survival—ignore it, and you might just find yourself with .06 seconds to think, "Oh my God, this can't be—"

OBSERVING YOUR ENVIRONMENT

Observing your environment is just as important as observing the people within it. Look for and avoid areas that might be attractive to criminals looking for easy victims, such as blind spots, areas away from the crowds, or areas of low light; but also look for things in your environment that can work to your advantage, such as barriers, concealment, cover, and escape routes.

Blind Spots

Criminals count on surprise when targeting prospective victims, and they'll be more than happy to have their victims approach them, rather than the other way around. When approaching blind spots at the corners of buildings, or when approaching trees, tall bushes, concrete pillars, or vehicles, give them a wide berth, and turn to observe the hidden area as you approach.

Away from the Crowds

Just as criminals count on surprise, they also count on an easy escape with no witnesses. Regardless of how convenient a shortcut might seem or however safe you might feel heading to your car late at night all alone, that's the kind of behavior that criminals count on to find easy victims.

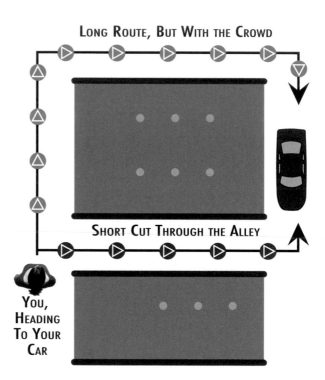

LONG ROUTE, BUT WITH THE CROWD

SHORT CUT THROUGH THE ALLEY

YOU, HEADING TO YOUR CAR

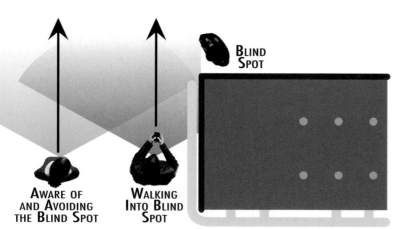

BLIND SPOT

AWARE OF AND AVOIDING THE BLIND SPOT

WALKING INTO BLIND SPOT

Be especially observant when approaching blind spots such as corners of buildings, tall vehicles, pillars, dumpsters, bushes, etc. Make a wide berth around these areas, and turn your head to look as you approach. Get ready to run.

Although you may be perfectly within your rights to walk down a dark alley all alone, you've already made two mistakes. This individual might be looking for a handout, or he might be looking for your money or your life. Fix your mistakes before it's too late by turning around and returning as quickly as possible to a crowded area.

Low Light Areas

Darkness is a criminal's friend. Back entrances of homes or businesses, dark alleys, parking areas with burned out lights; these are all areas where criminals may hover when looking for easy victims. Especially dangerous are areas with a rapid transition from bright lights to low light or darkness. It takes our eyes as long as 20 minutes to adapt to low light, and criminals who are stalking victims in these areas will be well adapted to the low light while our eyes are still adjusting. The parking garage on the opposite page is a good example—the garage contains plenty of well lit areas, but it also contains an area of low light, which should be avoided. When parking in a garage such as this, you should pick a spot that allows you to walk through the well lit areas in order to get to your destination, rather than a spot that requires you to walk through the areas with burned out lights. If a criminal is in the area looking for a victim, he's much more likely to hover behind a vehicle or pillar in the dark areas, than in the brightly-lit areas.

Barriers, Concealment, and Cover

When under threat, any barrier between you and the threat increases your ability to escape or evade the attack. Vehicles, tables, chairs, even a display case at a convenience store can help to foil an attacker with an edged or impact weapon. Concealment is anything that hides you from the threat (a closed door, a wall, or anything you can duck behind) while cover (things like concrete pillars, or the front of vehicles where the engine block is) protects you from incoming bullets. As part of your situational awareness when in public, you'll need to be aware of these objects within your environment, and make a mental note on how they can help to serve as barriers, concealment, or cover.

Escape Routes

In addition to looking for barriers, concealment, and cover, you should also identify at least two escape routes wherever you are, in case you need to quickly put distance between yourself and a threat. You'll recall from our topic on "Focus Level Orange," that if a situation doesn't feel right, you can choose to exit the area preemptively, even if you haven't positively identified a threat. If you *have* positively identified a threat, having identified escape routes in advance can save valuable time, when seconds will count. In particular, when under the threat of a firearm, you'll need to spoil your attacker's aim by increasing your distance as quickly as possible. Picture how the difficulty increases at your local range when you increase the distance between you and the target from 10 feet to 50 feet to 100 feet. How about pushing it out to 100, 200, or 300 feet? The attacker will find it just as aggravating.

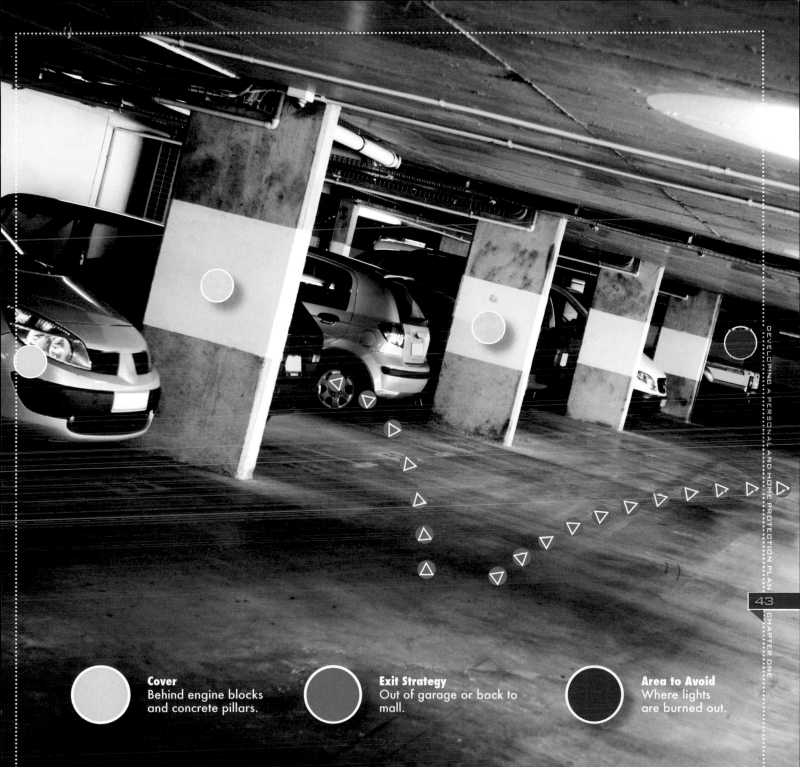

Cover
Behind engine blocks and concrete pillars.

Exit Strategy
Out of garage or back to mall.

Area to Avoid
Where lights are burned out.

HOME SECURITY

Students of self-defense can spend hours or days studying and training on methods of staying safe in public, including perfecting the skills of situational awareness and the use of a handgun in self-defense. Yet those same individuals can exhibit sloppy and unsafe behavior when it comes to securing the one place where we *should* feel safe, namely our homes. One reason for this disparity may simply be that when we're in our homes, our places of sanctuary, it becomes easy to slip back into "focus level white" and to believe that nothing bad can occur. Another reason may be that it's more difficult to quantify the dangers of a home invasion when compared to the risks of other crimes of violence. While the FBI maintains detailed crime data in their Uniform Crime Report (the source for most media reports on violent crime) including the crime of burglary, they do *not* differentiate between burglaries that occur in empty homes versus occupied homes. If a violent crime occurred during a home invasion, the FBI would categorize the crime under *two* headings such as burglary and rape, but with no separate category of "home invasion," it's impossible to determine, nationally or locally, just how common these "hot burglaries" are using the FBI data alone. Suffice to say, taking personal responsibility for our own safety, and the safety of our families, *cannot* stop at the front door.

Thinking Like a Criminal

When evaluating the security of your home, we suggest putting yourself in the mind of the criminal who wants to gain access to your home, and conducting a thorough inspection, inside and out. You should start from the outside of the home and make a methodical, 360-degree inspection starting from the ground up. During your inspection, you'll need to ask yourself the types of questions we've posed on the opposite page.

■ According to FBI statistics, burglars enter the front door of homes 34% of the time, and back or screen doors 22% of the time. The most common method of breaching the door? A good, swift kick. To test the security effectiveness of locks and doors, Consumer Reports has established a standard test, using a 100-pound battering ram capable of delivering varying degrees of force to the door. In a test conducted by the DIY Network's show Deconstruction®, a variety of door locks were tested to determine how long it would take to breach the door using the average strength of a kick. When testing a standard deadbolt and strike plate with standard length screws, the door was breached after just two impacts of the battering ram, at just 60 joules per "kick." When tested using the same dead bolt, but a reinforced strike plate ($10 – $15) and three-inch screws, the door was breached only after 13 impacts, at an average of 160 joules each, which equates to more than 17-times the force required to breach the standard door and lock.

Home Security Inspection Checklist

Windows:

- Identify all windows that are on the ground level that could potentially allow a home invader to fit through. Never mind determining if it would be *easy* for the home invader to do so; they've been known to do some pretty unorthodox things to gain entry to a home.

- Do they lock properly?

- Are they locked?

- Does anything block the view of the window from the outside such as a tree or shrubs?

- Is there anything outside the house that could potentially be used as a step stool to climb through the window? While home invaders aren't likely to carry their own ladder or step stool, they *will* take advantage of anything you've left outside that will make their job easier.

- Do you have alarm company stickers on your windows? New, fresh looking stickers—not stickers that look like they were put on by the previous occupant.

- Do your windows have plastic or metal locks?

- If you have standard hung windows, do you have a secondary security device, such as a bar stop?

- If you have casement windows, do you have standard or reinforced hinges?

- Do the windows have a protective laminate applied to the inside of the window, or baked inside? In other words, will your windows be shattered with a single blow, or are they designed to withstand repeated blows?

- On the first floor, what's in front of the windows? For example, are they blocked by a table or other barrier that a home invader would need to climb over, or is the area wide open?

Doors:

- What is the quality and strength of the front, back, side, and interior garage doors? It's natural to focus on the strength of your *front* door, but criminals will focus on whichever door is the weakest.

- What's the general appearance of the door? Does it look new, or is it old, faded, and looking primed for a good kick?

- Are the hinges on the outside or inside?

- Do you have an ability to see who is at the door without them seeing you?

- Do you use a deadbolt, chain lock, or throw-over lock?

- How long are the screws that are used to mount the strike plate? You'll actually need to unscrew the screws to answer this question.

Lights:

- Is your house well lit, or poorly lit on all sides? How about the adjoining neighbors' houses? Criminals will not only look for dark homes, they'll look for dark homes, *surrounded* by dark homes.

General Appearance:

- How close are trees or shrubs to your home? Is there anything that a criminal can hide behind while trying to enter a window or door?

- Do you have burglar alarm signs (in new condition) at all entry points?

Alarm:

- Do you have a security alarm, and do you set it? (Homes that have alarms are *three times* less likely to be burglarized.)

- Is it connected to an alarm service?

- Do you have motion detectors, glass break sensors, and sensors on the windows?

Making Your Home More Secure

Once you've completed a security inspection of your home, it's time to look at methods to make your home more secure. In the recommendations which follow, we've offered a variety of solutions costing just a few dollars at the low-end, to several thousand dollars at the high-end. The great news is that even the lowest cost solutions will dramatically decrease the probability that your home will be subject to a burglary or home invasion.

Windows

■ Replace any plastic locks with metal locks (about $2.50 each), and add a bar stop to each window ($20).

■ Treat the inside of windows with a plastic window treatment (the type of treatment used to insulate the windows), which will dramatically increase the effort required to break through the window (about $6.50 per square foot).

■ If you're *serious* about window security, invest in replacement casement windows with a reinforced hinge, metal locks, and a protective laminate that's baked into the window (about $350 per window).

Doors

■ Replace any doors that are not steel or solid core, including the door interior to the garage. Choose a door that doesn't contain clear windows that would allow a person outside the home to see in; instead, add your own hotel-style peephole ($6 – $11).

■ All exterior doors should have a deadbolt and/or a throw-over type lock (about $15).

■ Replace standard strike plates with reinforced strike plates, and use extra deep screws (at least three-inches long) which will anchor into the wall stud, rather than just the door frame ($12—$15).

■ If you're serious about door security, invest in a high-security lock ($180 or more), which defeats criminal's ability to use a "bump key" to pick the lock. High security locks use a unique pin configuration and hardened cylinders, which require 30—40 minutes to defeat, even for a trained locksmith.

■ If you're *really* serious about door security, invest in a solid steel door from Master Security (from $500 to several thousand dollars), which have five built-in deadbolts and an anti-pick lock. Master Security doors are designed to stop sledgehammer blows and even gunfire. In a test on the DIY Network's show Deconstruction®, four sledgehammer armed testers failed to breach the door even after ten minutes of repeated blows.

Exterior

■ Add exterior lights to all sides of the house, including the sides not containing doors. If you're concerned about electricity costs, put them on a motion detector circuit. Additional lights throughout the front and back yard will encourage a potential criminal to move further down the street to find a house that isn't so well lit.

As mentioned, FBI statistics confirm that about 56% of home entries are through the front door or back door, and those same statistics show that first floor windows are the next favored entry point at about 23%. In another Deconstruction® test, five different types of windows with varying security mechanisms were tested to determine how well they'd withstand a determined home invader or burglar. The testers discovered that a standard hung window with a single lock could be breached in less than a minute by breaking the lock, or in seconds by breaking the glass. Same for a basic casement window. By adding a bar stop ($20) and a plastic window treatment ($6.50 per square foot) to the standard hung window; or reinforced hinges to the casement window, the time to breach the window was increased dramatically. For real security, consider upgrading to high-security casement windows with reinforced hinges and metal locks, which also come with a protective laminate that's baked directly into the glass. Even after repeated strikes with a crowbar, the window failed to break during the Deconstruction® test. The cost? About $375 per window. The peace of mind? Priceless.

■As much as you might love the bushes and trees that have been growing around your house for years, if they're overgrown, they're going to provide cover for someone trying to break into your house, or lying in wait for you while you approach the door. Trim all bushes at least four-feet from the house, and trim any tree branch that blocks the view to your windows or doors.

■Place new alarm company signs at all doors, and stickers on all first floor windows.

Burglar Alarm

The first step in effectively using a burglar alarm, is to get the alarm. The second step is to set it, religiously. Insurance company surveys have shown that 60%—81% of people who have burglar alarms fail to set them when at home, or even when on vacation. The number one excuse (53%) for failing to set the alarm is because the homeowner leaves pets indoors, however, alarm manufacturers now offer "pet immune" motion detectors. By combining an infrared scanner with a motion detector, the systems are able to differentiate between the heat of a pet, and the heat of an intruder. In addition to the new "pet immune" features, security systems themselves have evolved from clunky systems requiring hard wiring at doors and windows (and slow law enforcement responses as alarm companies initiated "call backs" to determine if the alarm was an actual emergency or a false alarm), to state of the art systems like something out of a spy novel. Two-way systems are now available from

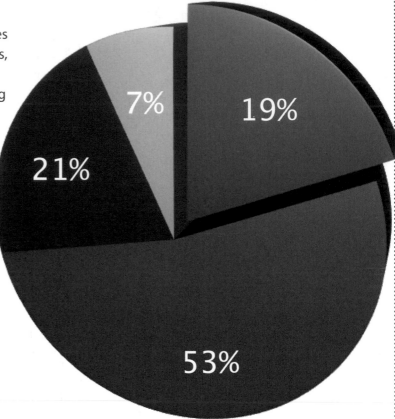

● Set Alarm
● Don't Set Because of Pets
● Don't Set Because of Children
● Forget to Set

companies such as AlarmForce®, which immediately opens a live channel between the home and the monitoring service when the alarm goes off. This allows the customer service agent to immediately differentiate between an actual emergency and a false alarm. Systems are also available with "glass break" detectors, which are more effective than simple window monitors that only sound if the window is opened (but wouldn't sound if the window was broken). The detectors are even tuned to differentiate between the sound of a broken window, and the sound of a broken glass.

Planning for Home Defense

In addition to taking steps to better secure our homes, we'll also need to take steps to plan for what to do if all of our security measures fail, and we still find ourselves in the middle of a home invasion. While you don't necessarily need to draw a floor layout of your home as part of your home invasion plan, you should at least *have* a plan and discuss it with everyone in your household, including your children. Think of this as no different than discussing a plan in

case of fire, tornado, hurricane, or earthquake. When discussing a home invasion plan with the family, we'd suggest reviewing the checklist items on the following page, and ensuring that all family members are aware of how to dial 911, and all age-appropriate family members are aware of the location of the home defense firearm and how to use it. Plan a route for all family members to head to the most secure areas of the home, and include in the plan who will get the phone and dial 911, who will access the defensive firearm, and who will assist loved ones.

In addition to planning for actively defending the home, we also suggest that you plan for retreat or escape, even if you're not legally obligated to do so. For example, if you needed to quickly retreat from a

■ Home security systems have evolved from clunky systems requiring hard wiring at doors and windows, and slow law enforcement responses as alarm companies initiated "call backs" to determine if the alarm was an actual emergency or a false alarm, to state of the art systems like something out of a spy novel. Two-way systems are now available from companies such as AlarmForce®, which immediately opens a live channel between the home and the monitoring service when the alarm goes off. This allows the customer service agent to immediately differentiate between an actual emergency and a false alarm. If an alarm is tripped when you are not at home, most systems can now alert you through an app on your smartphone, even sending you a text message with an image of the intruder. Systems are also available with "glass break" detectors, which are more effective than simple window monitors that only sound if the window is opened. The detectors are even tuned to differentiate between the sound of a broken window, and a broken glass. For pet owners, ADT® and other manufacturers now offer "pet immune" motion detectors. By combining an infrared scanner with the motion detector, the systems are able to differentiate between the heat of a pet, and the heat of an intruder.

room or from the home, what are the options? What rooms are the safest, and what doors are the closest? If you exit the house, in which direction do you run to find the closest neighbor? You can include older children as active participants in the plan by assigning them with simple tasks that can help keep themselves and their siblings safe. For example, their tasks could include:

■ Get out of the house and find a neighbor, and ask the neighbor to call 911.

■ Get the younger kids into the same bedroom, and close and barricade the door.

We suggest two or three small points for each child, such as, "If something bad happens, your job is to get out of the house, get to a neighbor, and have him or her call 911. Then your job is done."

Finally, it's important to discuss what *not* to do in the event of a home invasion. For example, if everyone in the family is in the same part of the house, then it is not necessary, prudent, or smart to "clear rooms" looking for the intruder. In addition, it's extremely important to discuss what to do if a family member is coming home late or unexpectedly, and how to communicate it if a guest will be in the home. The use of a family "code word" or "challenge and reply" can avoid tragedy if your teenage son or daughter has decided to sneak a significant other into the house for a late night rendezvous, or if your spouse has gotten up for a late night snack.

MENTAL EXERCISES

With enough time and money, dozens of advanced shooting schools are available to the average citizen, including advanced topics such as force-on-force, low light shooting, shoot/no-shoot scenarios, etc. In fact, we're sure that a school exists that would teach us to use infrared gear, rappel from a helicopter, breach doors, and rescue hostages, but let's face it—the

The Home Defense Checklist

- Are the front and back lights on?
- Is the alarm on?
- Are all doors locked (including deadbolt and/or throw-over lock)?
- Is the firearm appropriately staged to prevent unauthorized access? (Keep in mind that you'll need to follow federal and state safe storage laws.)
- Where is the phone and how do I dial 911 (in the dark, with a head full of cobwebs)?
- If the home is invaded, what room do we move to?
- If we need to exit the home, which neighbor's house do we go to?

- What commands do we give?
- How do I identify a friend from a foe?
- What's a family code word to identify whom and where you are?
- How do we inform our family that we'll be coming home late, or that a guest will be in the home?
- Does each family member know how to dial 911?
- Does each age-appropriate family member know how to use the home defense firearm?
- What do we do when the police arrive?

average permit holder is lucky to get to the range once a month. So how do we bridge the gap between the training that we *do* perform, versus the type of scenario we might find ourselves in if a critical incident does occur? One simple alternative we can do while sitting in our armchair at home is to run through a series of mental exercises.

Mental exercises shouldn't be confused with paranoia, or with a responsibly armed citizen fantasizing about getting in a shootout with a bad guy. It's simply a process to have a mental checklist of items that wouldn't normally be part of our time on the range. For example, when walking through a parking garage, picture what you would do if someone stepped out from behind a car with a knife. What commands would you give? Where would you find cover? What would be your mental trigger? At home, mentally walk through the step-by-step process that you would go through if you heard the front door being kicked down. These simple mental

exercises can help to avoid the, "Oh my God" reaction described by Cooper.

On the Range

Mental exercises can extend to our time on the range as well. One goal of mental exercises on the range may seem counterintuitive, which is to elevate our stress level to the point that our body will generate higher levels of adrenaline. This might be done by converting a relaxed round of shooting at 21-feet to an exercise where we imagine the target is an attacker, charging us with a knife. The goal should be to place several rounds into critical areas within one to two seconds (the time it would take for the attacker to reach us). The results might be lower accuracy when compared to a more relaxed practice round, but it will force us to learn to shoot safely and accurately, while having a pounding heart and shaking hands. When running mental exercises at home or at the range, you'll need to create hypothetical problems (such as the examples on the this page) that require a solution. Your solution will need to be a *complete* solution; that is, it should include the checklist items shown below, including evaluating your options and preparing for the aftermath.

At Home

■ What if I hear the front door being kicked down, or a window shattered?

■ What if my burglar alarm goes off in the middle of the night?

■ What if a stranger at the door suddenly produces a weapon?

■ What should I do if I hear someone outside of the house?

■ What if I believe they're stealing my property? (This is an easy one—stay inside, call 911, and be a good witness.)

■ What if I find the door to my house open upon arriving home? (Also an easy one—stay outside, call 911, and let the police do their job.)

■ What if I hear someone in the house at night? How do I distinguish a family member from an intruder?

In Public

■ What if I'm approached by one or more individuals who cause me concern?

■ What if I "step off the line" and they follow me?

■ What do I do if they produce a weapon? What if it's a knife? What if it's a gun?

■ What if a threat materializes between a loved one and me?

■ What if I see an attack in progress on someone else?

■ If I see someone that I believe has committed, or is about to commit a crime, what should I do? Should I follow them, or stay in a safe location and call 911?

Mental Exercise Checklist

- What are my options?
- What cover or barriers are available?
- How do I move "off the line?"
- How do I draw from the holster?
- What commands do I give?
- What balance of speed and accuracy would be required if I had to shoot?
- How do I work the physiological reactions into my response?

- How do I disengage/re-engage any safety devices including holster retention, manual safeties, or decockers?
- How do I clear a malfunction?
- How do I perform a reload?
- What do I do in the aftermath?
- Whom do I call and what do I say?
- What do I say to the police when they arrive?
- What will I do when I'm arrested?
- Where is my lawyer's contact information?

HOW DOES A CONCEALED CARRY PERMIT FIT?

When it comes to our personal protection plans, a "Concealed Carry Permit" simply provides us with one more option that might be used if we find ourselves unable to avoid or escape from a dangerous situation when out in public. But, as discussed on the opposite page, possessing a firearm actually *elevates* our legal and moral need to find ways to avoid or escape. A concealed carry permit should *not* be confused with any additional authority under the law, beyond the right to carry an object in public that might otherwise be illegal. In most of our experiences, the only individuals that we've known who have carried firearms on a daily basis have been law enforcement (who *do* have additional authority), so it's understandable that confusion can occur about what exactly our permit authorizes us to do. First, let's look at some things that our permit is *not*.

A firearm isn't a magic talisman that will protect you from harm, nor will simply displaying it defeat evil.

Rob Pincus

What a Permit is Not

An Invincibility Shield

We cannot look at our concealed carry permit as a permit to go to places, do things, or say things that we shouldn't otherwise. If we ignore the guidelines on conflict avoidance and allow ourselves to be placed in a dangerous situation that we could have avoided, we'll quickly discover that our permit does not stop incoming bullets, and it will *not* shield us from an aggressive prosecutor who believes that we were spoiling for a fight.

A Shield of ANY Kind

Never confuse a concealed carry permit with a "Junior Police Officer" badge. Police have specific responsibilities (such as chasing down bad guys) that could put us in legal peril if we tried to imitate them. For example, if we tried to prevent a property crime (such as attempting to stop someone from breaking into a car, or chasing down a purse thief), or if we followed an individual who we suspected was up to no good and the situation escalated to the point where we used force to protect ourselves, the prosecutor could argue that we've broken one or more of the rules governing the use of force or deadly force outlined in Chapter Four, and we may be charged with a crime. On the same topic, we'll occasionally hear of an enterprising organization selling "Concealed Carry Permit" badges, modeled after police badges. These are *really* bad ideas, not only because they could be confused with actual police badges (possibly resulting in a charge of impersonating a police officer) but they may also give the "holder" of the badge the incorrect impression that they have some special powers or authority. Save your money.

A "Fix" For Bad Attitudes

If you pull out your handgun and wave it at someone in an attempt to adjust his behavior (such as the guy who just cut you off in traffic), you'll quickly find yourself on your way to jail, charged with assault or worse.

If you're unlucky enough to see this charming fellow in the lane next to you, keep calm, don't react, and keep that middle finger to yourself.

SO WHAT'S IT GOOD FOR?

A concealed carry permit is just that—it's a permit to carry an object in public that might otherwise be illegal. *Every other law* that applies to non-permit holders also applies to us, including the rules governing the use of force and deadly force. In fact, our permit may put us in greater legal jeopardy compared to non-permit holders, since many state and federal statutes provide additional penalties when a firearm falls into the mix. For example, if a non-permit holder verbally threatens someone with death or great bodily harm for cutting him off in traffic, he might be charged with misdemeanor assault. Insert a permit holder and a firearm into the same situation, and he should expect to be charged with felony assault, and anything else the prosecutor can come up with. Remember—if you choose to carry a firearm, your level of responsibility to avoid conflict has increased, not decreased.

USCCA MEMBER
MELISSA NEUMANN
COLLEGE STUDENT
AND CONCEALED CARRY
PERMIT HOLDER.

MELISSA IS A SENIOR at the University of Minnesota, and will soon complete her degree in Electrical Engineering before continuing on with a graduate degree. In addition, Melissa is a contestant in the upcoming Miss Minnesota USA pageant.

EVERYDAY CARRY:
RUGER LC9 IN A TOP SPEED HOLSTER.

BACKGROUND: I grew up going to gun shows and shooting with my dad. Now I'm happy to say that I am a gun owner and USCCA member. I decided to get my permit to carry right away when I turned 21. My belief is that I should take steps now to protect myself instead of waiting for something bad to happen before taking action. Besides getting my permit to carry, I also take women's self-defense classes. I like that Concealed Carry Magazine contains many stories and tips that help me learn more about carrying responsibly. The magazine is especially helpful for me since I'm a new permit holder.

→CHAPTER 2

SELF—DEFENSE FIREARM BASICS

- Four Universal Safety Rules
- Properly Clearing Semi-Automatics and Revolvers
- Additional Safety Considerations
- Double Action vs. Single Action
- Detailed Revolver and Semi-Automatic Explanations
- Handgun Sizes and Weights
- Pros and Cons of Different Handgun Options
- Ammunition and Ballistic Basics
- Ammunition & Semi-Automatic Malfunctions and their Clearance
- An Introduction to Home Defense Shotguns, and the AR-15 Platform
- Tasers and Pepper Spray

Self-defense firearm basics should be an enjoyable topic for new and experienced shooters alike. In this chapter we'll start by reviewing what are called the "Universal Safety Rules" that are non-negotiable when it comes to safe firearm ownership, handling, and use. We'd love to say that the universal rules were our idea, but that's not the case. Like the color codes of awareness, the Universal Safety Rules were developed by Colonel Jeff Cooper and have been adopted by nearly every firearms training organization in the world. We'll also cover a number of other safety considerations that are part of safe firearm ownership including topics associated with firearm maintenance, safety on the range, and safety considerations when selecting a holster. We'll also cover the proper clearance (unloading) procedures for both semi-automatics and revolvers, including lots of good pictures to help you through the process.

In this chapter, we'll also explain the difference between double action and single action handguns. This might sound like kind of a technical topic, but it's an important one to understand because it not only affects the operation of your firearm, it's an important safety consideration when selecting a firearm. In our example, we'll be using a pistol called a SIG Sauer P229 (which happens to be the same pistol used by U.S. Air Marshals), but the theory is the same for both semi-autos and revolvers. Once we're through that topic, we'll be reviewing several different types of revolvers and semi-autos. Revolvers have been a mainstay of repeating handguns since Sam Colt developed the first modern design in 1836 with his Colt Patterson model. More than 180 years later, Colt would still recognize today's modern revolvers as having many of the same functional components as his designs, although he'd probably find them a bit less attractive than his beauties. As you'll see in our examples, revolvers have a revolving cylinder, which typically has between five and eight chambers, each capable of holding a cartridge.

Semi-automatics have been on the market since the late 1890s, but it took another famous inventor, John Moses Browning, to perfect the design with his Model 1911 (which was adopted by the U.S. Army as its standard sidearm in March of 1911). Since then, advancements have been made in handgun design, safety, and materials, leading to an entire class of firearms that didn't exist prior to the early 1980s, including polymer-frame handguns, striker-fired handguns, double-action-only handguns, and lightweight, pocket pistols. We'll cover plenty of detail on all of those options in this chapter.

Also included in this chapter are introductions to the home defense shotgun and the AR-15, including what options or features you should consider if picking out either of these platforms for home defense. We'll close this chapter with a short explanation of how Tasers and pepper spray work, and what you should know if you're considering these less-than-lethal self-defense choices.

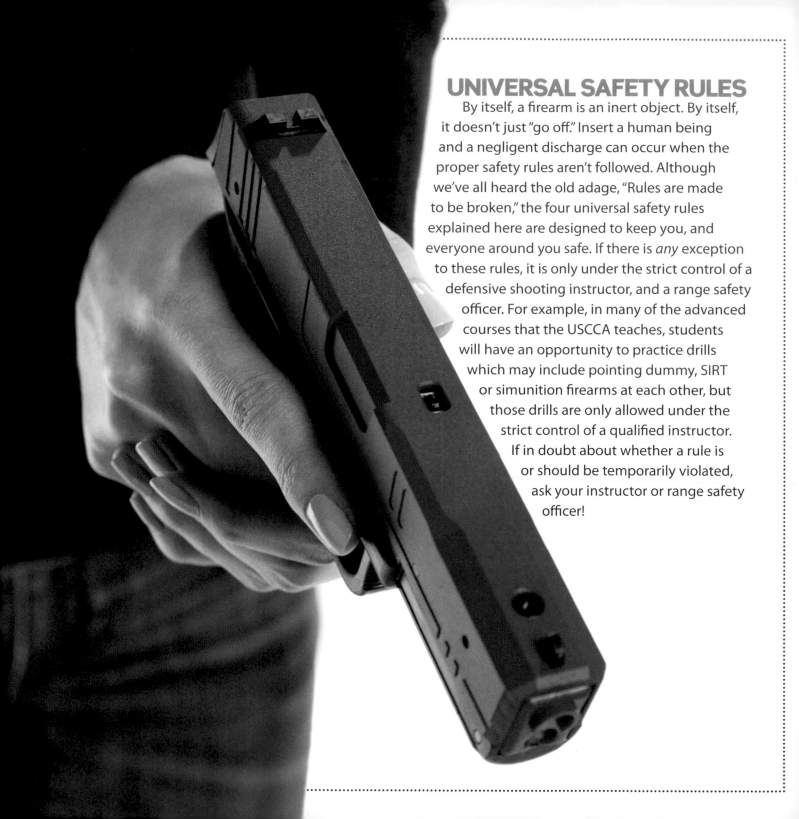

UNIVERSAL SAFETY RULES

By itself, a firearm is an inert object. By itself, it doesn't just "go off." Insert a human being and a negligent discharge can occur when the proper safety rules aren't followed. Although we've all heard the old adage, "Rules are made to be broken," the four universal safety rules explained here are designed to keep you, and everyone around you safe. If there is *any* exception to these rules, it is only under the strict control of a defensive shooting instructor, and a range safety officer. For example, in many of the advanced courses that the USCCA teaches, students will have an opportunity to practice drills which may include pointing dummy, SIRT or simunition firearms at each other, but those drills are only allowed under the strict control of a qualified instructor. If in doubt about whether a rule is or should be temporarily violated, ask your instructor or range safety officer!

Rule #1: Treat all guns as though they are always loaded. Most firearm "accidents" occur with firearms that the users had sworn were unloaded. Never, never, *never* grow careless with a firearm. Every single time you pick it up, perform the proper clearance procedure, and educate those in your household how to do the same. Treat a firearm that you've just unloaded with the *exact* same respect as one that you've just loaded.

Rule #2: Never point your gun at anything that you are not willing to destroy! Said another way, you should always be aware of the direction of your muzzle, and you should always keep that muzzle pointed in a safe direction.

Since your firearm has to point somewhere, you should always ensure that it's pointed in a direction that can serve as a backstop, and will not cause a dangerous ricochet if the firearm were to discharge. That criteria would indicate that pointing the firearm straight up or straight down would not be considered a safe direction, since a round negligently fired up may penetrate a ceiling; ricochet off the ceiling; or travel for thousands of feet if fired outside; and a round fired straight down can penetrate a floor or ricochet off the floor or ground.

A good method to practice this rule is to pretend that a laser extends out from the end of the barrel. You should NEVER let that imaginary beam touch anything that won't stop a bullet (that includes any wall, ceiling, or floor) or ANYONE (that includes your own hands, legs, or body) unless you are in a defensive situation and all criteria is present for the use of deadly force.

Rule #3: Keep your finger OFF the trigger and outside the trigger guard until you are on target and have made the decision to shoot! Until these criteria have been met, your trigger finger should be straight and placed firmly on the frame of the firearm. Your trigger finger should be in this location whenever you are not shooting, including when you are clearing a malfunction or reloading. The finger should be completely above the trigger area, not on the trigger guard, and not blocking the ejection port. In a defensive situation, do NOT put your finger in the trigger guard unless all requirements have been met for the use of deadly force. Training consistently with this method will avoid a negligent discharge in a stress situation, when your body's natural adrenaline dump will cause the strength of your grip to increase.

Rule #4: Always be sure of your target and beyond! Said another way, you must POSITIVELY identify your target before you shoot and you MUST be convinced that anything that you shoot at (a target on the range, or an attacker in a parking garage) must have an effective backstop to stop your bullet, otherwise you MUST NOT SHOOT! In addition to knowing what is behind your target, you must also know what is to the left, the right, in front of, above and below your target. Whether you're practicing at the range, hunting in the wilderness, or involved in a defensive situation, remember that every round you fire will continue in a straight line until it impacts into a target. You must be convinced that it will stop in the target of your choice, rather than a "target" that you didn't see, or weren't aware of.

CLEARING A SEMI-AUTOMATIC

As mentioned in Universal Safety Rule #1, we *always* do a clearance procedure *anytime* we pick up a firearm (other than the exceptions noted below). This might seem a bit ridiculous (as in "I *just* cleared the pistol, why would I clear it again?") but this habit will ensure that you avoid the, "I thought it was unloaded" type of accident. During the clearance procedures that follow, always remember all four Universal Safety Rules, including maintaining muzzle control and keeping your finger OUTSIDE of the trigger guard.

The *only* exceptions to this rule are: When operating on a "hot" range and picking up a previously loaded firearm from the benchrest in preparation to fire; when retrieving a loaded handgun from a gun vault to holster it for the day; or, when placing a loaded handgun in a gun vault at the end of the day.

To properly clear a semi-automatic handgun, follow the step-by-step procedure outlined to the right.

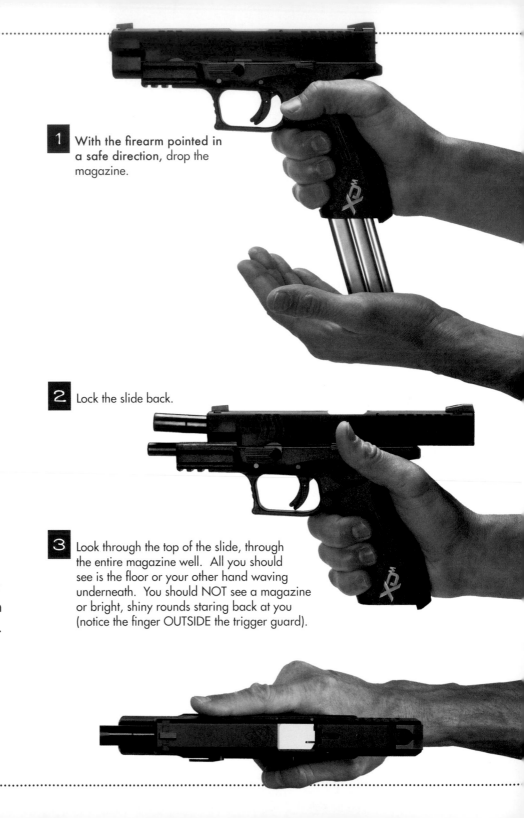

1 With the firearm pointed in a safe direction, drop the magazine.

2 Lock the slide back.

3 Look through the top of the slide, through the entire magazine well. All you should see is the floor or your other hand waving underneath. You should NOT see a magazine or bright, shiny rounds staring back at you (notice the finger OUTSIDE the trigger guard).

4 Observe the feed ramp and chamber of the barrel to ensure that no round is chambered, and double-check by sticking your pinky into the chamber. We know this sounds like we're getting a bit anal, but this is the best method to ensure that your firearm has been properly cleared.

One additional piece of advice—make sure that your fingers are nowhere near the slide release when your pinky is inserted into the chamber, otherwise you'll get a painful lesson on how quickly (and forcefully) the slide will slam closed. **Lastly,** whenever possible, a second person should confirm that the firearm has been cleared.

CLEARING A REVOLVER

Clearing a revolver is a simple procedure, but one that takes additional care when compared to clearing a semi-automatic, because the direction of the muzzle can tend to drift as any live rounds or empty casings are cleared from the chamber.

As with any firearm that you haven't operated before, take the time to read through the owner's manual, ask questions, and visually inspect the firearm before handling it. If at any point during the clearance procedure you become stuck, stop doing what you're doing and ensure that the firearm remains pointed in a safe direction. If you can't get unstuck, set the firearm down and ask for help.

To properly clear a revolver, follow the step-by-step procedure outlined to the right.

1 Open the cylinder by pressing the cylinder release button (located on the left side of the revolver), with the thumb on the strong hand.

2 While pushing the cylinder release button, swing the cylinder open by pushing it with the fingers on your support hand. Ensure that it is fully open, and that none of the chambers are visually blocked by the frame of the gun.

3 Press the ejection rod (the thin rode found on the front of the cylinder) to force any live rounds or empty casings out of the cylinder. If the rounds or casings don't fall free from the cylinder, the revolver can be tipped up slightly to allow gravity to assist (as long as Universal Rule #2 is followed), or the rounds/casings can be removed one by one with the fingers on the strong hand.

4 Rotate the cylinder with the thumb of the support hand, and visually check each chamber to confirm they are all empty. It's a good practice to count each cylinder as you check it—for example, on the revolver pictured to the right, we'd want to count out from one to six, to confirm that we've checked all six chambers.

ADDITIONAL SAFETY CONSIDERATIONS

In addition to the four Universal Safety Rules, we've added a few additional topics here to consider:

Safety

1. Educate others on the four Universal Safety Rules, and do not feel bad asking someone to, "watch your muzzle" or to take his finger out of the trigger guard.

2. Prior to handling any firearm, know how to operate it safely. If you're not sure, ask someone who does, but don't assume the guy behind the gun counter is an expert on each and every firearm. Most owner's manuals can also be downloaded from the manufacturer's website.

3. Never depend on safeties in place of the four Universal Safety Rules. Mechanical devices can and do fail! The ultimate "safeties" are your brain and trigger finger.

4. When handing a firearm to someone else, the action should be open.

5. Use only the correct ammunition for your gun, matching up the caliber on the barrel, the ammunition box, and the stamp on the bottom of the cartridge. In addition, prior to using any ammunition with a higher than normal pressure rating (indicated by a +P or +P+ designation) ensure that your firearm is rated for these pressures. A common error is in using .38 Special ammunition with a +P rating in an older .38 Special revolver, not rated for that pressure.

6. Never handle firearms when under the influence of alcohol or drugs (including prescription or over-the-counter drugs). If you wouldn't drive a car, you shouldn't handle (or carry) a firearm. That's common sense, but doing so may also put you in direct violation of federal and state law.

7. Removing the magazine from a semi-automatic will not remove the round that has been chambered, and most semi-autos will still fire without the magazine in place.

8. Be sure the barrel and action are clear of obstructions including dirt, mud, snow, squib loads, etc. If in doubt, perform the proper clearance procedure, then disassemble your firearm, removing the barrel so that you can perform a visual check.

9. Never shoot at a hard, flat surface; water; or any other object that can cause a shot to ricochet.

10. Store guns and ammunition so they are not accessible to minors (that's federal law) and unauthorized individuals.

Firearm Maintenance

1. Be sure your gun is safe to operate. If you're not sure, bring it to a qualified gunsmith. This is particularly important if you've purchased or inherited a used firearm, or if you notice any cracks, or any change in the firearm's operation (for example, a failure to eject, or a higher frequency of malfunctions).

2. Clean and lubricate your firearm promptly after use. The most common reason for a firearm malfunction is a dirty gun. Plus, these are expensive pieces of equipment. Cleaning your firearm after every use will help to ensure its value is maintained.

On the Range

1. Wear eye and ear protection every time out. If you can't hear instructions on the range, do not crack your ear protection, instead, cup your hand over the back of your ear to indicate that the commands should be repeated.

2. Know and observe all range rules. A key range rule frequently violated is the rule to case and uncase firearms on the firing line, rather than on the shelf or table behind the firing line. This is a major safety violation. In addition, ALWAYS follow the four Universal Safety Rules, and report any individual to the range officer who is not following these rules or who exhibits any unsafe behavior.

3. Never step in front of or behind the firing line unless upon the *specific command* of your instructor or an RSO.

Holster Safety

1. Ensure that your holster of choice completely covers the trigger and trigger guard. No exceptions.

2. Your holster should retain your firearm in place even if running or jumping. Select a rigid holster that is molded specifically for your firearm rather than a more general "one size fits all" holster.

Otis Cleaning Kit

From a single kit, nearly every firearm type and caliber can be cleaned with the Otis Cleaning Kit—everything from a .22 caliber handgun to a 12-gauge shotgun. Properly cleaning and lubricating your firearm after each use will maintain its value, and ensure that it works when you need it.

UNDERSTANDING A GUN'S "ACTION"

Understanding a handgun's "action" is one of the first steps toward understanding their function and in selecting one that meets your needs. Firearm engineers can argue for hours about the true definition of single action and double action, but functionally, it's a pretty simple concept. Firearms in single action mode will have a shorter, lighter trigger press, and firearms in double action mode will have a longer, heavier trigger press. Mechanically speaking, single action means that the trigger performs a single function, that is, it releases the hammer (which means that the hammer already has to be cocked), while double action means that the trigger press does two things— it first cocks the hammer, then it releases it. Feel free to ignore the mechanical definition and just remember that single action means a shorter and lighter trigger press and double action means a longer and heavier trigger press. Today, some pistols are single action only (SAO), some are double action only (DAO), and some can be fired in either mode like the example shown here, a SIG Sauer P229.

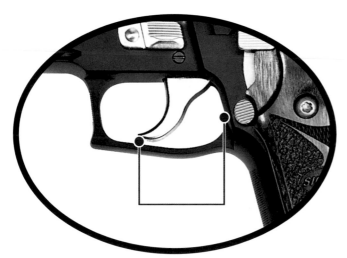

In double action, the distance of the trigger press is approximately ¾ of an inch.

Weight of press is approximately 12 pounds.

In single action, the distance of the trigger press is less than ½ of an inch.

Weight of press is approximately 4 ½ pounds.

The decocked hammer indicates that the firearm is in double action mode. The trigger is set fully forward.

The cocked hammer indicates that the firearm is in single action mode. The trigger is set farther back, closer to the break point.

Decocker

Many semi-automatics with an exposed hammer have a decocker, which allows the hammer to be decocked (lowered safely), placing the firearm back into double action mode. The presence of the decocker tells you that this is a DA/SA semiautomatic.

REVOLVERS

Revolvers operate with rounds loaded into a revolving cylinder. Pressing the trigger (in double action mode) or cocking the hammer rotates the cylinder, placing a new round in alignment with the hammer and barrel.

Modern revolvers with an exposed hammer (such as the Ruger LCRx revolver shown on the opposite page) are designed to allow the shooter to fire in either single action or double action mode. With the hammer forward (double action mode) a longer, heavier trigger press will rotate the cylinder and cock and release the hammer. Manually cocking the hammer with the thumb puts the gun in single action mode, which might have a trigger press as light as three pounds, and trigger travel as short as 1/16th of an inch. That's nice for accurate target shooting, but is less safe for a self–defense gun, which brings us to double action only revolvers.

You'll notice that the Ruger LCR revolver shown to the immediate right seems to lack a hammer spur—the hammer is actually still there, its just hidden within the frame of the gun which makes this revolver a double action only (DAO), which provides a consistent trigger press that is longer and heavier than a similar revolver shot in single action mode. This provides an additional level of safety, since a longer, heavier trigger press requires more intent than a short, light trigger press.

Front Sight

Muzzle

Barrel
The measured length of the barrel does not include the length of the cylinder.

Cylinder
Cylinders are designed to hold multiple rounds in separate chambers.

Cylinder Release
Allows the cylinder to be opened for loading and unloading.

DAO Revolver
The lack of an exposed hammer spur indicates that this revolver is double action only (DAO).

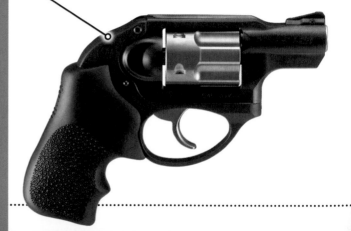

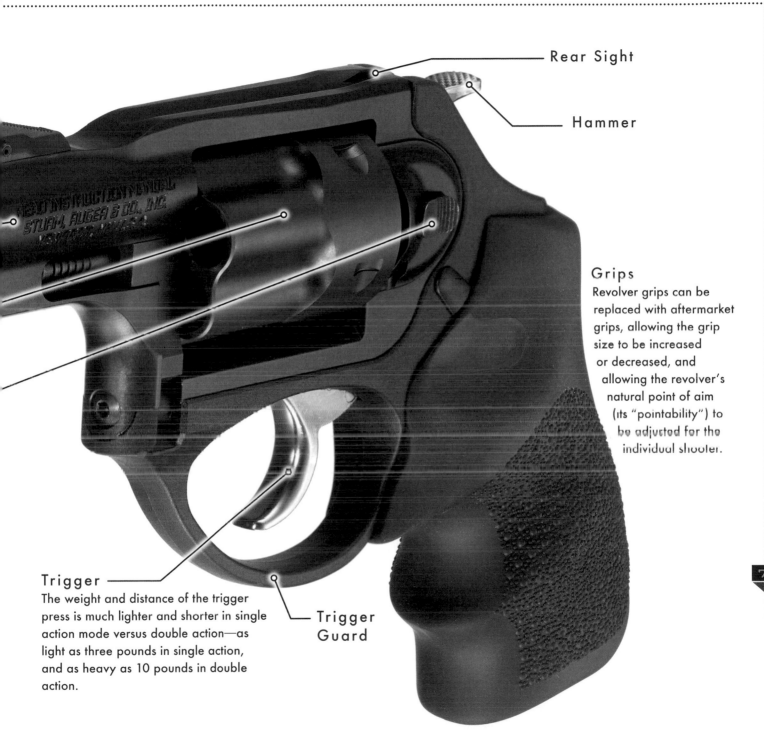

Rear Sight

Hammer

Grips

Revolver grips can be
replaced with aftermarket
grips, allowing the grip
size to be increased
or decreased, and
allowing the revolver's
natural point of aim
(its "pointability") to
be adjusted for the
individual shooter.

Trigger

The weight and distance of the trigger
press is much lighter and shorter in single
action mode versus double action—as
light as three pounds in single action,
and as heavy as 10 pounds in double
action.

Trigger Guard

SEMI-AUTOS

Semi-autos utilize a moving slide, which slides back using the power of the pistol's recoil (or the blowback of the expanding gases), ejecting the empty casing and re-cocking the hammer or striker. A powerful spring then reverses the direction of the slide, causing it to strip a new round off the top of the magazine, chambering it, and putting the slide back into battery. Like revolvers, semi-automatics come in a variety of actions, including those that will fire only in double action, and those that can fire in either single or double action. Like a double action only revolver, DAO semi-automatics have only one firing mode, which will consistently be a longer, heavier trigger press when compared to a similar model shot in single action mode. The Ruger LCP shown to the right is a DAO semi-automatic.

DA/SA semi-automatics (such as the SIG SAUER P229 profiled earlier) are normally carried with the hammer forward, so the first shot will be a double action shot and all subsequent shots will be in single action (since the moving slide automatically cocks the hammer/striker during the firing cycle). Most DA/SA semi-autos have a decocker, which allows the hammer to be lowered safely, placing the firearm in double action mode, which is considered to be a safer method for carrying.

Slide
The moving part of the pistol that slides to the rear, ejecting a spent case and loading a new round.

Take Down Lever/Rod
This control allows the slide to be removed from the frame, allowing the barrel and recoil spring to also be removed for cleaning.

Slide Lock
When the slide is manually retracted to the rear, it can be locked in the open position by pushing the slide lock upward, catching it in the small notch in the slide (seen just below the LCP initials in this photo).

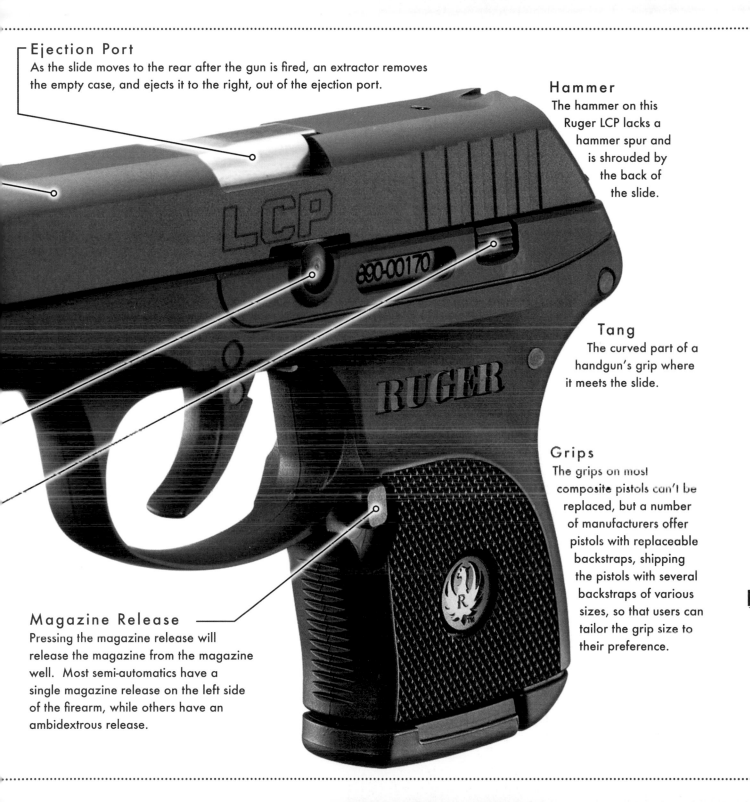

Ejection Port
As the slide moves to the rear after the gun is fired, an extractor removes the empty case, and ejects it to the right, out of the ejection port.

Hammer
The hammer on this Ruger LCP lacks a hammer spur and is shrouded by the back of the slide.

Tang
The curved part of a handgun's grip where it meets the slide.

Grips
The grips on most composite pistols can't be replaced, but a number of manufacturers offer pistols with replaceable backstraps, shipping the pistols with several backstraps of various sizes, so that users can tailor the grip size to their preference.

Magazine Release
Pressing the magazine release will release the magazine from the magazine well. Most semi-automatics have a single magazine release on the left side of the firearm, while others have an ambidextrous release.

STRIKER FIRED SEMI-AUTOS

The actions described on the previous pages all have one thing in common—the firearms are all hammer operated; that is, regardless of whether or not the hammer is exposed or hidden, it's the hammer that drives the action. Hammer operated firearms fit more neatly into the "single action only, double action only, or DA/SA action" categories than do many popular firearms, including Glocks, Springfield XDs, and many other modern firearms which are striker fired, and utilize a striker/firing pin held back under the tension of a spring. The cutaway illustration to the right, highlights the striker and spring utilized by these striker-fired handguns, as well as a number of other internal components (such as rifling, recoil springs, magazine components, etc.) which are shared with hammer operated semi-automatics.

Rifling
Rifling is the name for the spiral grooves cut into the inside of the barrel (referred to as "lands" and "grooves") which bite into the bullet as it speeds down the barrel, forcing the bullet to spin, which stabilizes it in flight.

Recoil Spring
While physics (an equal and opposite reaction) causes the slide to move rearward after a round is fired, the powerful recoil spring causes the slide to reverse direction, forcing the slide to strip a new round off of the top of the magazine, chambering that round, and locking the slide and barrel back into "battery."

Trigger Safety
The trigger safety is nothing more than a blade that juts forward of the trigger itself, with the back of the blade dangling down behind the trigger. During a proper trigger press, the trigger safety is depressed from the front, which raises the back of the trigger safety allowing it to clear the frame of the firearm, and allowing the trigger to be fully depressed.

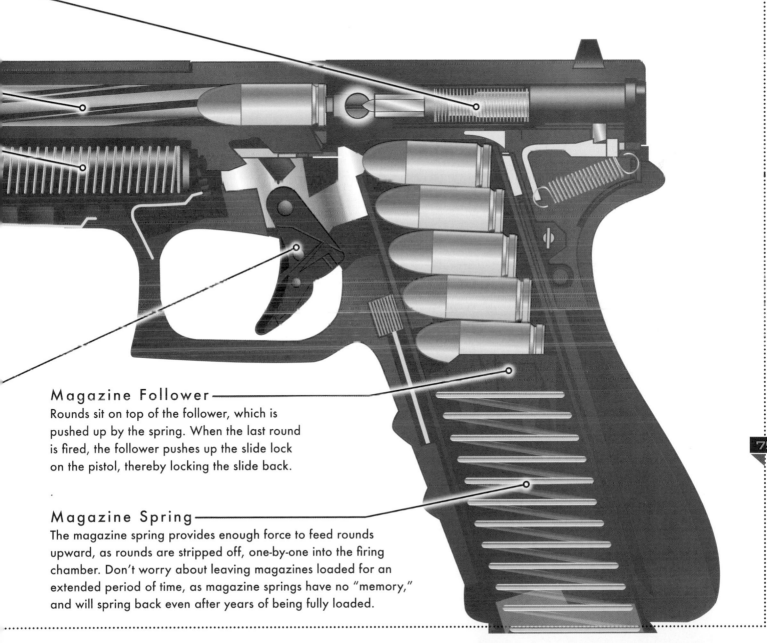

Striker (Firing Pin) and Spring

As the trigger is pressed on this striker-fired Glock, the firing pin or "striker" moves rearward, increasing the tension on the firing pin spring. When the trigger bar releases the firing pin lug, the striker moves forward with enough force to indent the round's primer, igniting the round's propellant.

Magazine Follower

Rounds sit on top of the follower, which is pushed up by the spring. When the last round is fired, the follower pushes up the slide lock on the pistol, thereby locking the slide back.

Magazine Spring

The magazine spring provides enough force to feed rounds upward, as rounds are stripped off, one-by-one into the firing chamber. Don't worry about leaving magazines loaded for an extended period of time, as magazine springs have no "memory," and will spring back even after years of being fully loaded.

WHAT HAPPENS WHEN THE TRIGGER IS PRESSED?

When the trigger is pressed on a semi-automatic, a bullet leaves the barrel and the slide cycles, ejecting the empty casing and loading a new round, all faster than the eye can see. The step-by-step operations shown here follow the mechanics of a Glock pistol in action.

1 When at "rest," the Glock's firing pin is half-cocked, and the firing pin channel is blocked by the firing pin safety (highlighted). The barrel is "locked" to the slide by the tight fit of the barrel's square chamber, and the slide's square ejection port (visible in the diagram just above the chambered round).

2 When the trigger is pressed, an extension of the trigger bar pushes the firing pin safety up, clearing the firing pin channel. As the trigger continues rearward, the firing pin (highlighted) is fully cocked, then released. The firing pin hits the chambered round's primer with enough force to cause a small explosion, creating a small shower of sparks, which ignite the round's propellant. The solid propellant rapidly turns gaseous, and the expanding gases force the bullet from the casing and accelerate it down the barrel. The barrel's "rifling" (the spiral grooves) causes the bullet to spin, which stabilizes it in flight.

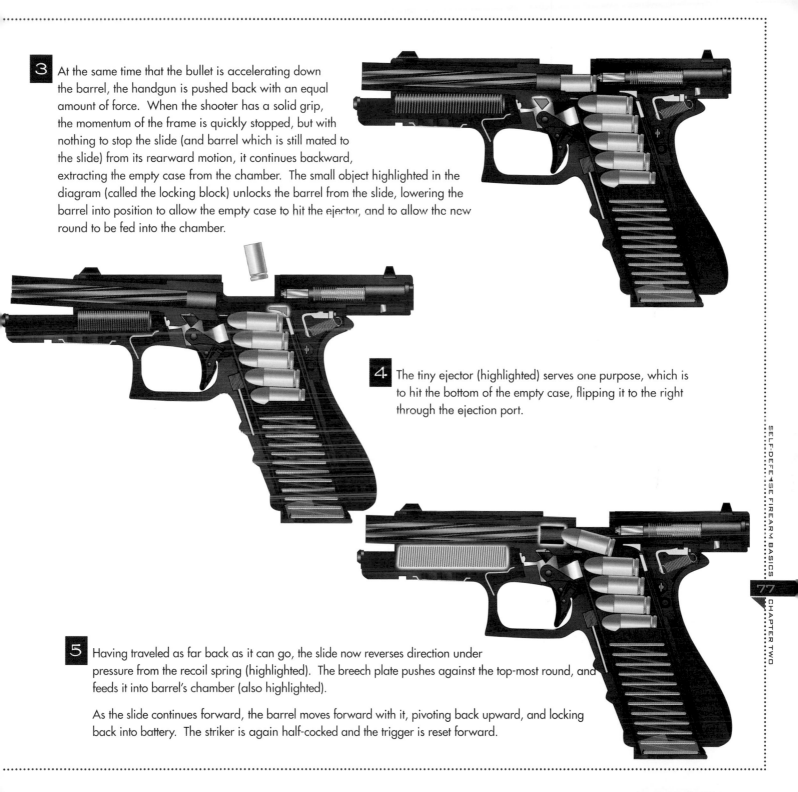

3 At the same time that the bullet is accelerating down the barrel, the handgun is pushed back with an equal amount of force. When the shooter has a solid grip, the momentum of the frame is quickly stopped, but with nothing to stop the slide (and barrel which is still mated to the slide) from its rearward motion, it continues backward, extracting the empty case from the chamber. The small object highlighted in the diagram (called the locking block) unlocks the barrel from the slide, lowering the barrel into position to allow the empty case to hit the ejector, and to allow the new round to be fed into the chamber.

4 The tiny ejector (highlighted) serves one purpose, which is to hit the bottom of the empty case, flipping it to the right through the ejection port.

5 Having traveled as far back as it can go, the slide now reverses direction under pressure from the recoil spring (highlighted). The breech plate pushes against the top-most round, and feeds it into barrel's chamber (also highlighted).

As the slide continues forward, the barrel moves forward with it, pivoting back upward, and locking back into battery. The striker is again half-cocked and the trigger is reset forward.

SEMI-AUTO MAGAZINES

While revolvers have a built in device to hold multiple rounds (the cylinder), semi-automatics have rounds fed from a detachable magazine. Magazine types and styles vary, but all can be categorized as single-stack or double-stack. Single-stacks store rounds one on top of the other in a single, straight line, while double-stacks store rounds in two staggered rows, allowing more rounds to be stored but resulting in a wider magazine (and larger pistol grip.) The magazine style you end up with is dictated by your handgun of choice—for example, if you choose a Model 1911, a Springfield XD(S), or a Glock 43 as your carry gun, you'll end up with single-stack magazines. On the other hand, if you choose a Springfield XD(M) or the full-sized Glock 17 as your handgun of choice, you'll end up with double-stack magazines. Loading a magazine is a simple process, in fact, it could be compared to loading a Pez dispenser, but the spring pressure of some magazines (in particular, double-stack magazines with a capacity of 15 or more rounds) can make getting the last few rounds into the magazine a bit tough, so you might consider using a speed loader, which is a plastic device which surrounds the magazine itself, and uses an internal rod, rather than using your thumb, to push the rounds down. See the opposite page for simple step-by-step instructions.

Double-Stack Magazines

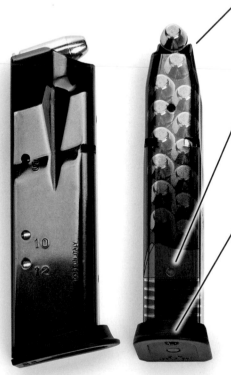

Single-Stack Magazines

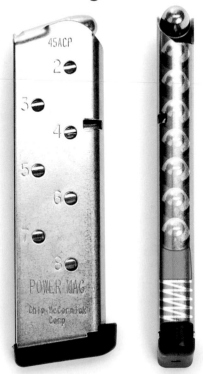

Magazine Lips
The width of the lips is slightly smaller than the diameter of the round, holding the round in place until it's stripped off and loaded into the chamber. When the gap widens on a worn magazine, double-feeds can result.

Follower and Spring
Rounds sit on top of the follower, which is pushed up by the spring. When the last round is fired, the follower pushes up the slide lock on the pistol, thereby locking the slide back.

Base Plate and Base Pad
The base plate secures the spring to the bottom of the magazine, while the pad gives more area when slapping the magazine into the magazine well and also protects the magazine when it hits the floor during a speed reload.

1 Pick up the magazine with your support hand and hold it firmly in place, high enough on the magazine so that your support thumb can easily reach the top of the magazine. Resting the magazine against your hip or on a solid surface (such as your countertop at home or a benchrest at the range) will assist in the loading process.

2 With your support thumb, push down on the magazine's "follower" (the plastic or metal plate inside of the magazine). Pick up one round and push it into the magazine from the front, using a downward and backward motion to push the follower down. The round should slide all the way to the back of the magazine, and be held in place between the follower and the magazine's lips at the top (the width of the lips will be slightly smaller than the round you are loading, to hold it in place).

3 After the first round is loaded, use your support thumb to push down on the round you just loaded, and slide a new round in. Continue this procedure until the magazine is full. As mentioned, on double-stack magazines, you may find that it becomes more and more difficult to push the top round down, once the magazine gets closer to capacity. Using a magazine speed loader can give you the extra leverage to get the last few rounds loaded.

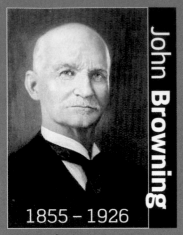

CHOOSING THE RIGHT GUN FOR YOU

In addition to considering whether you'd like to gravitate toward a revolver or a semi-automatic (plus all of the other features such as the action and additional safety components), you'll also have to consider what size and weight of firearm is right for you, based upon:

- The caliber range that you are comfortable shooting.
- Your size and the way you normally dress.
- Holster options that work for you.
- When and where you plan to carry.
- The weather and time of year.

Due to the factors above, you'll very likely need to make some compromises on your firearm choice when it comes to comfort, capacity, and shootability. What may be right for one person, may not be right for *you*.

Trade-Offs

Lighter, smaller firearms usually mean a smaller caliber (and less stopping power) or a more punishing recoil, which might lead to less time on the range. Larger firearms, on the other hand, never get any lighter as the day goes on, which may cause you to leave it at home.

Other Criteria to Consider

■ **Grip size, shape, angle, and material.** Determine how well the grips allow the firearm to properly "point" for you and whether or not your knuckles properly align to the front strap. Grip material and texture are important elements to consider to ensure a solid grip that won't slip.

■ **Grip length:** Short grips are more concealable and "print" less on covering garments, but they provide less space to fit all four fingers of your support hand.

■ **Proper placement of your finger on the trigger:** The trigger should rest comfortably in the range between the pad of your finger and first knuckle crease.

■ **Balance:** Revolvers and composite framed semi-autos can sometimes feel nose heavy. Always test balance with a fully loaded firearm (make sure this is done on the range, and not on the sales floor).

SAMPLE HANDGUN SIZES AND WEIGHTS

Smith & Wesson
Model 27
Length: 9.25"
Frame Material: Steel
Caliber: .38/.357
41 Ounces

Smith & Wesson
Model 60
Length: 7.5"
Frame Material: Steel
Caliber: .38/.357
24 Ounces

Smith & Wesson
Model 36
Length: 7"
Frame Material: Steel
Caliber: .38 Special
20.4 Ounces

Smith & Wesson
Model 442
Length: 6.4"
Frame Material:
Aluminum Alloy
Caliber: .38 Special
15 Ounces

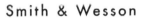

NAA Mini-Revolver
Length: 4"
Frame Material: Steel
Caliber: .22 LR
4.5 Ounces

Springfield
1911 Loaded
Length: 8.5"
Height: 5.5"
Frame Material: Steel
Caliber: .45 ACP
41 Ounces

Smith & Wesson
M&P
Length: 7.75"
Height: 5.5"
Frame Material: Composite
Caliber: 9mm/.40 S&W
30 Ounces

SIG SAUER
P229 Equinox
Length: 7.1"
Height: 5.4"
Frame Material: Steel
Caliber: .357 Sig/.40 S&W
32 Ounces

Springfield XD
Sub-Compact
Length: 6.25"
Height: 4.75"
Frame Material: Composite
Caliber: 9mm/.40/.45
26 Ounces

Ruger LCP .380
Length: 5.2"
Height: 3.6"
Frame Material: Composite
Caliber: .380 ACP
9.4 Ounces

As mentioned, when choosing a personal carry firearm, there are going to be trade-offs. To best understand those trade-offs, our suggestion is to rent a few firearms of different sizes to try them out on the range, and then test them with a holster option that works for *you*. You might discover that you prefer the heavier gun on the range because it withstands recoil better, but that trying to carry that same gun in a concealed holster just isn't going to work. The good news is that many of the most popular manufacturers offer a whole range of handguns that are virtually identical in look, shape, and function, but that come in two or three different sizes. Glocks and Springfield XDs or XDMs are great examples—both manufacturers offer full-sized handguns that you'd see on the hip of a police officer, but they also offer versions that look like they were hit with a shrink ray, making them small enough to fit into a front pocket, or that will virtually disappear in an inside-the-waistband holster. We'll talk more about those "pocket pistols" in a moment.

Choosing a Revolver

If you'd still like a bit more advice, we're big fans of two handgun options. If you're just starting out and you are unsure of how much time you can actually dedicate to training, a double-action-only revolver might just be a perfect choice. You don't have to worry about extra controls like manual safeties or decockers, and malfunctions are almost unheard of. If you have a misfire, you simply press the trigger again, while the clearance procedure on a semi-automatic is more involved. If you can withstand a moderate recoil, then a DAO

■While semi-automatics are arguably more popular for concealed carry when compared to the revolver, the operator must become comfortable not only with the firearm's operation, but also with how to field strip the firearm for cleaning and maintenance.

revolver chambered in .38 special is a good choice. Our final advice on that particular revolver, is don't listen to your friends at the range who tell you to put .357 magnums in it instead of 38 specials. A .38 special round has plenty of stopping power, and if you are new to handguns, shooting a .357 magnum won't be a lot of fun, and it might dissuade you from further practice, or further carrying.

REVOLVERS	
Pros	**Cons**
<ul><li>Simple to load and unload.</li><li>Mechanically simple, resulting in a lower likelihood of malfunctions when compared with a semi-automatic.</li><li>Typically more reliable with many different types of ammunition.</li><li>Easier to clean, and easier to maintain than semi-automatics.</li></ul>	<ul><li>Typically hold less ammunition than a semi-automatic of comparable size.</li><li>The bulky cylinder may make it harder to conceal than a thinner semi-automatic.</li><li>Revolvers often weigh more than a semi-automatic of comparable size.</li><li>Some may find revolvers to be more difficult to shoot than a semi-automatic because of a heavier trigger weight, a double-action trigger, or because of the shape of the grip.</li></ul>

SEMI-AUTOMATICS	
Pros	**Cons**
<ul><li>Larger magazine capacity (more ammunition).</li><li>Faster to load and reload than revolvers.</li><li>More options: styles, shapes, sizes, calibers, including choosing a hammer or striker-fired, etc.</li><li>Flatter shape is easier to conceal than a revolver.</li><li>Many options are available with lower calibers (and lower recoil) than a revolver chambered in .38 Special.</li></ul>	<ul><li>Malfunctions are more common when compared to using a revolver. The operator must learn how to clear these malfunctions!</li><li>Field stripping for cleaning and maintenance is more complex and involves multiple parts that must be removed (see the opposite page).</li><li>Based on size or hand strength, some people may find it difficult to rack a semi-automatics slide which will be required for initial loading and when clearing malfunctions.</li></ul>

Choosing a Semi-Automatic

If you're ready to step up to a semi-automatic, we're big fans of striker-fired handguns, in particular, Glocks, Springfield XDs or XD(M)s, Smith & Wesson M&Ps and the new Ruger LCP II. These guns mimic the longer, heavier trigger press of a double-action-only handgun, and they are typically *incredibly* reliable guns.

Can't Find a Gun in Your Size?

Would you be surprised to find out that fewer than 20 percent of licensed permit holders actually carry their gun with them when out in public? While reasons for that abound, the number one reason mentioned is that the license holder's firearm of choice ended up being too heavy and too uncomfortable. While we could argue that personal protection doesn't need to be comfortable, a better answer has evolved during the last decade, as gun manufacturers have continued to make smaller and smaller versions of their most popular firearms. This has created an entire class of handguns referred to as "pocket pistols" which can be so small and so light, that the license holder nearly forgets the gun is there, that is, until they need it. As mentioned earlier, smaller pistols do tend to offer smaller calibers (usually .380 ACP and below) which historically have been knocked for their lack of stopping power, but most permit holders have discovered that carrying a pocket pistol is so easy that carrying becomes almost second nature, as easy as slipping a wallet into your pocket. And while a .380 caliber or smaller certainly does have less stopping power than a 9mm or larger, it has infinitely more stopping power than that 9mm, .40 S&W, or .45 ACP that was left at home because it was too bulky or too heavy. If that answer doesn't satisfy you, then you'll be happy to hear that a number of manufacturers have even produced these pocket sized pistols in 9mm and even .45 ACP, although the recoil on those guns might make practice on the range a bit less enjoyable.

We've highlighted a few of our favorite pocket pistols here, including options from Ruger, Glock, and Smith & Wesson. One last comment—NEVER slide a pocket pistol into your pocket without a pocket holster. Loose change, keys, or fingers can easily slip into the trigger guard unless the pistol is properly secured in a holster that completely covers the trigger and trigger guard. See Chapter Six for a couple of ideas on pocket holsters.

MANUFACTURER / MODEL / CALIBER	WHAT WE LIKE
Ruger LCP II .380 ACP	A beautiful redesign of the original and hugely popular Ruger LCP, the LCP II has a more manageable recoil than the original, and a shorter, crisper trigger. Besides that, it looks great.
Glock 43 9mm	In 9mm, the Glock 43 provides a larger caliber in nearly the same size package as other pocket pistol options, and it boasts the same great reliability as its bigger brothers.
Smith & Wesson Bodyguard .380 ACP	The Bodyguard comes in two configurations, with an integrated Crimson Trace laser, and without. Unlike most other pocket-sized pistols, the Bodyguard is also available in two-tone, and in flat dark earth as shown on the opposite page.

■ At just over 10 ounces and three-quarters of an inch thick at the slide, the new LCP II is adding to an already impressive line-up of concealed carry options from Ruger. Holster options for the LCP II include a variety of inside- and outside-the-waistband options, and an innovative and minimalistic pocket holster from BORAII, which is profiled in Chapter Six.

Model: *Ruger LCP II*
Weight: *10.6 ounces*
Overall Length: *5.17 inches*
Slide Width: *0.75 inches*
Caliber: *.380 ACP*
Capacity: *6+1 rounds*

■ Weighing in at just 1.7 ounces heavier than the LCP II, the M&P Bodyguard has gained popularity as one of the most sought after pocket pistols. As with the LCP II and other pistols considered in the "pocket" size, the Bodyguard has dozens of out-of-pocket holster options available including inside-the-waistband and outside-the-waistband. See Chapter Six for a few ideas.

Model: *M&P Bodyguard*
Weight: *12.3 ounces*
Slide Width: *0.75 inches*
Overall Length: *5.25 inches*
Caliber: *.380 ACP*
Capacity: *6+1 rounds*

AMMUNITION COMPONENTS

What you see below are not bullets; they are more properly called cartridges, rounds, or ammunition. The bullet is the conical-shaped object sitting on top of the propellant (in other words, it's the part of the round that shoots down the barrel). As simple as the self-contained cartridge sounds, it wasn't until 1847 that a practical, self-contained cartridge was patented, with credit going to a French gunsmith by the name of B. Houllier. In 1855, Sam Colt made a major blunder when he rejected an employee's idea to bore completely through a revolver's cylinder, which would have allowed these new self-contained cartridges to be dropped in from the rear. Rollin White subsequently had the idea patented, and licensed the patent to Horace Smith and Daniel Wesson.

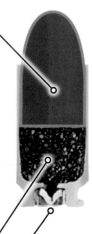

Bullet
This "full metal jacket" (FMJ) bullet shows how the copper sheath covers a lead core

Propellant
Modern propellants have a high amount of surface area to ensure a rapid, stable burn, ensuring a maximum expansion of gases.

Primer
When struck by the firing pin, the round's primer causes a small explosion, showering sparks into the round's casing, igniting the propellant.

Semi-Automatic Round
On rounds designed for semi-automatics, the rim at the base of the round is no wider than the cartridge case, which allows the rounds to stack easily within a magazine and also allows the round to feed and extract smoothly. The purpose of the rim is to provide a location for the extractor claw to grab on to as it's feeding and extracting the round.

Revolver Round
On rounds designed for revolvers, the rim is wider than the cartridge case, which allows the rounds to drop in the revolver cylinder, without falling all the way through.

DEFINING CALIBER AND OTHER MEASUREMENTS

The name of ammunition is typically its caliber (the diameter of the bullet) in either 100ths of an inch or in millimeters, and some other designation such as the company that holds the original patent on the round.

For example, the name .45ACP (Automatic Colt Pistol) tells us that this round is forty-five one-hundreds of an inch in diameter, and that Colt originally patented this round. The round carries the same name regardless of whether it's being shot in a Colt, a Kimber, a Springfield, etc.

Caliber measurements are sometimes inexact; for example, the .38 Special has an actual measurement of 357/1000ths of an inch. That's a holdover from the days of muzzle loading firearms, when the actual diameter of a ball had to be slightly smaller than the barrel in order to allow the ball to fit.

Grains

Grains are a unit of weight, with 7,000 grains per pound, or 437.5 grains per ounce. That means that a 230 grain bullet is just over half an ounce.

Caliber

Caliber is a measurement of the diameter of the bullet (not the casing). The caliber designation has nothing to do with the round's power, it only defines how big of a hole it will make (see the illustration below).

Bullet Weight

The bullet's weight is indicated in grains. There are 7,000 grains in a pound, and handgun bullet weights range from about 40 grains to 230 grains or more.

Case Volume

The relative volume of the case is a good indication of how much propellant the round has. The greater the volume, the more propellant. The more propellant, the faster the bullet will leave the barrel.

Is Caliber all that Matters?

Each of the three rounds to the right are .22 caliber, that is, they'll all make exactly the same size hole in their target. They also happen to all have a 40 grain bullet, yet the differences in case volume (i.e. volume of propellant) makes dramatic differences in the relative velocity of each bullet, translating to dramatic differences in the "power" of each round.

.22 INCH

.22 Long Rifle
Best known as a "plinking" round, the .22 shouldn't be discounted as a self-defense round.

Bullet Weight:
40 Grains

Muzzle Velocity:
1060 FPS

.22 INCH

5.7MM FN
Designed by FN as an alternative to the 9mm, the 5.7MM FN is blazing fast at nearly 2,000 FPS.

Bullet Weight:
40 Grains

Muzzle Velocity:
1950 FPS

.22 INCH

.223 Remington
Best known as the standard NATO round for light rifles, it has a velocity more than triple the .22LR.

Bullet Weight:
40 Grains

Muzzle Velocity:
3330 FPS

STOPPING POWER

Stopping, or "knock down" power is a hot topic of discussion at any gun club—some people will argue for hours that stopping power is directly related to a bullet's kinetic energy, while others will argue that a bigger hole is all that matters. Kinetic energy is measured using the following formula:

Kinetic Energy = ½ MV²

In this formula, M = the mass of the bullet, and V = the speed of the bullet in feet per second. Calculating the mass of a bullet involves converting the weight of the bullet from grains to pounds (there are 7,000 grains in a pound), and needs to figure in gravity (32 feet per second per second). This formula has been the standard for computing a bullet's energy, but it favors velocity over weight, which can result in some oddities. For example, it shows the 9mm bullet having more energy than the .45ACP, which tends to fly in the face of real world military, police, and self-defense statistics. That problem has caused many people to disregard the kinetic energy formula in favor of the Taylor Knockout Factor (TKOF), developed by John Taylor. In addition to using the bullet's velocity and weight, the TKOF formula also includes the bullet's diameter (the size of the hole the bullet will make). Unlike the kinetic energy formula, the TKOF provides *equal* weighting to the bullet's weight, speed, and diameter. The Taylor Knockout Factor is measured using the following formula:

TKOF = (MVD) / 7,000

In this case, M = the weight of the bullet in grains (without calculating in gravity), while V = the speed of the bullet in feet per second, and D = the diameter of the bullet in inches. The Taylor KO Factor tends to favor heavier, larger caliber bullets when compared to the kinetic energy formula. While either formula provides valuable information, we tend to favor the TKOF measurement (which is how we've placed the rounds to the right), since it seems to better reflect real world statistics.

Feel free to ignore the debate and the formulas—our advice is to simply select the biggest caliber you can shoot well and load it with good self-defense ammunition.

Oh, and for you Dirty Harry fans who might be wondering where the venerable .44 Magnum is on our scale to the right. We'd love to add it, but we'd have to *double* the height of our book—the .44 Magnum has a TKOF factor of 18.55, nearly double the .357 Magnum.

Self-Defense Caliber Options

We recommend that your self-defense firearm falls within the green or yellow scale to the right (preferably the green), as long these rules apply:

Rule #1: You select a gun that you'll actually carry (that is, it isn't too heavy).

Rule #2: You select the largest caliber that you're comfortable shooting (and comfortable paying for practice ammunition!)

Remember that a .22 caliber in your holster is infinitely more valuable than a .45 left at home.

For a bit more advice from one of our favorite defensive shooting instructors and why he favors the 9mm, see the commentary from Rob Pincus on the next two pages.

10mm
Bullet Weight: 200 Grains
Muzzle Velocity: 1200 FPS
Energy: 635 Ft. Lbs.
TKOF: 13.49

.45 ACP
Bullet Weight: 230 Grains
Muzzle Velocity: 835 FPS
Energy: 356 Ft. Lbs.
TKOF: 12.35

.357 Magnum
Bullet Weight: 158 Grains
Muzzle Velocity: 1235 FPS
Energy: 535 Ft. Lbs.
TKOF: 9.95

.40 S&W
Bullet Weight: 180 Grains
Muzzle Velocity: 990 FPS
Energy: 390 Ft. Lbs.
TKOF: 10.18

.357 SIG
Bullet Weight: 125 Grains
Muzzle Velocity: 1350 FPS
Energy: 506 Ft. Lbs.
TKOF: 8.55

.38 Special +P
Bullet Weight: 130 Grains
Muzzle Velocity: 925 FPS
Energy: 247 Ft. Lbs.
TKOF: 6.13

9mm Luger
Bullet Weight: 124 Grains
Muzzle Velocity: 1140 FPS
Energy: 358 Ft. Lbs.
TKOF: 7.14

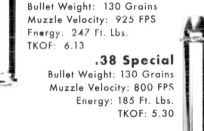

.38 Special
Bullet Weight: 130 Grains
Muzzle Velocity: 800 FPS
Energy: 185 Ft. Lbs.
TKOF: 5.30

.380 ACP
Bullet Weight: 95 Grains
Muzzle Velocity: 955 FPS
Energy: 190 Ft. Lbs.
TKOF: 4.93

.32 ACP
Bullet Weight: 71 Grains
Muzzle Velocity: 905 FPS
Energy: 129 Ft. Lbs.
TKOF: 2.94

.22 Long Rifle
Bullet Weight: 40 Grains
Muzzle Velocity: 1060 FPS
Energy: 100 Ft. Lbs.
TKOF: 1.33

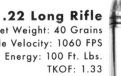

.25 ACP
Bullet Weight: 50 Grains
Muzzle Velocity: 760 FPS
Energy: 64 Ft. Lbs.
TKOF: 1.36

TAYLOR KNOCKOUT FACTOR

15 14 13 12 11 10 9 8 7 6 5 4 3 2 1 0

ACTUAL SIZE
1:1
Rounds shown in actual size

SELF-DEFENSE HANDGUN
& CALIBER RECOMMENDATIONS, BY ROB PINCUS

1. Bigger is not better: Carryability

When it comes to a personal defense gun for concealed carry, neither the gun itself nor the round being loaded into it need to be the stuff of 1980's action movies or 1970's police dramas. The days of the .45 ACP and the magnum revolver being the image of defensive handguns are gone. There is no doubt that the new crop of first time guns owners, the large number of women obtaining concealed carry permits and the incredible amount of information and education to the gun-buying public can all be credited with the establishment of the 9mm as the most preferred personal defense caliber and the increase in interest for mid-sized and compact single stack firearms. Today, the person who carries regularly is very likely to not be a life-long gun enthusiast. They may only own one gun for a specific purpose: Personal Defense. They aren't shooting on the weekends with their family, they aren't hunters and they aren't willing to wear a tan vest every day or otherwise dress around their gun. They want something with a high degree of what I call carryability, and slim 9mm's are very carryable.

2. Fit is Paramount: Shootability

Manufacturers are realizing that their guns need to fit as many types of hands as possible. Thankfully, the ego-driven days of "any gun will do, if you will do" have also passed. While that sentiment may be fundamentally true, if we get to pick the gun we'll be using days, months, or even years in advance of our defensive shooting, we should pick a gun that fits our hand well. That means two things: Smaller grips that will accommodate both small and large hands and modular grips that can be quickly and easily adjusted to a more perfect fit for everyone. When it comes to holding a gun intuitively, after thousands of students in thousands of classes, I can assure you that smaller grips can be held by larger hands much more easily than small hands can manage a large gun. Manufacturers have been responding not only with single stack designs, but also with less girth in the area of the grip that is held between the thumb and index finger of the strong hand and with deeper in-cuts at the top of the back of the grip area. The Springfield XD and the Smith and Wesson M&P firearms exemplify these traits and tend to fit more people well because of them. Fit is the primary driver of shootability. If a gun doesn't fit a person's hand well, they will not be able to shoot it intuitively or naturally. Their shooting will be forced and mechanical, which means that their efficiency will suffer.

3. There is no Replacement for Reliability

People are making excuses for their guns less and less often—and this is critical. If a gun isn't reliable, you shouldn't be carrying it for personal defense. I often make the comparison between guns and cars with my students. People generally need their cars every day. People rely on their cars to get them to work, to move their families around and to meet their obligations. Cars must be reliable and functional. You may want a 1968 Corvette Stingray, but if you live in New Hampshire and have a family of four, there is no way that you will have that car as your primary vehicle. Thankfully, we don't need our guns every day—but, that means that people can choose to buy and carry eccentric choices that they "like" and they will probably never have to confront their decision. But as I mentioned earlier, fewer and fewer people carrying guns for defense today are gun collectors.

Modern Bonded Hollow Point 9mm Ammunition:

Today's 9mm defensive ammunition generally meets the criteria that most experts would agree are needed in a defensive round. The top of the line offerings in this caliber (standard and +P) from most major manufacturers are going to reliably penetrate about 15" of 10% Ballistic Gelatin after going through heavy and light clothing. These tests are conducted regularly by many entities, most notably by the FBI. The FBI performs these tests through a variety of barriers under very controlled conditions so that they can chose the best ammunition for their agents and for the benefit of law enforcement agencies around the country trying to do the same. Of all the calibers that regularly meet the minimum criteria (9mm, .40 S&W, .357 Sig, etc.), 9mm offers the following advantages:

1. Lower recoil. Lower recoil means faster follow-up shots and less punishment during training and practice when compared to larger rounds.

2. Higher capacity: The smaller 9mm round means more ammunition can fit into any given size package, which means more shots can be fired during a defensive gun use before you need to reload.

3. Lower cost: Training and practice ammunition in 9mm costs less than the other larger calibers, which means return on your ammunition budget investment.

WHY USE HOLLOW-POINTS FOR SELF-DEFENSE?

So far, our discussion of ammunition has focused on nomenclature and caliber size, but we haven't yet talked about what *type* of ammunition you should consider for personal protection. Ammunition types tend to fall into two major groups (although there are others), including **ball** ammunition and **hollow-point** ammunition. Think of ball ammunition as being one solid mass, while hollow-point ammunition has a hollowed-out cavity at the tip, and usually has the jacketed edges of the cavity "scored" into four to six segments. The cavity and scored edges allow the round to dramatically expand, in particular, when the round has entered a fluid filled object at high speed. While that might sound like the round is designed with one purpose only (to inflict maximum damage on a human being), the purpose of the round's expansion is to reduce the possibility of the round passing through one object, and striking something, or someone, on the other side. While ball ammunition is a perfect choice for punching holes through paper at the range, it's *less* safe for bystanders if you choose to carry it in your defensive firearm. While you'll need to make an individual decision as to whether or not hollow-point ammunition is the right choice for you, your decision might be made a bit easier by contacting your local police department and asking them what *they* carry (today, nearly every police department in the United States issues hollow-point ammunition as standard issue). Note that hollow-point ammunition is *not* legal in all states.

Hollow-point
This cutaway of a hollow-point round shows how a section of the projectile has been removed (or hollowed out) from the center. This design allows the bullet to expand on impact, which slows the bullet down inside your target, preventing it from passing through (in most cases).

■ Hollow-points operate on hydraulics—that is, the fluid contained within a body provides adequate pressure within the hollow-point's cavity to rapidly expand the cavity, and fold back the lead core and pre-scored copper jacket. While this is occurring, the increased diameter causes a rapid deceleration of the bullet, eventually slowing and stopping it. This deceleration occurs much more rapidly in a hollow-point bullet that has fully expanded, when compared to a bullet that is not designed to expand (such as ball ammunition), or a hollow-point that fails to expand because of a lack of velocity, or one that has become clogged with heavy clothing, which can cause the hydraulic process to fail.

SELF-DEFENSE AMMUNITION OPTIONS

There are too many self-defense rounds for us to comment on, but we've described a few of the most popular below. You'll notice that we've focused on "traditional" hollow-points (the EFMJ aside), rather than more exotic rounds such as frangibles, which are designed to shatter on impact to avoid overpenetration.

ROUND	DESCRIPTION	CHARACTERISTICS
Hornady TAP FPD (For Personal Defense)	Uses "low flash" powder to protect night vision. Also has black nickel plating to provide better feeding and eliminate corrosion.	Both the low flash characteristics and nickel coating make this a great home defense round. The black case color is also pretty cool, and actually feels slick to the touch.
Federal Hydra-Shok	Copper Jacketed Hollow-point, with unique center post to provide controlled expansion.	Until recently, the Hydra-Shok was almost universally adopted as the ammunition of choice for police departments across the U.S. Federal recently released an update to the Hydra-Shok, called the HST, which seems to offer more consistent expansion than its predecessor and is quickly replacing the Hydra-Shok as the ammunition of choice for law enforcement.
Federal EFMJ (Expanding Full Metal Jacket)	Looks like a full metal jacket, but has a scored copper jacket covering an internal rubber nose and lead core.	The full metal jacket look and characteristics allow this round to feed much more reliably than traditional hollow-points, yet the expansion is still impressive. We've personally tested the expansion of a .45 ACP that mushroomed to .70. Unlike traditional hollow-points which rely on hydraulics to expand, the EFMJ operates on deceleration, with the scored jacket collapsing over the rubber nose upon impact, resulting in a pancaked bullet.
Hornady Critical Defense	Contains a rubber core within the hollow-point cavity.	Some handguns are prone to jamming as the edge of hollow-point rounds gets hung-up on the bottom of the feedramp during the loading cycle. The rubber core of this round can help to solve that problem.
Speer Gold Dot	Copper Jacketed Hollow-point with a wider and deeper cavity than traditional hollow-points.	With so many "shall issue" states, firearm manufacturers have been selling more short barrel pistols than ever before. Those short barrels result in lower muzzle velocities, which can result in hollow-points failing to open. The Gold Dot line has much larger and deeper hollow-point cavities, resulting in positive expansion, even with short barrel handguns.

WHY DOES BARREL LENGTH MATTER?

Why does barrel length matter? A longer barrel will result in a higher velocity bullet, since there is more time for the bullet to accelerate before the gases dissipate. For the same model pistol with different barrel lengths (for example, Springfield XDs with 3", 4" and 5" barrels) velocity can vary by as much as 300 feet per second for the same weight bullet.

So why does that matter? When it comes to punching holes through paper, it really doesn't matter. When it comes to using a firearm for self–defense, it *does* matter. A higher velocity round is more likely to stop a violent attacker because of deeper penetration of the bullet and a higher probability that hollow-point bullets will expand. There used to be a "magic number" of about 1,000 feet per second before a hollow-point bullet would expand, but with newer hollow-point bullets with larger cavities, that barrier is no longer critical.

Feet Per Second

Sample Muzzle Velocities by Barrel

CALIBER	5 INCHES	4 INCHES	3 INCHES	2 INCHES
.38 Special	1062	1014	878	733
9mm Luger	1233	1173	1105	1019
.40 S&W	1193	1136	1071	985
.45 ACP	1047	1003	911	857

Source: ballisticsbytheinch.com

AMMUNITION CARE AND STORAGE

Taking care of your ammunition (including storing it safely) is as important as caring for your firearm. Here's what you should remember:

■ Keep ammunition in a cool, dry area and store it separately from your firearm.

■ Keep ammunition in its original factory box or carton.

■ Do not expose ammunition to water or any gun solvents or oils. They can leak into the seam between the bullet and the casing, allowing the propellant to become damp and unreliable, possibly leading to a hang fire.

■ As mentioned in our "Additional Safety Considerations" section, use only the correct ammunition for your gun, matching up the caliber on the barrel, the ammunition box, and the stamp on the bottom of the cartridge. In addition, prior to using any ammunition with a higher than normal pressure rating (indicated by a +P or +P+ designation), ensure that your firearm is rated for these pressures.

■ Inspect ammunition prior to loading. Discard rounds with damaged cases, corrosion, or loose bullet.

■ Replace personal protection ammunition at least once a year (ammunition that has been loaded into your firearm, but not fired). That's not because the ammunition goes bad (we've fired .38 Specials that were found in the in-law's basement and were at least 40 years old). It's because repeated heating and cooling of your firearm and ammunition can lead to condensation, which can lead to corrosion of both.

■ Understand that not all types of ammunition will feed reliably in your firearm. In particular, for self-defense ammunition, you should practice with at least 200 to 250 rounds before selecting your personal protection ammunition of choice.

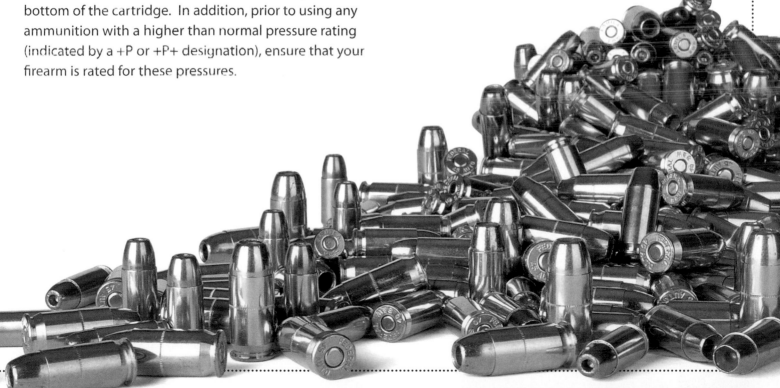

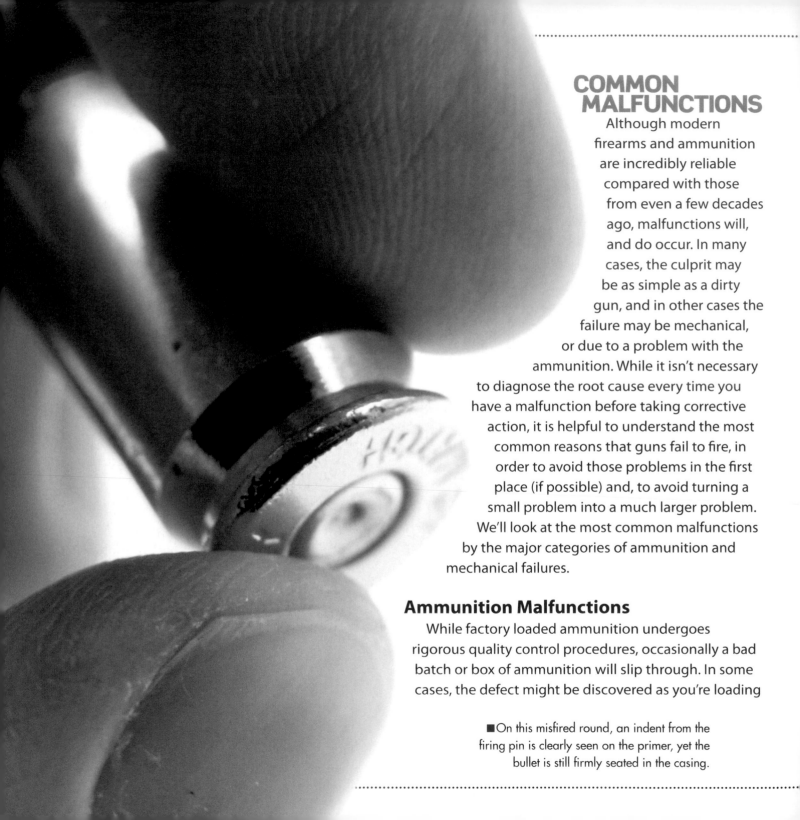

COMMON MALFUNCTIONS

Although modern firearms and ammunition are incredibly reliable compared with those from even a few decades ago, malfunctions will, and do occur. In many cases, the culprit may be as simple as a dirty gun, and in other cases the failure may be mechanical, or due to a problem with the ammunition. While it isn't necessary to diagnose the root cause every time you have a malfunction before taking corrective action, it is helpful to understand the most common reasons that guns fail to fire, in order to avoid those problems in the first place (if possible) and, to avoid turning a small problem into a much larger problem. We'll look at the most common malfunctions by the major categories of ammunition and mechanical failures.

Ammunition Malfunctions

While factory loaded ammunition undergoes rigorous quality control procedures, occasionally a bad batch or box of ammunition will slip through. In some cases, the defect might be discovered as you're loading

■On this misfired round, an indent from the firing pin is clearly seen on the primer, yet the bullet is still firmly seated in the casing.

the ammunition or otherwise inspecting it, but in most cases the failure won't be discovered until you're actually shooting it at the range, or, in a defensive situation. Ammunition malfunctions fall into three major groups:

Misfire: Misfires occurs when the primer fails to ignite after being struck by the firing pin. As shown on the image on the opposite page, the impact of the firing pin may be enough to actually dent the primer, but the round fails to fire. The usual suspect in misfires is a dirty firearm, rather than a bad round. When the inner workings of a firearm have become clogged with dust and oil, it can interfere with the smooth movement of the firing pin or striker, resulting in a reduced impact on the primer. You'll recognize this type of malfunction if you've pressed the trigger and all you hear is the "click" of the hammer or striker, but no "bang." You'll clear this type of failure with the *Tap and Rack* procedure demonstrated on the next page.

Hangfire: This type of malfunction is *extremely* rare, and typically only occurs in very old ammunition where moisture or oil has found its way inside the cartridge. The wet propellent can ignite very slowly, with any dry propellant effectively acting as a "fuse." If that fuse burns its way to a concentration of dry

propellant, the round can fire up to a full minute after the trigger was pressed.

Squib load: Although squib loads are also rare, they are the most dangerous of all ammunition malfunctions, and must be watched for (and listened for) closely. Squib loads are often caused by a round that has no propellant, either because of a failure at the ammunition plant, or because the round was hand loaded at home, and the individual doing the hand loading was daydreaming instead of conducting their own quality control. When the trigger is pressed on a squib load, the primer will still ignite and its small explosion is often enough to drive the bullet from the casing, but not all the way down the barrel. You'll recognize this type of malfunction if you've pressed the trigger and you hear a "pop" instead of a "bang," and you feel a reduced or no recoil. Immediately stop firing, and put the firearm down. At the direction of a range safety officer, you should then disassemble the firearm, including removing the barrel. If a bullet is lodged in the barrel, it can usually be removed with a wooden dowel or cleaning rod. Do *not* fire the gun again if you suspect you've had a squib load, or you risk a damaged gun, damaged hands, damaged eyes, etc.

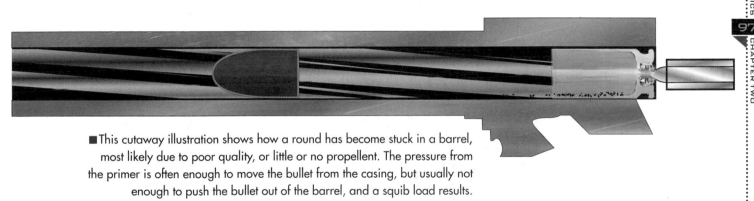

■ This cutaway illustration shows how a round has become stuck in a barrel, most likely due to poor quality, or little or no propellent. The pressure from the primer is often enough to move the bullet from the casing, but usually not enough to push the bullet out of the barrel, and a squib load results.

SEMI-AUTO MALFUNCTIONS

Semi-autos can have failures for a variety of reasons:

1. A round has misfired and remains chambered.
2. The ejected casing has failed to completely eject and is caught between the slide and the barrel, known as a "stovepipe" malfunction.
3. The lack of a solid grip allows the entire gun to shift rearward, resulting in the slide's failure to separate from the frame far enough to eject the empty casing, and the empty casing is reloaded in the chamber.

If you find yourself on the range or in a fight and your firearm malfunctions, you should use the **TAP and RACK** clearance procedures (steps #1 and #2) shown to the right.

If you've completed those two steps and discover that the slide isn't going forward, you most likely have a more significant malfunction which may include a failure to feed or a failure to eject. These malfunctions are usually caused by one of two culprits:

1. A worn extractor, which can leave the empty case in the chamber of the gun after the slide cycles.
2. A bad magazine, which can cause two rounds to be fed at the same time.

Either failure will try to force two objects into the chamber at the same time, in effect, locking the slide in place and disabling the firearm. In order to clear this type of malfunction, you'll need to complete steps #3 through #5 on the opposite page.

1 **TAP** the bottom of the magazine to fully seat it.

2 **RACK** the slide fully to the rear by grasping the slide between the palm of the hand and all four fingers, while simultaneously rolling the firearm to the right, to dump out the bad round.

3 If the slide fails to lock into battery after steps #1 and #2, you should **LOCK** the slide to the rear.

4 Then **DROP** the magazine (it may be necessary to pry it from the gun if a double-feed has it locked in place). Once the magazine is dropped, more often than not, you'll see two rounds hit the floor.

4 **RACK** the slide three times to remove any additional obstructions.

5 **REINSERT** the magazine (or insert a spare, since the magazine itself might be causing the problem) and rack the slide to chamber a new round.

SHOTGUNS

Conventional wisdom is that a shotgun is the best firearm for home defense when compared to a pistol, but that "wisdom" is usually based upon the incorrect theory that you can't miss with a shotgun since they create a "pattern" of shot, rather than a single hole. At 20 to 30 yards that matters, but at seven feet, a shotgun pattern will typically be no larger than a baseball, and at 21 feet, it will typically be no larger than a basketball. That means that shotguns still require deliberate aiming, and that shooting from the hip or selecting a shotgun with just a pistol grip and no buttstock might result in a missed shot. Where shotguns *do* give us an edge is in the load that they deliver.

At close quarters, even #6 or #7 shot loads will stop or disable an attacker, and 00 or 000 buckshot will fire the near equivalent of six to eight .380 pistol rounds, all delivered within that baseball sized pattern. Shotguns, like any long gun, also give us a much longer sight radius (the distance between the rear sight and the front sight), aiding in accuracy. Options for home defense shotguns range from your granddaddy's old side-by-side, to autoloaders like the Benelli M4 shown in the middle image on the right, but reliability counts more than the action you choose.

As we did with handguns, we'll spend the next few pages explaining some of the nomenclature surrounding shotguns, including explaining exactly what "gauge" means and how it's calculated, we'll explain what is meant by different shot sizes (including bb-shot, buckshot and slugs), and we'll explain what a shotgun "choke" is, and why it matters when it comes to home defense.

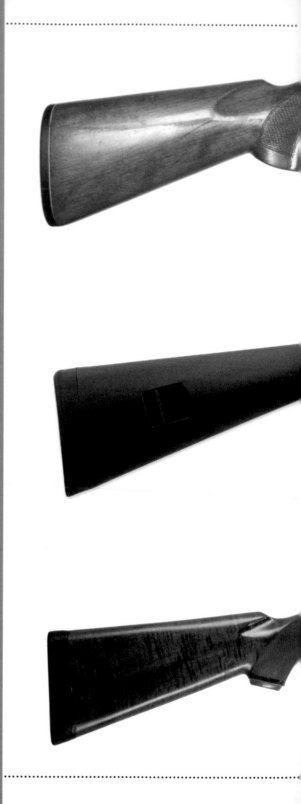

PUMP ACTION

■ Pump action shotguns have a single barrel, with a moveable forestock which is used to manually eject spent casings and to reload a new shell into the chamber. Most pump action shotguns are loaded from below (between the forestock and the trigger guard), with rounds being stored in the tubular magazine, which extends past the end of the forestock. The length of the tubular magazine will dictate how many shells can be held, which is typically between three and six.

SEMI-AUTOMATIC

■ Unlike the pump action shotgun above, semi-automatic shotguns use the firearm's inertia to automatically retract the bolt, eject the spent shell, and reload a new shell into the chamber. Like the pump action, most semi-automatic shotguns are loaded from below, with rounds stored in the tubular magazine visible beneath the barrel. Other semi-automatic shotguns use a magazine loaded from below, similar to how an AR-15 magazine is inserted.

DOUBLE-BARREL

■ Like they sound, double-barrel shotguns have two barrels. Their configuration is appropriately called over-under (shown above) or side-by-side. Although double-barrel shotguns are limited to just two rounds, they are able to be reloaded quickly by swinging the barrels open which automatically ejects the spent casings, before two new shells can be loaded.

What Does "Gauge" Mean Anyway?

Unlike the unit of measurement used for bullets (caliber), shotgun sizes are measured in gauge. The gauge of a barrel is equal to the number of solid spheres of lead, each having the same diameter as the barrel, that would in total weigh a pound. For example, a solid sphere of lead weighing exactly 1/12th of a pound, would fit perfectly into the barrel of a 12 gauge, and a sphere of lead weighing 1/20th of a pound would fit perfectly into the barrel of a 20 gauge. A .410 shotgun is the exception, which is actually a caliber measurement (the barrel is 41/100ths of an inch in diameter).

12 Gauge

Lead Ball with a Perfect Fit = 1/12th Pound

Shotgun Chokes

A shotgun's choke constricts the end of the barrel to one degree or another, which affects the pattern size (the total area hit by the pellets). The tighter the choke, the tighter the pattern. Other things that can affect the pattern size are the length of barrel, shot size, and the composition of the shot, such as lead, steel, tungsten composites, etc.

The pattern will open up twice the size at twice the distance. For example a pattern of 3 inches at 7 feet, will be 6 inches at 14 feet. For home defense, we'd recommend a modified or improved cylinder choke.

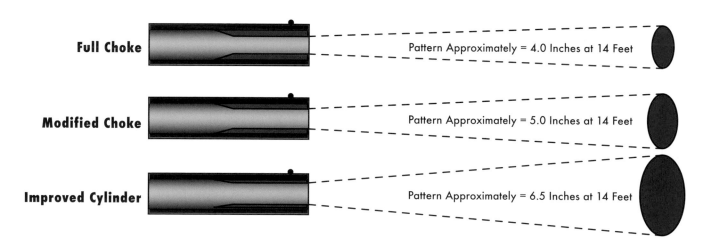

Full Choke — Pattern Approximately = 4.0 Inches at 14 Feet

Modified Choke — Pattern Approximately = 5.0 Inches at 14 Feet

Improved Cylinder — Pattern Approximately = 6.5 Inches at 14 Feet

There's a reason that police officers prefer shotguns when defending themselves in the close quarters of a home. A typical 000 load will contain the near equivalent of six to eight .380 ACP pistol rounds, all delivered in a five to six inch pattern.

Shot Size

Shot size ranges from #12 at .05 inches in diameter through 000 (pronounced "triple-ought") at .36 inches in diameter. For home defense, anything from #6 on up is up for the task, but our choice would be a 00 or 000 low-recoil load, which contains six to eight pellets, just smaller than a .380 ACP, and similar in weight to a .25 to .32ACP (at between 54 and 72 grains).

Lead Shot Size	7 ½	6	5	BB	00	000
Diameter (Inches)	.095	.11	.12	.18	.33	.36
# Per Ounce	350	225	170	50	8	6
Actual Size	●	●	●	●	●	●

Below, we've recommended two low recoil buckshot loads which are appropriate if you have at least two to three layers of drywall between yourself (the defender) and any loved ones or neighbors. Otherwise, we'd recommend backing up to a #4 load or smaller. Steer clear of magnum loads—you're delivering those pellets tens of feet, not hundreds.

ROUND	DESCRIPTION	CHARACTERISTICS
Federal Low-Recoil 000 Buckshot	Contains eight .36 caliber pellets, weighing between 70 and 72 grains apiece.	The low recoil aspect allows a rapid recovery between shots, and with eight .36 caliber pellets, it's the near equivalent of delivering eight .380 ACPs all in one shot.
Hornady TAP-FPD 00 Buckshot	Designed for both pump and semi-autos, it provides very tight patterns with eight .33 caliber pellets.	TAP-FPD (For Personal Defense) buckshot is designed with home defense in mind and provides the tightest pattern on the market.

BB Shot
Contains 50 pellets per ounce of shot.

00 Buckshot
Contains 8 pellets per ounce of shot.

Slug
At one ounce, a typical shotgun slug equates to 437.5 grains, or almost twice the weight of a .45 ACP pistol round.

AR-15 PLATFORM

A favorite punching bag of the anti-gun movement, the semi-automatic AR-15 rifle is often referred to by the popular media as an "assault rifle" or a "machine gun." The AR-15 is neither of those things. While the AR-15 is tailored after the light rifle carried by American soldiers and Marines (the M16), that doesn't mean that the AR-15 is a machine gun (we should also note that the M16 isn't even a machine gun, since it's only capable of firing three-round bursts, rather than full automatic fire). Additionally, the fact that the AR-15 stock is made from black plastic and composite materials, doesn't mean that it's any more powerful than the average hunting rifle with a wooden stock. In fact, the AR-15, chambered in the Remington .223, is considered too *light* a caliber to be legal in many states for deer hunting, with less than half of the kinetic energy as the .30-06 (pronounced "thirty-ought-six"), the most common deer hunting round on the market. The attractiveness of the AR-15 for someone considering a firearm for home defense (or just for plinking), is the same thing that continues to attract the U.S. military to the M16 more than forty years after it was first adopted as its standard light rifle, and that's the rifle's utter reliability; its low recoil and light weight; and its almost unlimited ability to be customized with hundreds of accessories. However, as reliable and ubiquitous as the AR-15 is considered today, it wasn't always that way.

A Short History of the AR-15

The brainchild of Eugene Stoner, chief engineer at the Armalite Division of Fairchild Engine and Airplane Corporation, the AR-15 (AR stands for "Armalite Rifle"), was conceived as a short range, light-weight replacement to the M14 (the U.S. Military's standard battle rifle from 1959 to 1970), after statistics from World War II and the Korean War confirmed that most combat occurred at far less than 100 yards, and that the heavy M14, weighing in at 12.75 pounds and firing the powerful .308 round, could prove unwieldy for the average infantryman. Although the U.S. Army first tested the AR-15 during a set of trials in 1959, it was actually the U.S. Air Force that first adopted the rifle in 1962 with an initial order of 8,500 rifles, designating the new rifle the M16. During their tests, the Air Force found that 43 percent of testers were able to qualify as "experts" with the AR-15, while only 22 percent of testers on the M14 were able to do so. They also found that the AR-15 had a failure rate of just 2.5 rounds per 1,000 rounds fired, compared to the M14, which experienced a failure rate of 16 per 1,000. U.S. Special Forces operating in Vietnam soon followed suit, ordering 85,000 by 1963, with more than 1,000 destined for the South Vietnamese Army. In 1963, Secretary of Defense Robert McNamara suspended production of the M14 rifle, and in 1966, concluded that the AR-15/M16 was to be the new, standard issue rifle for the U.S. Military.

Second Lieutenant Thomas Schweizer, Platoon Commander of the 2nd Platoon, Echo Company, 1st Marine Division, Vietnam, in 1967. Coincidentally, Schweizer's father commanded the same platoon during World War II. While the father would have carried an M1 Garand, the son carried the new M16.

Reliability Problems in Vietnam

While the Air Force trials in 1960 showed a failure rate of just 2.5 per 1,000 rounds fired, a series of small errors led to a much larger failure rate in the harsh conditions of Vietnam. Chief among the errors was the military's failure to provide adequate cleaning kits with the rifles, and a failure to provide adequate training on how to keep the rifles clean. By 1967 that error was corrected, and new rifles began to be shipped with more complete cleaning kits. In a nod to the average age of U.S. Soldiers and Marines in Vietnam, the military even went as far as commissioning Mad Magazine artist Will Eisner to create a comic book, explaining exactly how to properly maintain the M16 rifle in the field.

The Modern AR-15

While the early failures in Vietnam stuck with the AR-15's reputation for the next two decades, today, AR-15s are widely considered to be one of the most reliable platforms on the market. While AR-15s can be bought off-the-shelf fully configured, most aficionados prefer to order the upper, lower, and accessories separately, so that the rifle can be tailored specifically to the purchaser's needs. In that way, the AR-15 is really the "erector set" of firearm platforms, with literally thousands of variations available from the base platforms. If you'd like to take the DIY approach, it's important to know that the AR-15's "lower" (the portion of the firearm containing the trigger control group) is what's actually considered the firearm, so you'll need to make that purchase through a licensed dealer. All other components can be picked up off the shelf to create an AR-15 all your own. Options and accessories for the AR-15 platform include red dot and telescopic sights; mountable lights and laser sights; adjustable or fixed stocks; and forward grips including vertical grips, grips that include a light and/or laser, or versions that rake back at an angle designed to perfectly fit the human hand. Many options and accessories are mounted with nothing more than a screwdriver and a bit of Loctite, while others are designed to easily attach and remove using spring-loaded, knurled screws or using the latest innovation, which is a key or slot-based attachment method which makes attaching or removing dozens of accessories a breeze. Although it's impossible to show you all of the options that are available, on the next two pages we'll introduce you to the basic components and nomenclature of a stripped down AR-15 just waiting for dozens of accessories to be attached, after which we'll introduce you to some of our favorite accessories and manufacturers.

Collapsible Stock

Unlike a fixed stock, collapsible stocks allow the user to tailor the length of stock for their specific height, neck length, etc. Most shooters will collapse the stock much shorter than a stock length they'd use on a traditional hunting rifle—the shorter length allows them to take up more of an isosceles stance (with both shoulders squared to the target), rather than a traditional rifle stance, which would angle the shooting shoulder to the rear.

Folding Rear Sight

This folding rear sight allows the sight to be dropped out of the way when using a red dot scope, yet quickly raised if the battery in the scope fails.

Rail System

Selecting an AR-15 with a "flat top" picatinny rail system, will allow you to mount your optics of choice and/or a folding rear sight.

Magazine Release

Similar in function to a pistol magazine release, pushing this button will drop the magazine, allowing for a rapid reload.

Pistol Grip

Like it sounds, the AR-15 pistol grip allows the shooter to take up a grip reminiscent of shooting a pistol, rather than a traditional rifle grip, which forces the hand back at an odd angle. Like all AR-15 accessories, pistol grips can be purchased in all shapes and sizes, including this example from Magpul, which has a small storage compartment in the bottom.

Magazine

AR-15 magazines are traditionally made from steel, but plastic magazines like this one from Magpul are gaining in popularity. Personally, we're huge Magpul fans.

Expandable Handguard

While the picatinny accessory rail system shown on the opposite page remains the standard for mounting accessories, it's no longer standard practice to utilize a foreend/handguard completely covered in the heavy rail system and instead, it's now common practice to use adaptable handguards using the **M-Lok** or **KeyMod** systems (shown here) which allow small sections of picatinny rail to be added wherever needed, by using key-shaped mounts or slots.

Fixed Rear Sight

This front sight happens to be fixed in place, while other models allow a folding front sight to be added using a section of picatinny rail on the handguard.

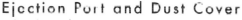

Ejection Port and Dust Cover

When firing the AR-15, empty casings are ejected to the right through the ejection port, aided in part by the "shell deflector," which is the small, pyramid shaped piece just behind the ejection port. When not using the AR-15, the dust cover (which is shown hanging open below the ejection port), can be closed to keep dust and grime from entering the bolt assembly. It isn't necessary to open the dust cover before using the AR-15, that will happen all on its own when the first round is fired.

Flash Suppressor or Compensator

Fixed to the end of the barrel, flash suppressors are intended to reduce the size of the "flash" that can occur as burning propellent leaves the barrel. That flash can be particularly irritating when firing in low light, since it can disrupt your night vision. Compensators look similar to suppressors, although rather than having horizontal channel cuts, they'll typically have angled holes, which will direct the dissipating gases in a direction opposite the rifle's natural muzzle rise.

Magpul CTR™
Designed for light, fast action. The streamlined A-frame profile avoids snagging and shields the release latch to prevent accidental activation.

Magpul MOE™ SL
Uses dual-side release latches and an angled rubber butt-pad which is optimized for use with body armor or modular gear.

Magpul ACS™
Includes duel, rear accessible, water-resistant battery storage tubes and an integral storage compartment in the butt of the stock.

Magpul BAD Lever
With the twist of a hex key, the BAD (Battery Assist Device) attaches to your bolt release, giving you an ability to release the bolt ambidextrously by pressing down on the bottom of the lever with your trigger finger. This allows the shooting and support hands to remain in place.

VLTOR BCM Charging Handle
The latch on an off-the-shelf charging handle is relatively small, requiring the operator to use the index and middle finger on the shooting hand to retract the bolt. The BCM charging handle uses a larger, extended latch, which allows the shooter to leave the shooting hand on the pistol grip, and retract the bolt using the heel of the support hand.

Aimpoint CompM4

Utilizes a single, two minute of angle (MOA) red dot, which will work for both close in and distance shots. The battery is rated to last an amazing 80,000 hours on the daylight setting. Submersible to 150 feet.

Magpul AFG (Angled Fore Grip)

Mounts to the bottom of the hand guard via a picatinny rail or by using the Magpul M-Lok mounting system. Unlike a traditional forward pistol grip, the AFG is ergonomically designed to match the natural angle of the support hand, and places that hand much higher on the centerline of the bore, which reduces recoil and fatigue.

Holosun Micro Optic

Extremely light weight optic, at just over three ounces. Allows user to adjust the size of the dot at 0.5 MOA per click. No need to turn it on, as it automatically activates with a slight movement of the firearm.

EOTech Model 512

Unlike the Aimpoint and Holosun optics which utilize single dots for their reticle pattern, the EOTech reticle is composed of a large outer ring with a diameter of 65 MOA, surrounding a single dot which is one MOA. Fans of the EOTech reticle appreciate the fact that the large outer ring allows for faster target acquisition, while the inner dot allows for precise shots.

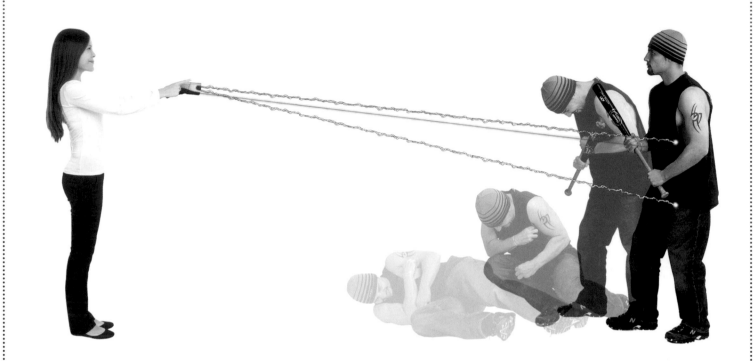

OTHER USE OF FORCE OPTIONS

As part of our personal protection plans, we may want to consider other "use of force" options which have a lesser chance of killing an attacker, and a lesser chance of putting us in legal peril, such Tasers, pepper spray, knives, and impact weapons. When considering these other options, it's important to remember that while a firearm can have a disabling or deterrent effect out to dozens of feet, these other devices will require you to be within 10—15 feet of the attacker for a Taser or pepper spray, and within arm's reach for an edged or impact weapon.

How Do Tasers Work?

More properly called an electronic control device (Taser® is a brand name), these devices are designed to send a high-voltage, low-amperage electrical charge through the body of an attacker. The charge confuses the body's own natural electrical signals, incapacitating the attacker. Consumer models, such as the Taser Bolt, utilize cartridges that when fired, release compressed air to shoot two probes connected to wires in the direction of the attacker (up to 15 feet), which then embed themselves in the attacker's clothes or skin. The device is designed to deliver a 30 second shock, allowing the victim to drop the Taser, and retreat to cover. Detractors have claimed that criminals will use Tasers to incapacitate their victims, however, Taser has developed an innovative device within the Bolt, which showers the ground with 20 to 30 "confetti like" tags, containing an identification number that can be traced by police. Taser also requires that purchasers pass a background check prior to device activation.

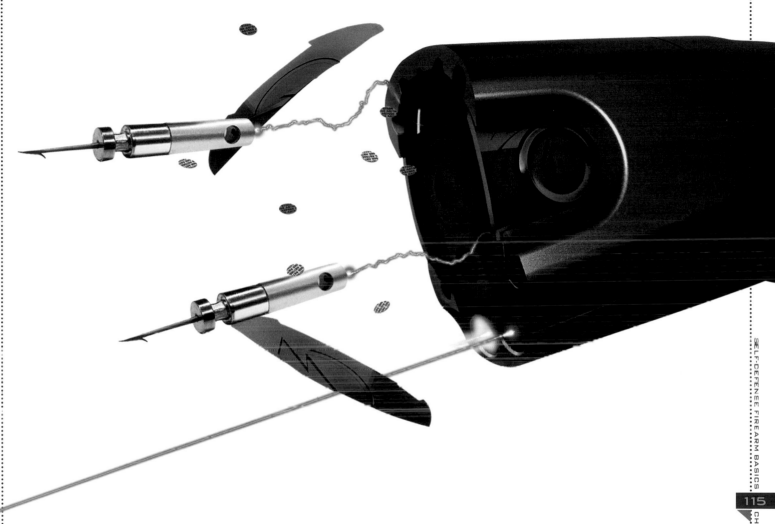

■The Taser Bolt comes in a small package with replaceable cartridges, and a built-in laser and LED light to assist in aiming. If the user misses an attacker with the ejected probes, the device can also be used in a direct contact mode, using built-in contacts on the face of the device. Taser has a lifetime guarantee and will replace the device for free if it is used in a defensive situation. When fired, the Bolt releases compressed air to shoot two probes connected to wires in the direction of the attacker (up to 15 feet), which then embed themselves in the attacker's clothes or skin. The device is designed to deliver a 30-second shock, allowing the victim to drop the Taser, and retreat to cover. To avoid misuse, the Bolt showers the ground with 20 to 30 "confetti like" tags, containing an identification number that can be traced by police.

Pepper Spray

The active ingredient in pepper spray is oleoresin capsicum (OC), a chemical found in cayenne peppers (hence the name "pepper" spray). OC affects mucous membranes like the eyes, nose, throat, and lungs, and causes instant capillary dilation, causing the eyelids to shut. The bronchial tubes may also swell tightly, making it hard for the attacker to breathe. Sprayed into an attacker's face, pepper spray may incapacitate an attacker for as long as 45 minutes. Pepper spray potency can be measured in a variety of ways, including showing the percentage of OC contained in the spray (although this makes no statement about the potency of the OC itself); or "heat" can be measured in Scoville Heat Units (SCU) which is a subjective measurement of the dilution required before no heat is detectable (although some manufacturers will show the SCU of the base OC, while others will show the SCU of the diluted OC); or potency can be expressed in CRCs (Capsaicin and related Capsaicinoids) which measures the actual percentage of heat and pain producing active ingredients. Our advice is to take a look at all three numbers, but use the CRC rating as the final determining factor when picking out a pepper spray that works for you. As a quick litmus test, the U.S. Government requires a CRC rating of at least one-percent for bear deterrent pepper spray.

Think it's not possible to practice with pepper spray? Think again—nearly every manufacturer sells training canisters which contain an inert liquid for use during training exercises. If you train with this method, just be sure to *triple* check that the canister you are using is labeled "Inert, for training use only," otherwise, your training companion will have some choice words for you.

Kimber Pepperblaster

The PepperBlaster from Kimber, stores OC and benzyl alcohol in separate tubes, which are mixed when the trigger is depressed. The PepperBlaster delivers its spray at 90 miles an hour. The Pepperblaster has a CRC rating of 2.4%.

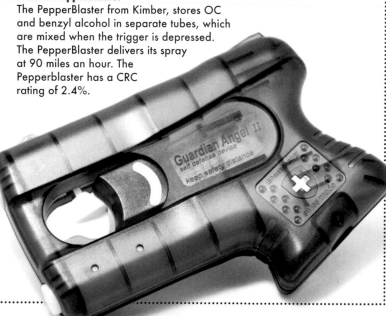

Sabre Inert Training Spray

This practice canister from Sabre is identical to the active canister, which allows the user to build the proper muscle memory for deployment, and, it gives the user the opportunity to see just how far the canister can spray. Just triple-check that the canister is indeed inert, *before* you spray it into the face of a training partner.

USCCA MEMBER
RICK GREEN
CHIEF DEVELOPMENT
OFFICER, RANGE
SYSTEMS, INC.

RANGE SYSTEMS DESIGNS, builds, and ships shoot houses and modular live fire ranges to law enforcement, military, and special forces training groups around the world. Based upon a proprietary, bullet defeating solution based on ballistic rubber, Range Systems provides training solutions to groups as diverse as foreign governments, military, and state and local law enforcement.

EVERYDAY CARRY:
A LARRY YATCH SIGNATURE SERIES GLOCK 22, AND AN EMERSON MINI-CQC 15 TACTICAL KNIFE.

BACKGROUND: I'm an ordinary business guy with a family, not a gun enthusiast who grew up around guns. My first shot fired was in a basic handgun class held by Michael Martin, author of Concealed Carry and Home Defense Fundamentals. Shortly after getting my permit to carry, I joined the USCCA to learn as much as possible about how to become a responsible permit holder, and I found Concealed Carry Magazine much better aligned to the interests of permit holders, rather than the traditional gun magazines. In particular, I enjoy the new gear section as well as Mark Walter's column, and I never miss an episode of Armed American Radio!

CHAPTER 3

SHOOTING FUNDAMENTALS

- Muscle Memory Explained
- Proper Grip
- Stance or "Shooting Platform"
- Point Shooting
- Flash Sight Picture
- Sighted Fire
- Trigger Control

During the defensive firearms courses that we teach, we'll continually differentiate between the skills required for defensive shooting, and the skills required for being a good "marksman" on the range. Unlike relaxed exercises on the range with paper targets at 50 feet, dynamic critical incidents are usually fast, and they're usually close. Nationally known instructor Tom Givens has gathered data confirming that nearly ninety percent fall between 9 and 15 feet. In addition, when we're under the extreme stress of a violent attack, our higher brain will very likely check out, and to one degree or another, automated responses will take over. Because of that, if we have a choice between a complex method of doing things and a simple method, we're going to have to pick simple. If we have a choice between a method that embraces those automated responses or fights them, we need to pick the method that embraces them.

As you'll see in this chapter, we're going to look at these defensive shooting fundamentals as a set of building blocks—if you can master one skill, the next skill becomes easier to accomplish. On the other hand, if we blow one of the skills, it will affect the rest. Mastering these fundamentals won't qualify you for the U.S. Shooting team or win you the Bianchi Cup, but they will provide the proper building blocks to work toward defensive accuracy, which we'll further define in this chapter.

Our goal when practicing these skills should be consistency, which allows us to effectively bake the fundamentals into the neural pathways of our brain (creating what most people would call "muscle memory"), which we'll explain further in this chapter. Whatever skill or task isn't previously hardwired into those pathways, is probably not a task that we'll be able to accomplish during a violent attack. They say that "practice makes perfect," but that's not quite true. Practice makes *permanent*, so for every evolution of these fundamentals that you conduct on the range, take the time to make them, well, perfect. The reality is, you should think of defensive shooting is an athletic endeavor. You will need to learn to establish a consistent grip; learn to stand in a way that is in harmony with how humans fight (and provides a good shooting platform); and learn to press your trigger smoothly. We'll help you to do *all* of those things in this chapter.

We're going to start with what we consider to be the basis of all other shooting fundamentals, namely, taking up a proper shooting grip. This section not only explains why we think a proper grip is so important, it also provides a number of illustrations showing exactly how to get your grip right.

In our section on shooting platforms, we'll introduce you to the shooting stance that was a staple of nearly every police academy for nearly four decades, but we'll go on to explain why most police academies and civilian training courses have moved beyond the Weaver stance, and are now teaching a more natural and neutral shooting platform, designed to match the body's and the mind's automated responses to the extreme stress that will accompany any violent attack.

Our topic on target alignment will discuss the balance of speed versus accuracy, and what our options might be when moving from one end of the scale to the other. Those topics will include using unsighted fire or "point" shooting, using a flash sight picture, and using precise sight alignment, which are the three major options when it comes to aligning our barrel to the target. We'll also discuss when one option might be preferable over the other, but we'll also discuss why the automated responses that we'll very likely experience might just choose the method for us. We'll wrap up this chapter with a topic on trigger control where we'll explain how you can train yourself to press the trigger smoothly and efficiently, without disrupting target alignment.

WHAT EXACTLY IS "MUSCLE MEMORY?"

We've all tossed out the phrase "muscle memory" when talking about learning a repetitive skill, regardless of whether that "skill" is playing golf, playing the piano, or drawing from the holster. Unfortunately, muscles themselves have no "memory," so, where exactly are these repetitive skills being stored? The answer is the cerebellum, which is the brain's memory center. When a certain skill or movement is practiced repeatedly, pathways are actually modified in the cerebellum to store and link individual movements, similar to how individual still frames are stored and linked on a spool of film. The more the skill or movement is repeated, the stronger the pathways linking the individual steps. The result can be near automatic playback of the stored memory of movements. As an example, new students learning to draw from the holster will learn that there are four steps involved, and they'll practice those movements in four distinct steps. But after thousands of repetitions, those four movements will have become fluid, and the "experts" may not even be able to answer the question, "How many steps does it take to draw the handgun from the holster?" To them, the process is fluid and automatic (they might even say, "It takes just one step.") No one knows just how many times a task or series of tasks will need to be repeated before it's ready for "automatic playback," but suffice to say, it's going to be more than plinking at the range a couple times a year. Dry firing, drawing from the holster with a cleared firearm, and virtual simulations are all ways that these pathways can be built, all without a shot being fired.

Making Pathways Permanent

The basic and advanced drills that we'll discuss in Chapter Seven all have one thing in common—they're all fundamentally rooted in the building blocks discussed in this chapter. Regardless of how fast you might draw from the holster, if you haven't mastered trigger control, all you'll end up with is a very fast miss, and that won't impress anyone, especially a bad guy. If you've mastered unsighted fire, but you haven't put in thousands of repetitions disengaging your gun's safety, you might find yourself with an inoperable gun when it counts, because the situation didn't give you time to *think*, it only gave you time to *act*.

When Can you Quit Practicing the Fundamentals?

That begs the question, "When can you quit practicing the fundamentals, and just focus on the advanced stuff?" The short answer is, never. One of our good friends who happens to be a retired Navy SEAL, once took the time to estimate how many rounds he'd fired in his Navy career—his conservative estimate was somewhere above one-and-a-half *million* rounds. Yet if you asked him how he started each range drill to this day, he'd tell you that he always starts with dry firing (explained in Chapter Seven), and a number of basic drills to reinforce the fundamentals, before he moved on to more complex exercises. Regardless of whether his training exercise for the day was rappelling from a helicopter into a fortified compound, or landing a zodiac onto an oil platform, he'd start and end the day with dry firing, and a review of the fundamentals. If that's good enough for the Navy SEALS, it's good enough for us.

Whether you're learning to draw from the holster or learning the Macarena (you know who you are), repetition of any task begins to build new pathways into the cerebellum, connecting individual movements into a continuous series of movements for near automatic "playback." Similar to how a film projector can take individual still frames and make them appear as though they flow together into continuous movement, the cerebellum can do the same thing with these repetitive tasks. The key here is that you'll need to practice them until they become repetitive.

PROPER GRIP

Although all of the shooting fundamentals we'll cover in this chapter are important, we're going to start with what we consider to be the fundamental of all shooting fundamentals, namely, learning how to take up a proper grip when using a handgun. If you've never had formal handgun instruction, it may sound a little basic to discuss the proper way to "grip" a handgun—in other words, don't you just pick it up, point it down range, and start pressing the trigger? Well, in a way, it isn't any more complicated than that, but before stepping into *how* to take up a proper grip, it's probably a fair place to start by talking about what the *goal* of a proper grip is. If your answer is to hold the handgun, you'd only be half correct.

When setting up your grip, the pistol should be placed firmly into your firing hand like you are making a fist, with the web of your hand high and centered on the back strap. The firing hand thumb should be high, to create a space for the support hand.

The trigger finger is OUTSIDE THE TRIGGER GUARD and is pressed on the frame or slide, and the middle finger is bumped up against the bottom of the trigger guard.

The ultimate goal of a proper grip is creating and maintaining *control* of your handgun during the firing cycle. Other instructors might take issue with our choice of grip as the most important fundamental over other shooting fundamentals. That's a debate we recently had with a fellow instructor, who argued that precise trigger control had to be more important than grip. To demonstrate this, he had a number of us stand on the firing line and fire one round at a target at 50 feet while daintily holding our pistol with our thumb and middle finger, and slowly pressing the trigger, all while maintaining perfect sight alignment. Of course, most of us hit fairly close to our point of aim. His point was that if you could make an accurate shot at that distance with almost no grip pressure at all, then

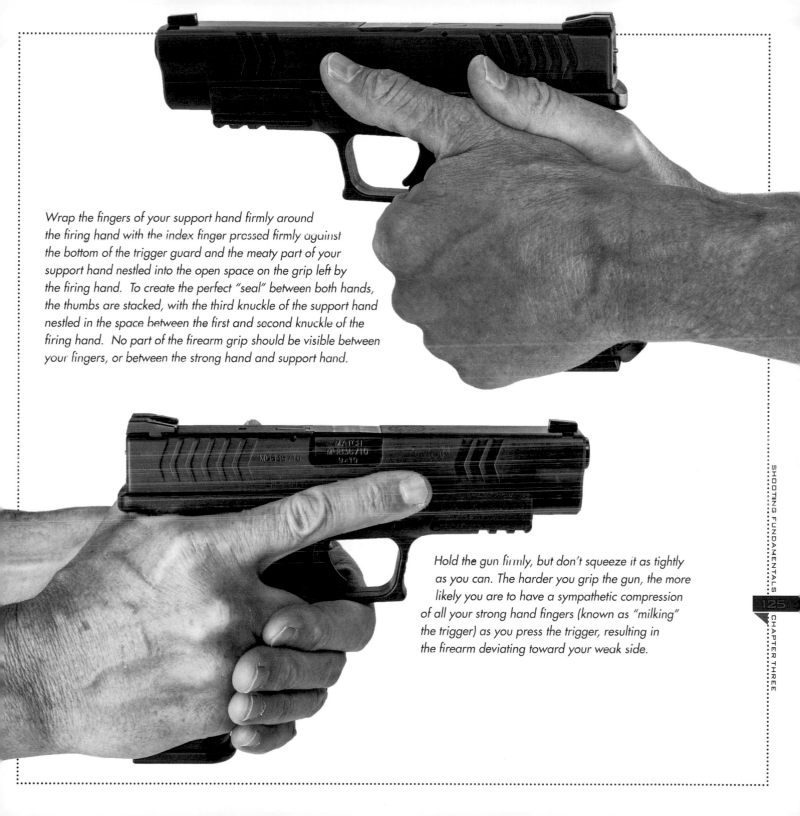

Wrap the fingers of your support hand firmly around the firing hand with the index finger pressed firmly against the bottom of the trigger guard and the meaty part of your support hand nestled into the open space on the grip left by the firing hand. To create the perfect "seal" between both hands, the thumbs are stacked, with the third knuckle of the support hand nestled in the space between the first and second knuckle of the firing hand. No part of the firearm grip should be visible between your fingers, or between the strong hand and support hand.

Hold the gun firmly, but don't squeeze it as tightly as you can. The harder you grip the gun, the more likely you are to have a sympathetic compression of all your strong hand fingers (known as "milking" the trigger) as you press the trigger, resulting in the firearm deviating toward your weak side.

trigger control *must* be more important than grip. While it was a cute trick to show at the range, taking four or five seconds to fire one round at a stationary target 50 feet away, had about as much to do with an actual critical incident as Wii Sports Resort has to do with competing in the Ironman Triathlon. Here's why. Unlike relaxed exercises at the range, critical incidents are usually *fast*, they're usually *close* (with nearly ninety percent falling between 9—15 feet), and when rounds are fired, *multiple* rounds are usually fired—in other words, the mythical one shot stop was usually just that, a myth. So much for one round fired at 50 feet having any meaning. If multiple rounds might be necessary to stop a bad guy from stabbing you, beating you, choking you, or raping you, then it stands to reason that the faster you can put those rounds on target, the sooner the stabbing, beating, choking, or raping will stop. Two things are going to affect your ability to deliver rounds quickly—first, how quickly you can bring your firearm back on target after the muzzle flips during recoil; and second, how quickly you can cycle the trigger.

As seen from above, the tip of the trigger finger, when placed on the slide, should be directly across from the tip of the thumb on the support hand. Most new shooters will find their support thumb being much farther back than the tip of the tip of the trigger finger— this is corrected by rotating the support hand farther forward, resulting in what's referred to as a "thumbs forward" grip.

That theory also finds its way into competitive shooting. While comparing choreographed competition to an actual critical incident can only go so far, this comparison might be worth it. When asked how they're able to deliver so many rounds on target so quickly, many competitors will explain that a good solid grip and full arm extension allows them to press the trigger as fast as they are physically able, in fact, they'll often refer to that technique as "mashing" the trigger (which is not exactly the kind of trigger control that our colleague had in mind). If we bring that theory back to how it might apply to surviving a critical incident, a solid grip means more rounds on target in a shorter amount of time. Any sloppiness in your grip means a lack of control during recoil, a higher muzzle flip, and slower follow-up shots. Think about it this way. Instead of the range exercise that our colleague used in an attempt to prove that trigger control was more important than grip, let's try a new exercise, but this one with a different set of rules. Instead of firing one round at a target 50 feet away, let's place the target at 12 feet (right in the heart of where most defensive shootings occur), and fire as many rounds as we can into the target's center of mass in three seconds. Using our colleague's technique, you'd be lucky to place more than one round on target, as you fought to bring the handgun back under control after the first round was fired. On the other hand, if you fired using a good solid grip and your arms at full extension (both techniques combining to manage your firearm's recoil as much as possible), you'd be able to press the trigger as fast as humanly possible, and accurately deliver, well, a lot of rounds in that same three seconds.

So if we agree that the primary purpose of a solid grip is to create and maintain control of the firearm during the firing cycle (thereby allowing the most rapid follow-up shots), then it's going to be important to have as much physical contact between your hands and the firearm as possible, and to do that consistently, as outlined in our step-by-step illustrations.

SHOOTING STANCE

In the classroom or on the range, the term "shooting stance" usually implies a specific position for the arms, the head, the upper body, the legs, and the feet. When it comes to the "perfect" stance, instructors can argue for hours about the optimal angle of the shoulders to the target (if any), how far apart the feet should be, and whether the arms should be flexed a little, flexed a lot, or not flexed at all. While you might have the luxury of perfecting each of those body positions when standing on the firing line at your local range, under the extreme stress of a violent attack, you're not going to have the time or the luxury. In fact, we'll often mention in our classes that the only "perfect" shooting stance occurs at the range, and that during a dynamic critical incident, you'll have to be prepared to shoot from whatever awkward position you find yourself in, which might include being seated, rapidly retreating, or lying flat on your back. In addition, there is now ample evidence from a decade of police dash cam videos that suggest that the "automated responses" that occur during violent attacks, will have more of an effect on our body position, than will dozens or even hundreds of hours spent on the range. While it's often said, "we'll fight the way we've trained," those dash cam videos suggest that we should, "train the way we'll fight." So let's talk about those automated responses, which originate within an almond sized structure in the brain called the amygdala.

Jack Weaver

The Weaver stance was developed by L.A. Deputy Sheriff Jack Weaver, in an effort to win Jeff Cooper's "Leatherslap" competition in Big Bear, California in 1959. At that time, the typical competitive shooter shot from the hip or one-handed from the shoulder, and according to Jack, "What started out as serious business soon produced gales of laughter from the spectators as most of the shooters blazed away..." and "with guns empty and all 12 rounds gone but the 18-inch balloons still standing, they had a problem: load one round and take aim or load six and blaze away again." By the time the 1959 Leatherslap rolled around, Jack had realized that "A pretty quick hit was better than a lightning-fast miss," and decided to bring the pistol up using both hands and use the pistol's sights, rather than just shooting from the hip. Jeff Cooper commented, "Jack walloped us all, decisively. He was very quick and he did not miss."

The Weaver stance was a staple for nearly four decades at police academies across the world, and takes up a "bladed" body position, with the strong side foot placed to the rear and the body bladed at approximately 45 degrees to the target. The arms create solid isometric pressure with the strong arm slightly flexed and pushing forward, and the support arm elbow down, and pulling back. The theory behind the Weaver stance was that the isometric pressure between the two arms helps to manage recoil, and the arm position places the firearm in a location which allows the shooter to easily focus on the front sight. If your shooting requirements were limited strictly to marksmanship at the range, those theories would be meaningful. The problem is, dozens of dash cam videos have proven that regardless of how often police officers had trained on the Weaver, the body's and the mind's natural reaction to face the attacker head on with the arms at full extension took over during dynamic critical incidents. That evidence was enough to cause most police academies (and most civilian schools) to gravitate toward a more natural and neutral shooting platform, which we'll discuss next.

As we'll explain in Chapter Five, the amygdala contains most of the brain's alarm circuits designed to react to any imminent threat, which would include a violent attack. When its alarm circuits are tripped, the amygdala has a direct connection to the motor cortex (that is, it skips the reasoning and planning part of the brain) in order to take immediate action, such as: freezing our legs if we were about to step in front of a speeding bus; raising our hands to protect our head from a flying rock; or ducking into a crouch, orienting toward a threat, and pushing the arms out to full extension to defend against the threat. It's that last automated response that has been recorded time and time again on dash cam videos during police shootings, and it's the stance that we're going to focus on when it comes to discussing two stances that closely match that automated response.

ISOSCELES STANCE

The Isosceles (which gets its name from the perfect triangle formed by the squared shoulders and straight arms) squares the body to the target, with both arms at full extension, pointed directly at the target. The stance is designed to match the body's and mind's natural reaction to face an attacker head on and to push the

■ Taking up the Isosceles stance is simple, and only requires that the body be squared to the target, with the arms pushed out to full extension. The arms and shoulders will form a perfect isosceles triangle.

arms out defensively, which allows shooters to "train the way they'll fight." In addition, since both arms are at full extension, recoil and follow-through are easily managed—shooters will find the firearm dropping back on target immediately after the muzzle rise. Since the arms point at the target using the Isosceles, it also provides a simple, repeatable method of using unsighted fire in a stress situation. You'll notice that we didn't refer to any specific position for the legs and feet—in a perfect situation, the feet would be firmly positioned under the body, but the Isosceles doesn't require that, in fact, the only real focus on the Isosceles is to face the target, and push the arms out to full extension (or as far as possible) which creates a natural, straight line from the shoulder to the fingertip. We're born with the ability to point that straight line with a high degree of accuracy, especially when we're talking about the distances of most self-defense shootings, with nearly ninety percent falling between 9—15 feet. Stepping back to the original theory behind the Weaver stance, it was believed that the Weaver allowed the shooter to position the firearm for easier acquisition of the firearm's sights, leading to more accurate fire. That's a great argument if you're trying to make a silver dollar sized hole at 50 feet, but it's less meaningful if you're trying to hit an attacker a dozen feet away (or one who's already on top of you), when speed will typically be critical, and trying to align your front sight, rear sight, and the attacker will be the last thing on your mind.

NATURAL AND NEUTRAL

The "Natural and Neutral" stance could be considered a more aggressive version of the Isosceles. Like the Isosceles, this stance positions the feet, shoulders and hips squared to the target, but the Natural and Neutral stance flexes the upper body forward at the waist, placing the shoulders above the knees or toes (not the hips); and the body's center of gravity is lowered, with the knees bent. This stance offers a great combination of being athletically neutral; it provides good support for recoil management and the presentation and retention of the firearm; and it works well with what the body will do naturally during a critical incident.

In training, a great way to get into this stance is to make a quick lateral movement. From a defensive standpoint, it makes practical sense to get off the line of attack, and moving laterally will automatically lower your center of gravity. This lateral movement should be quick, and take no longer than the time it takes to present your firearm on target, from either the high-compressed ready position (explained next) or from the holster. The movement itself should be about one body width. During an actual critical incident, the distance and direction of your movement will be based upon the environment and circumstances you find yourself in. For example, if you are standing next to the corner of a brick building that will provide cover, you'd want to move in that direction as opposed to the opposite direction which would leave you more vulnerable to the attacker. During your training (on a range that allows movement), you should get used to moving during the presentation of your firearm from the holster or ready position, and then plant your feet as you reach a shooting position. Since it's impossible to predict the exact position you'll be standing in (or if you'll be standing at all) during a critical incident, it's important to vary the direction you move and the position of your feet during training.

The **Natural and Neutral** stance matches the body's and mind's natural reaction to take up a low crouch, face the attacker head on, with the arms at full extension.

Shoulders and Hips
Shoulders and hips are squared to the target.

Arms
Both arms are at full extension, forming a perfect isosceles triangle.

Flexed at the Waist
The upper body is flexed forward at the waist, placing the shoulders above the knees or toes (not the hips).

Knees Bent
The body's center of gravity is lowered, with the knees bent.

Feet
Feet are shoulder-width apart and are squared to the target.

READY POSITIONS

As we'll discuss in Chapter Five, just because you've drawn your gun from the holster, does *not* mean that you need to press the trigger, or even point it at your potential attacker, unless you have no other choice. The two "ready" or "safe" positions shown here and on the opposite page, including the *Low Ready*, and the *High-Compressed Ready*, are designed for a variety of situations where it is appropriate to have the firearm out of the holster, but where it is not yet appropriate to take up a shooting stance, or to reholster. Regardless of the position, the trigger finger should remain outside of the trigger guard. From either of these ready positions, you can quickly transition to a shooting stance, or you can reholster if the threat has passed.

Low Ready Position

The low ready position squares the body to the target, with the firearm in a proper grip (and the finger outside the trigger guard) pointed to the ground. This position allows the defender to evaluate the situation while maintaining tight control over his firearm, and allows him to rapidly bring the firearm into action if required.

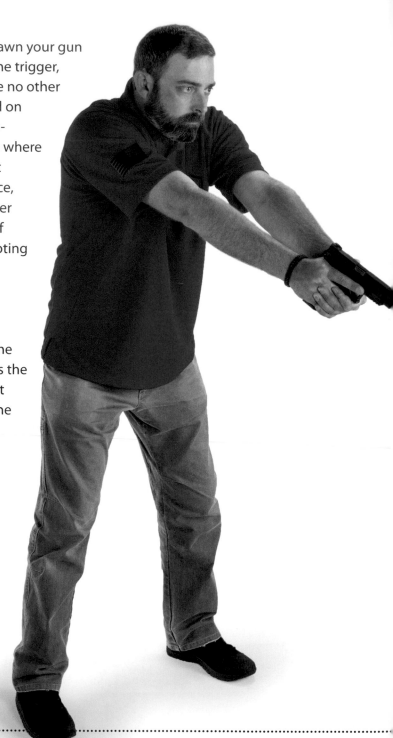

High-Compressed Ready Position

The high compressed ready position is a stance that brings the gun in close to the chest, with the muzzle oriented below the line of sight, elbows tucked at the shooter's side and the shoulders, with the hips and feet oriented towards the front. From this position, the shooter can easily reload, clear a malfunction, assess his or her environment, present the weapon toward the threat, protect the weapon from being grabbed and move it into an extreme close quarters shooting position.

Firearm Close to the Chest

This means very specifically the chest, not the belly. This is the "high" part of the high compressed ready. By keeping the gun up high in front of the body, you maintain more strength (arms bent, rather than extended) and control (it is harder for someone to reach the gun when it is tucked against the chest). It is also easier to present the gun consistently and efficiently if the gun is held high in front of the body. Keeping the gun close to your chest also keeps it out of your field of vision, allowing you to assess the environment around you.

Muzzle Down

Orienting the muzzle in a downward direction when using the high compressed ready position isn't just a safety issue, this orientation provides a number of other benefits including: The firearm will be in an appropriate position for reloading, malfunction clearance or other manipulation of the firearm; the firearm will be in a tighter retention position in the event that an attacker attempts to grab the muzzle; and it also matches the orientation that will occur when presenting the firearm on target from the holster.

Elbows In

By keeping your elbows tucked into your side, you create more of a barrier from an attempt to grab your gun from outside of your field of vision. Remember that your field of vision will be diminished during a critical incident, so having a physical barrier to someone grabbing your gun can help counteract your decrease in peripheral visual acuity. With your elbows in this position, you are also able to extend the gun out into a shooting position.

Oriented Toward the Front

By keeping your body (and field of vision) squared to the front, you will be able to respond to any threat that you've identified in an efficient manner, rather than reorienting your body toward a threat as you'd be required to do if you had taken up a bladed body position, such as the Weaver stance.

TARGET ALIGNMENT

On a typical day at the range or in the field, we'll usually measure the effectiveness of the shots that we've fired based upon their accuracy, rather than on how quickly we were able to get off the shot (missing fast when you were hoping to get that trophy buck won't impress anyone, including the buck). In a defensive situation however, we won't have the luxury of taking an unlimited amount of time to get the "perfect" shot, instead, we'll need to balance the *two* factors of speed and accuracy. Those two factors will constantly be in balance, and we'll need to make a split second decision on which factor is *most* important for the specific circumstances we find ourselves in. For example, if we're trying to hit an active shooter in the middle of a crowded mall, *accuracy* will be ultra critical; but if a knife wielding attacker is already stabbing us, then *speed* will be critical, and a margin of error of ten or even fifteen degrees will still mean a hit. Your decision on speed versus accuracy will not only affect the outcome of the situation, it will also affect how you choose to align your muzzle to the target. Three primary methods are used for target alignment—using unsighted fire, (also referred to as kinesthetically aligned shooting, which prioritizes speed over accuracy); using a flash sight picture (which provides an equal balance of speed and accuracy); or using sighted fire (which prioritizes accuracy over speed). You shouldn't necessarily think of each of these methods as being absolutely distinct, instead, you can think of them as being on a sliding scale. On one end is unsighted fire (which is not the same thing as un-aimed fire), which literally ignores the sights and gets the firearm up on target as quickly as possible, and at the other end is sighted fire, which requires us to focus on the front sight, and precisely align the front sight, rear sight, and target, for as accurate a shot as possible. Everything in-between, including a flash sight picture, is a combination of the two to one degree or another. Here's the catch—during a violent attack, the brain's automated "fight or flight" responses (which we'll discuss in more detail in Chapter Five), might just limit how far we can move toward the accuracy end of the scale, since one of those automated responses will most likely include the motor cortex locking our head and eyes on what the *brain* perceives as the most critical part of the attack. Evolutionarily speaking, that might have meant the teeth of an attacking wolf; today, that might mean the knife or gun in the hand of the attacker. The net effect means that it may be difficult, or even impossible, to see our firearm's sights, eliminating sighted fire as an option. That's actually okay—unlike a scored competition on the range, the goal of defensive shots isn't to place rounds into a dime-sized hole. Instead, our goal is what's referred to as **defensive accuracy**. Defensive accuracy can be thought of as *any round that significantly affects the attacker's ability to continue his attack.* Defensive accuracy doesn't mean that we need to place our shots in the same dime-sized hole that we might go for when we're trying to impress our friends at the range, but it also means that we can't simply "spray and pray," with no regard for where our shots land. The great news is that even when using unsighted fire, our accuracy can still be amazingly impressive at the close distances (with nearly ninety percent falling between 9—15 feet) that would typically accompany a violent attack. Working up the scale from speed to accuracy, let's take a look at each of the three methods of target alignment one at a time.

Unsighted Fire
Violent attacks will be *fast*, and they'll be *close*. Your motor cortex will very likely lock your eyes and your focus onto the weapon in the attacker's hands.

Sighted Fire
Forcing your eyes to change focus from a six foot tall attacker to a three millimeter wide front sight, *may simply not be possible.*

UNSIGHTED FIRE

When using unsighted fire, we're not discarding the idea of alignment, and instead, we're simply using another set of references to align our muzzle to the target, rather than using the firearm's sights. The fact is, the human body is *designed* to point. With the arm, hand and finger at full extension, the body has a natural, straight line from the shoulder to the fingertip, and we're born with the ability to point that straight line with a high degree of accuracy. With practice, you can become familiar with how your firearm feels in your hand when the firearm's muzzle is following that same straight line, rather than being too high or too low, or turned to the left or right. That knowledge of hand and body position is referred to as *kinesthetics*, and is a key factor in accurate unsighted fire, more accurately referred to as *kinesthetically aligned shooting*. When using this method, our advice is to focus on the *exact spot* where you want your rounds to land, rather than focusing on the entire target. Just like pointing your finger at a spot on the wall is more specific than pointing at the entire wall, focusing on a spot on

The shot groupings to the right will be achieved even with a three-degree margin of error from center. ▶

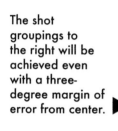

15 Feet
Shot grouping
9.3 inches across

10 Feet
Shot grouping
6.2 inches across

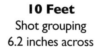

5 Feet
Shot grouping
3.1 inches across

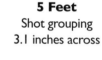

What's Arc of Movement?

Watch any movie where a laser sight is being used and the red dot doesn't waver a millimeter once it's on target. If you're the Terminator it might work that way, but in real life it doesn't. The body's natural movement, including heartbeat and breathing, and the effects of adrenaline on your muscles, will limit your ability to hold your firearm perfectly on target and a small amount of waver is expected. That's actually okay—at close distances (15 feet or less) a small amount of waver still allows accurate unsighted fire. In the calculated groupings on the opposite page, we're showing an arc of movement of three degrees, which equates to your muzzle wavering by an inch and a half in any direction, which is exactly the size of a silver dollar. Double the waver and you'll double the margin of error.

the target will enable more accurate unsighted fire. Speaking of accuracy, the average person's margin of error with unsighted fire will deviate by only a few degrees from his or her natural point of aim, allowing for tight shot groups at 10 to 15 feet, and even tighter groups at closer distances. Finally, think about point shooting in the same way you "shoot" a squirt gun—you don't use the squirt gun's sights and yet, more often than not, you can hit your "target" center of mass.

Whether we're pointing a finger, pointing a dart gun, or pointing a firearm, the human body is designed to point. With the arm, hand and finger at full extension, the body has a natural, straight line from the shoulder to the fingertip, and we're born with the ability to point that straight line with a high degree of accuracy. When pointing a firearm, we should train to elevate the firearm up into our line of sight (regardless of our method of target alignment), which allows even more accurate pointing than if the firearm is below our line of sight. When using unsighted fire, the firearm's sights will be out of focus, but should be visible on our target's center of mass. Transitioning between unsighted fire and sighted fire (when our brain allows us) is then a matter of changing our focus from the target to the front sight.

TARGET FOCUS

When using unsighted fire (aligning your firearm to the target kinesthetically), you should focus on the target with both eyes open. Although you won't be using your firearm's sights as a primary visual reference, you may still see the sights overlaying the target, although they will be blurry and out of focus. As mentioned earlier, when using unsighted fire, it's important to look at the *exact spot* where you want the round to impact.

Unsighted Fire Visual Reference
Although you're not depending upon your firearm's sights to gain proper alignment on your target when using unsighted fire, your firearm's sights will be in your line of sight, and you'll see a blurry overlay of the sights on the target, while you focus on the target, with both eyes open.

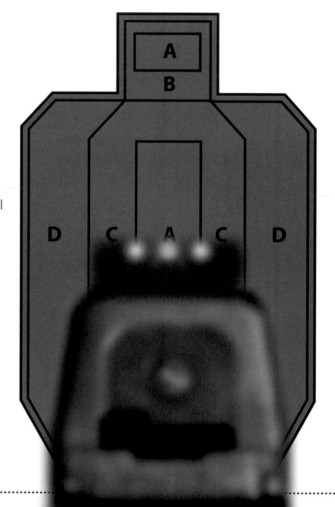

FRONT SIGHT FOCUS

When the situation you find yourself in pushes the requirements away from speed and toward accuracy, sighted fire will be necessary. When using sighted fire, three indexes must be aligned—the front sight, the rear sight, and the target, while focusing on the front sight. When focused on the front sight, it will be in complete focus, the rear sight will be semi-blurred, and the target will be the blurriest thing in your sight picture. The ability to shift from unsighted fire to sighted fire, and the knowledge of when one method should be used over another for a specific shooting problem, will come through consistent practice, and a varied training regimen, which we'll address in Chapter Seven.

Sighted Fire Visual Reference
When the requirements for precision require that you must use sighted fire, it's important to focus on the front sight rather than the target for the most precise shot. The front sight will be in complete focus, the rear sight will be semi-blurred, and the target will be the blurriest thing in your sight picture. Depending upon your eye dominance, it may be necessary to close one eye to obtain this perfect sight picture.

When targets are up close (9—15 feet), misaligned sights are more forgiving, but as your target pushes out beyond typical attack distances, even an alignment error of 1/16 of an inch will translate to more than 12-inches of error at 50 feet. Double the error in sight alignment (or double the distance), and you'll double the error on target.

Sighted Fire: Sight Alignment
Equal amounts of spacing should be visible on the left and right of the front sight.

Sights must be in a perfect horizontal line.

At 10—15 feet, these misaligned sights can still mean a hit, but an alignment error as small as 1/16 of an inch will translate to more than 12-inches of error at 50 feet.

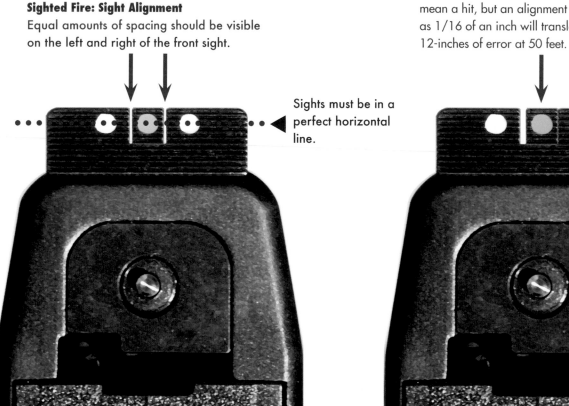

TRIGGER CONTROL

In the topic on proper grip, we pointed out that since dynamic critical incidents are usually fast, they're usually close, and when rounds are fired, multiple rounds are usually fired, that it stands to reason that the more rapidly and accurately we place rounds on target, the faster the violent attack will end. If a proper grip and full arm extension solves half of that equation, then the second half of the equation is solved by a smooth and efficient trigger cycle.

You'll notice we said trigger "cycle" rather than trigger "press." That's because in order to deliver multiple rounds quickly, you'll not only need to efficiently press the trigger to the rear, you will also need to efficiently and smoothly release the trigger to its reset point, before once again firing the gun.

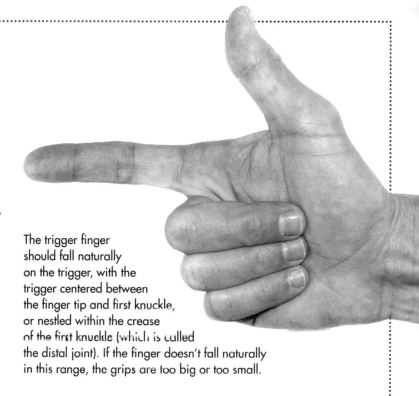

The trigger finger should fall naturally on the trigger, with the trigger centered between the finger tip and first knuckle, or nestled within the crease of the first knuckle (which is called the distal joint). If the finger doesn't fall naturally in this range, the grips are too big or too small.

This Ain't Camp Tomahawk

Back in Boy Scouts, we were taught that for accurate shooting (from the prone position, with sandbag support), we should breathe in, let it part way out, hold it, and then slowly *squeeeeze* the trigger in order to avoid anticipating the recoil. While that worked at Camp Tomahawk, it's not going to work in the chaos of a violent attack with adrenaline screaming through your body, and an attacker just seconds from reaching you, or already upon you. In the time it would take you to "breathe in and let it part way out..," the fight might be over, yet many training organizations continue to teach the same type of trigger cycle for their defensive handgun courses as they do for their basic firearms familiarization courses or their hunter safety courses, and that's a mistake. New shooters (especially new hunters) are often taught that the trigger should be

Wherever the trigger is placed, the finger must be pressed STRAIGHT to the rear so that the muzzle alignment is not disturbed.

sqeeeezed, and that the shooter should be "surprised" when the gun fires in order to avoid anticipating the recoil. While that might work from a prone position with sandbag support, it's bad advice for defensive shooting, most importantly, because an attacker can cover 10 feet or more for every second that you take to slowly squeeze the trigger. Secondly, trying to avoid anticipating the recoil causes you to, well, anticipate the recoil.

Trigger Break Point

Where many students get tripped up in learning a smooth trigger cycle is because they haven't built their firearm's break point or reset point into their "muscle memory" (actually, the neural pathways in the cerebellum). Without knowing exactly where the break point is (the point at which the gun will fire) shooters might begin their trigger press smoothly, and then "jerk" the trigger in the final stages of the trigger press. In other words, the shooter is guessing where the break point is, rather than knowing where it is, which can cause the shot to pull in the direction of the shooting hand.

To avoid the trigger "jerk" problem, we recommend including the "Ten-to-the-One" drill (as explained in Chapter Seven) in your training regimen. The "Ten-to-the-One" drill is designed to force an intense concentration on learning exactly where a pistol's break point is, and to keep the trigger press nice and smooth from the trigger's rest position to the break point where the pistol will fire, without jerking the trigger. When conducting this exercise, students begin to realize that when they maintain a solid grip and flexed wrists and arms (as explained in the sections on grip and stance), the trigger finger can be pressed smoothly, but

deliberately to the rear, without affecting the alignment on the target. That is, nothing will move accept for the trigger finger.

Trigger Reset

Without knowing exactly where the trigger's reset point is (the point at which the trigger will reset, and may once again be pressed to the rear), shooters will typically allow the trigger finger to travel much too far forward (sometimes even off of the trigger itself), resulting in slower follow-on shots, and a tendency to "slap" the trigger on subsequent rounds, disrupting target alignment.

The reset point of a trigger is easily identifiable by a tactile and audible "click" as the trigger is traveling forward. At that reset point, the trigger can once again be pressed to the rear, instead of allowing it to travel all of the way forward. You'll find dramatic differences in how far forward the trigger must travel before it resets when comparing different types of firearm actions, so you'll need to learn the reset point for your particular carry gun of choice. While practicing trigger reset should definitely be part of your dry firing exercises, we've found that one of the most effective ways of demonstrating when a proper trigger reset is not being performed, is to have an assistant videotape you during a range exercise. Most shooters are surprised to find out that not only are they allowing the trigger to travel all the way forward, in many cases, the trigger finger may be traveling so far forward that it literally comes completely off the trigger, even bumping up against the trigger guard itself.

When cycling the trigger, the most important things to remember are:
Smoothly press the trigger through the break point without
staging the trigger, and keep your finger on the trigger
while it resets, making sure that the trigger moves forward
past the reset point so that it can be pressed again.

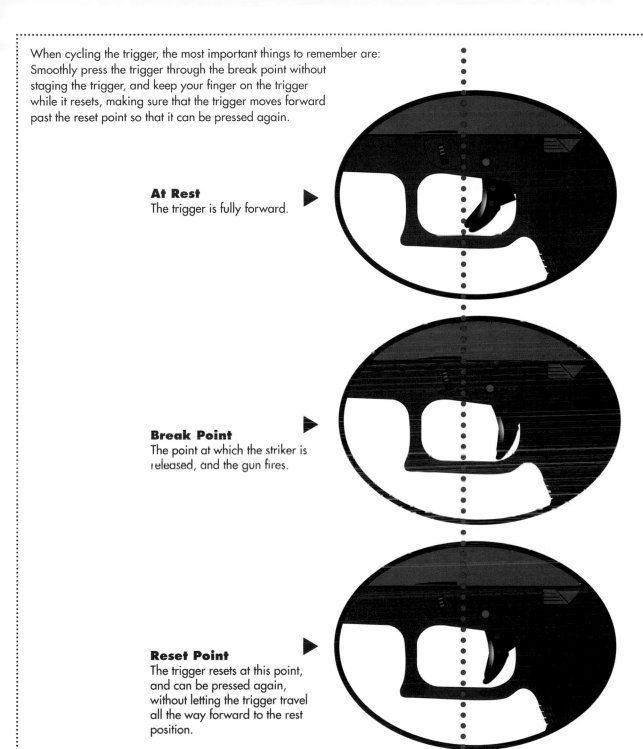

At Rest
The trigger is fully forward. ▶

Break Point
The point at which the striker is
released, and the gun fires. ▶

Reset Point
The trigger resets at this point,
and can be pressed again,
without letting the trigger travel
all the way forward to the rest
position. ▶

That's inefficient, and doesn't meet the goal of quickly delivering rounds on target. To avoid that problem, we recommend the "Push your Limit" drill (also explained in Chapter Seven), designed to not only build the neural pathways for knowing exactly where your trigger's break point is, but to also build the pathways for knowing where your trigger's reset point is, and to bring the two parts of the process together in an ever accelerating series of stages. The exercise is broken into three stages, with the first string of fire allowing the shooter to concentrate on the trigger's break point and reset point separately. The second string of fire will force the shooter to bring the two parts of the process together, and the third string of fire forces the shooter to push the trigger cycle time to the limits of his or her ability.

THE "RUBBER BAND" EXERCISE

While the "Ten-to-the-One" and "Push your Limit" drills require live firearms and ammunition, this last exercise can actually be done while sitting in front of your TV set at home. Like the "Push your Limit" drill, the "Rubber Band Exercise" is designed to build up muscle memory for a full trigger cycle from start to finish. Since a rubber band offers smooth resistance with no increase or decrease in resistance, it affords a simple method to practice your trigger cycle over and over again, while concentrating on a smooth trigger finger movement. Our suggestion is to start this exercise by performing each trigger "cycle" by counting "one-one-thousand, two-one-thousand," etc., which will require a "cycle" approximately every second. You can then pick up the speed with a count of, "one and two and three and four and five." This will require a trigger "cycle" approximately every half-second. When doing this exercise, you should release your finger at the same speed and smoothness as you use to press it to the rear.

The setup for the "Rubber Band Exercise" is simple–it's the same setup you'd use when shooting a rubber band across the room. In this case however, you'll simply flex your trigger finger from a starting point of 90-degrees, and end with it at approximately 60-degrees. Concentrating on a smooth, even "trigger cycle," will build those neural pathways, and will translate to the range and dynamic critical incidents.

USCCA MEMBER
HANNAH LEEPER
COLLEGE STUDENT, HUNTER,
HOME DEFENDER

■ AT JUST NINETEEN YEARS OLD, Hannah Leeper is two years shy of the legal age to obtain a permit to carry a firearm in Minnesota, but that doesn't stop her from training frequently with a variety of handguns, her shotgun, or one of the family AR-15s. Hannah is also an accomplished hunter, and is attending college with plans to get a degree in Forestry and Wildlife from Bemidji State University in northern Minnesota.

EVERYDAY HOME DEFENSE:
REMINGTON 870 EXPRESS 20-GAUGE SHOTGUN.

■ BACKGROUND: Even though I'm not old enough for my permit to carry, having grown up in a gun family, it's a normal step when we turn 21. My dad is a permit to carry instructor, and we all grew up shooting at the family farm, including target shooting, trap shooting, and deer hunting. I come from a big family with almost 30 cousins, and all of us got into the hunting and shooting sports at a pretty young age. We're lucky enough to have a couple hundred acres of land in the family just south of Osceola Wisconsin, so we have plenty of space to shoot. Other girls my age might read Glamour, but I read Concealed Carry Magazine. Knowing the hottest shoes of the season won't do me any good, but the great information in Concealed Carry Magazine, might just save my life.

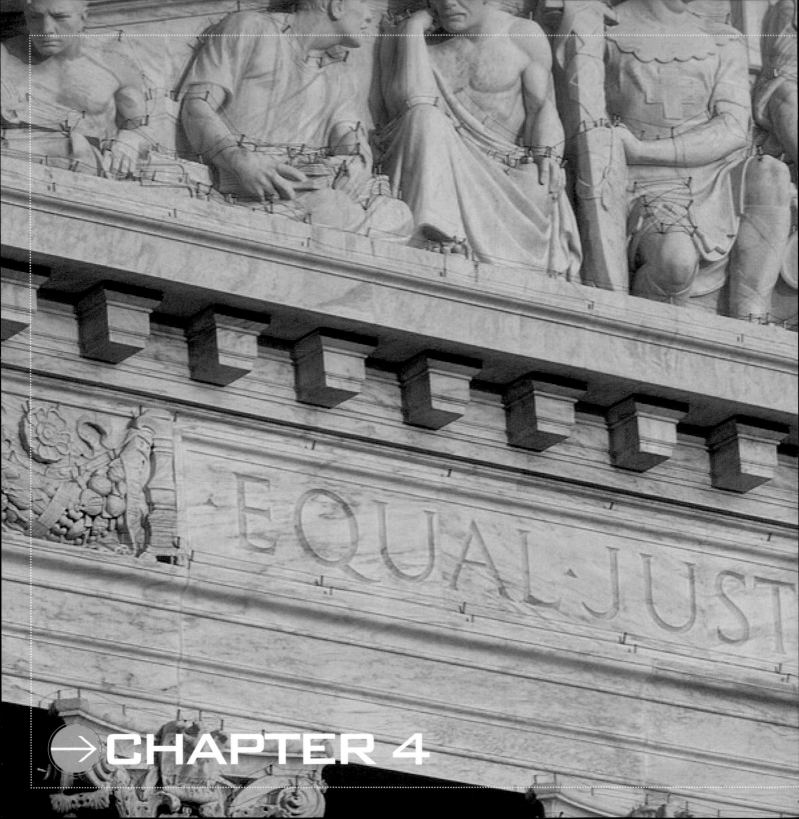

→CHAPTER 4

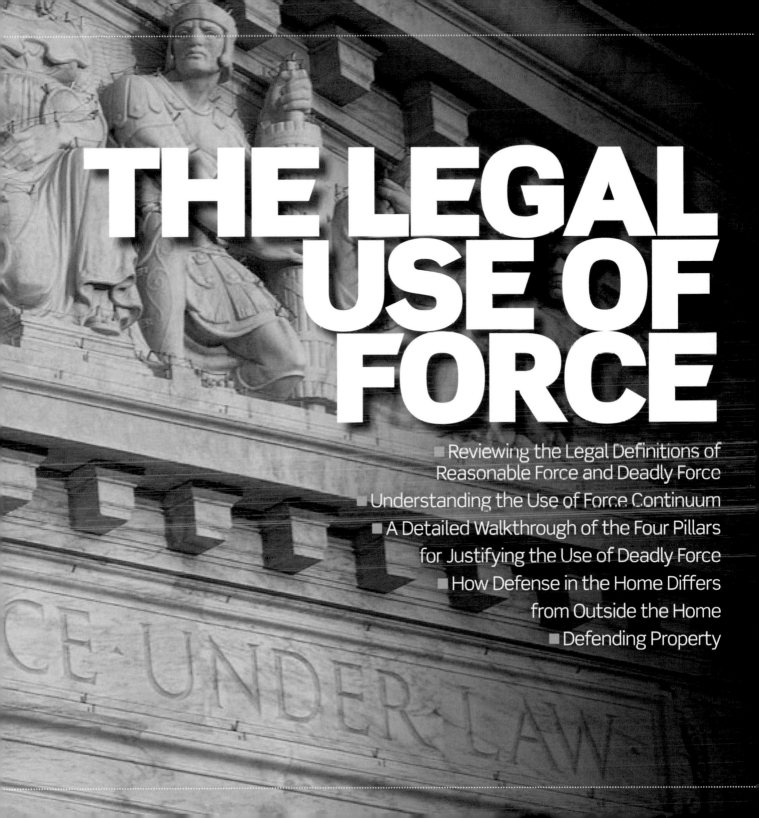

THE LEGAL USE OF FORCE

- Reviewing the Legal Definitions of Reasonable Force and Deadly Force
- Understanding the Use of Force Continuum
- A Detailed Walkthrough of the Four Pillars for Justifying the Use of Deadly Force
- How Defense in the Home Differs from Outside the Home
- Defending Property

Every state in the U.S. has definitions, statutes, and case law defining when civilians may legally use force (up to and including deadly force) to protect themselves, their families, and their homes. Although statutes and case law vary from state to state, most laws are based at least in part on the "reasonable person" test discussed in Chapter One. That means that whenever any level of force has been used, the prosecutor may second guess your decision, using 12 jurors to decide whether or not they believed your actions were reasonable under the circumstances. We'll start this chapter by looking at our "Use of Force Continuum," which provides examples of escalating levels of force that might be used when defending ourselves from a violent attack. As you'll see on the continuum, each progressive level of force will be viewed with a higher level of scrutiny. Depending upon the circumstances, a jury might decide that it would have been reasonable for you to point your firearm at an attacker, but it was unreasonable to shoot and kill him. When deadly force has been used, in addition to the "reasonableness" test, the courts will ask the jury to ensure that you've met other requirements which we'll also discuss in this chapter.

In addition to discussing your right to use force outside of your home, we'll also discuss your right to use force (up to and including deadly force) when defending your home. This aspect of the law is getting a fresh look in many states. To date, 26 states have passed what are generally referred to as enhanced "Castle Doctrine" laws, which in part, remove the obligation to retreat or escape when you're in a place where you have a right to be; and, they make the legal presumption that someone who has entered your home or occupied vehicle by stealth or force is there to do you harm, allowing you to use deadly force to stop that individual. Since not all states have passed strengthened Castle Doctrine laws, we've included the "obligation to retreat" in our topic on a use of force outside the home.

We'll wrap up this chapter with a discussion on "defense of property." As with the other use of force laws, defense of property laws will vary from state to state, but regardless of your state's laws, we'll discuss whether or not we think using force to defend property is a good idea.

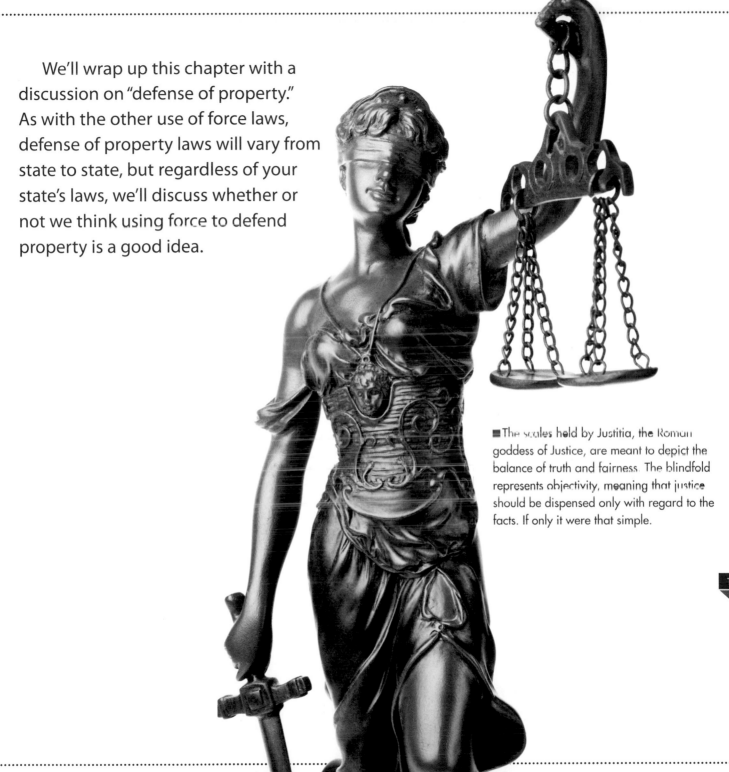

■ The scales held by Justitia, the Roman goddess of Justice, are meant to depict the balance of truth and fairness. The blindfold represents objectivity, meaning that justice should be dispensed only with regard to the facts. If only it were that simple.

THE USE OF FORCE CONTINUUM

When discussing a use of force and the legal consequences that you might face, it isn't as simple as looking at force as an "either/or" decision (i.e. you used force, or you didn't). The reality is, any use of force on your part will be viewed along a progressively steeper continuum (think of it as climbing a mountain), with multiple levels of force which will be viewed with greater and greater degrees of scrutiny. For example, at the lowest end of the spectrum, a decision on your part to expose your firearm to deter an attack (even if your gun never came out of the holster) will still be viewed as "force" by the prosecutor. If you can't prove that your actions were reasonable, you should expect to be charged with assault. One step above that, would be the decision to remove your firearm from its holster, and a step above that, would be a decision to point the firearm at the (alleged) attacker. The prosecutor won't necessarily view each of these levels of force linearly, and instead, he or she might consider each progressive level of force as being an exponential jump on the scale. Near the top of the continuum would be the decision to shoot at the alleged attacker (even if they didn't die), and at the very top of the continuum is a level of force where the attacker (or an innocent bystander) was shot and killed by you. The two horizontal bars on the bottom of the continuum indicate the legal definition that your use of force will be viewed under. We'll review both the "reasonable force" and "deadly force" definitions next, and you'll understand why we've placed those bars where we have.

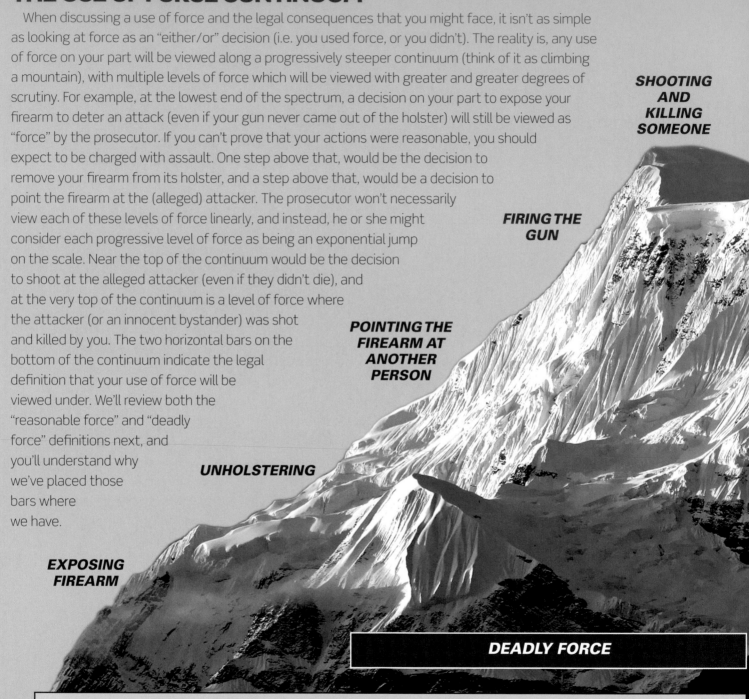

SHOOTING AND KILLING SOMEONE

FIRING THE GUN

POINTING THE FIREARM AT ANOTHER PERSON

UNHOLSTERING

EXPOSING FIREARM

DEADLY FORCE

REASONABLE FORCE

THE LEGAL USE OF FORCE

Although laws vary from state to state when defining our legal right to use force to protect ourselves, others, our homes, and our property, at their heart, most states' laws require that any use of force be "reasonable for the circumstances." That is, in addition to any specific rules outlined in statutory or case law, we must also pass the "reasonable person" test described in Chapter One. When deadly force has been used, we'll not only need to pass the "reasonable" test, we'll also need to pass other test criteria, which we'll explore in a moment.

Reasonable Force

Although laws vary, most states will define "reasonable force" as the minimum level of force required to end a threat, without going beyond that level. Said another way, reasonable force can be thought of as a level of force that does not *exceed* the threat. For example, if a threat to you included the possibility that you'd be bruised or receive a bloody nose, it wouldn't be considered "reasonable" for you to respond with a level of force that could break bones or permanently disfigure your attacker. That's the theory at least—you'll have seconds (or less) to decide whether or not your attacker will be satisfied with bloodying your nose, while the prosecutor gets days or months to make the same determination.

Deadly Force

Each state's laws also define when it is permissible to use what is generally referred to as "deadly force," "lethal force," or "the justifiable taking of a life." To simplify this topic, we'll refer to this level of force as "deadly force." While specific state laws vary, a common standard for the use of deadly force exists, which is:

Deadly force may only be used when there is an immediate, and unavoidable danger of death or great/grave bodily harm to an innocent person, where no other option exists other than the use of deadly force.

As simple as that statement may sound, each state will provide further legal definitions or interpretations for each component of that statement, including what it means to be "innocent," what "immediate" means, and what "great" (or "grave") bodily harm means. To help, we've summarized what those definitions *typically* mean and don't mean, into four key rules outlined on pages 154—157. After any use of deadly force, the prosecutor and/or jury will get a chance to determine whether or not they agree with your interpretation of those definitions, and of course, they'll get to conduct their thought experiment over the course of hours or days, and in the relative safety of a courtroom, while you'll need to make your decision in seconds, while under attack. The phrase "deadly force" itself can also be misleading—based upon the name alone, one might assume that if the attacker didn't die, then the deadly force rules wouldn't apply, but that's actually not the case. Typically, the term "deadly force" means a level of force which is likely to cause, or *could* cause the death of the other person, regardless of whether or not they actually did die. Therefore, the prosecutor gets to decide whether or not he or she thinks death could have resulted, and whether or not the deadly force rules should apply. (Hence the extension of the

"Deadly Force" bar on the continuum beyond "Shooting and Killing Someone.") That fact alone causes us to strongly recommend against warning shots. Prosecutors can easily refer to your warning shot as a "miss," and they can make a case to the jury that you actually *did* attempt to kill the alleged attacker, even if you claim that you only fired into the ground (a bad idea) or into the air (an even worse idea since you'll have the responsibility for wherever your bullet eventually lands.) If the judge instructs the jury to view your case under the deadly force rules rather than just the reasonable force rules, you'll suddenly have a much, *much* steeper hill to climb (remember that mountain on the "Use of Force Continuum"), since you'll need to prove that all of the deadly force rules were true, in addition to the reasonable force rules. Finally, it's important to understand that for us to be legally authorized to use deadly force, each of the deadly force rules must be in place and must remain in place at every single moment when we use, or attempt to use, deadly force. As an example, in the opening stages of an attack we may have no ability to escape (rule #4) because the attack may have occurred so quickly and at very close quarters. But, if we are able to wound the attacker such that an opening to escape suddenly becomes available, we must retreat at that point, rather than continue our use of deadly force. On the following pages, we're going to look at each of the deadly force rules in detail, including what the rules typically mean and don't mean. We'll also use a real life scenario to illustrate how each rule might be followed or broken.

THE RULES GOVERNING THE USE OF DEADLY FORCE OUTSIDE THE HOME

1. Must be in immediate fear of death or great/grave bodily harm for yourself or another person. The threat must be immediate and must be so serious that a reasonable person would fear death or great/grave bodily harm. Great or grave bodily harm is a significant or life-threatening injury.

2. Must be an innocent party. You cannot be seen as the person who started or escalated the conflict.

3. No lesser force is sufficient or available to stop the threat. If you can stop a threat with something less than deadly force, you are required to.

4. Must have no reasonable means of retreat or escape. If you can retreat, you must. However, you are not required to place yourself or a loved one in greater danger by retreating.*

   *The obligation to retreat has been removed in a number of states through enhanced "Castle Doctrine" laws, however, it is <u>your obligation</u> to understand your rights and obligations under your state's laws.

The four deadly force rules must be in place during every single moment when you attempt to use deadly force. As scary and as threatening as this individual looks, count on the prosecutor to second guess your decision whenever deadly force is used.

■ Pulling into your apartment complex, you notice a neighbor standing on his third floor balcony.

■ You exit your vehicle and head toward the front door of your first floor apartment.

■ Leaning over his balcony, your neighbor (who has threatened you in the past) pulls a knife from his waistband and shouts, "You're a dead man!"

■ Fearing death or great bodily harm, you shoot your neighbor.

While you could claim that you feared death or great bodily harm, you'd fail on the "immediate" portion of this rule. Since your neighbor was on the third floor and you were on the first, the threat most likely would not be perceived as "immediate" by the prosecutor.

1 REASONABLY IN IMMEDIATE FEAR OF DEATH OR GREAT/GRAVE BODILY HARM FOR YOURSELF OR ANOTHER PERSON

What it Usually Means:

■ You must pass the reasonable person test. The prosecutor must agree that a "reasonable person" would have also felt that he or she would have been in immediate fear of death or great/grave bodily harm in the same situation.

■ This rule applies whether protecting yourself or another person.

■ The threat must be immediate. The attacker must have the immediate means and opportunity to carry out his threat. A verbal threat to injure or kill you is not enough.

■ Great or grave bodily harm is a legal measurement that implies injuries so great that death is likely or possible, or that you'll be disfigured or crippled permanently or for a significant period of time.

■ The condition of the victim matters. For example, in most cases, if a smaller man is punching a larger man in the chest, it would not be considered great/grave bodily harm. However, if the larger man had a pacemaker, the criteria might be met, even though the attacker had no knowledge of the condition.

What it Usually Doesn't Mean:

■ It is not necessary that the attacker(s) have a weapon. Depending on the relative number, size and/or strength of the attacker(s) and the victim (what would be called a "disparity of force") the measurement of great/grave bodily harm might be met even though the attacker is unarmed.

■ Distance is not critical. If you cannot retreat, you are not required to wait until an attacker is close enough to injure or kill you before you are authorized to use deadly force. Remember the "Tueller Drill" (and remind your lawyer about it).

2 MUST BE AN INNOCENT PARTY

What it Usually Means:
■ In a deadly force situation, you must be the innocent party—you *cannot* be seen as the aggressor. That is, you must not be the person who started or escalated the conflict.

■ Shoving someone at a bar obviously violates this rule, but how about flipping someone off on the freeway? If the situation escalates, don't be so sure what the prosecutor will think.

■ The prosecutor will not only analyze the timeline of the incident itself, he'll also want to go back in time before the incident occurred to understand whether or not you knew the attacker, whether there was bad blood between you, and if there are any witnesses or evidence (prior arrests, etc.) to suggest that you're not as innocent as you claim to be.

What it Usually Doesn't Mean:
■ It doesn't mean that you are barred from everyday disagreements, but it does mean that if you see the situation escalating, you must disengage, allowing the situation to de-escalate.

■ You are not barred from coming to the defense of another person, but unless you can clearly identify who is the attacker and who is the innocent victim, a prudent course of action would be to call 911 and be a good witness. Don't assume that the guy who has the upper hand in the fight is the bad guy.

■ After entering a bar, another individual steps on your toe.

■ You mutter "asshole" under your breath.

> You failed the "innocent party" rule.

■ The individual bumps into your shoulder, knocking you back.

■ You shove the individual to the floor.

> You failed the "innocent party" rule again.

■ The individual jumps up from the floor and charges you with a knife.

■ You shoot the individual charging you with the knife.

> At this point, you are in immediate risk of death or great bodily harm, but since you've broken rule #2, you should expect to be charged with a crime.

155

THE LEGAL USE OF FORCE : CHAPTER FOUR

SCENARIO #3

You leave a busy city street and turn down an alley to take a shortcut to your car.

An individual approximately half your size steps from behind a dumpster and pulls his shirt aside, while reaching for a semi-automatic tucked into his waistband.

Your first mistake. While you haven't broken one of the rules yet, you've put yourself in a risky situation that could have been avoided if you'd stayed with the crowds.

You shout, "don't hurt me!" and draw your firearm from the holster. You leave your pepper spray in your pocket.

The individual draws his firearm from his waistband, and elevates it in an effort to shoot you.

You fire two rounds at him and one strikes him in the shoulder. He immediately drop his firearm and it slides under the dumpster.

At this point, you would probably get most prosecutors to agree that you had no alternative other than to immediately resort to deadly force, and that you would not have been expected to try your pepper spray first.

Bleeding, the individual stumbles toward you.

The individual refuses your further commands to stay back, and he steps into what you consider to be your "danger zone" so you shoot him again.

However, at this point, the individual no longer had control of his firearm (and was injured) and your pepper spray would most likely have sufficed to have stopped the continued threat. In addition, a prosecutor might argue that you've also broken rules #1 and #4 as well.

3 NO LESSER FORCE IS SUFFICIENT OR AVAILABLE TO STOP THE THREAT

What it Usually Means:

If you can stop a threat with something less than deadly force, you are required to. For example, if a reasonable person would have expected that you could have stopped an attack with your hands (or the pepper spray that you chose to carry) the prosecutor may not agree that deadly force was authorized..

You are required to stop using deadly force as soon as the threat of death or great/grave bodily harm has ended. If three bullets stop an attack, the fourth bullet could be considered a crime.

Relative size and strength of the attacker(s) and/or victim matter. For example, a large man being attacked by an unarmed, much smaller woman, may have lesser-force alternatives rather than resorting to deadly force. In the reverse scenario, the disparity of force may mean that the smaller woman might have no alternative other than immediately resorting to deadly force.

What it Usually Doesn't Mean:

You are not required to try other methods before using deadly force, you are simply expected to consider alternatives, and to only use deadly force when no other option is sufficient or available.

4 MUST HAVE NO REASONABLE MEANS OF RETREAT OR ESCAPE

What it Usually Means:

■ Many states' laws require that if you can do so safely, you are expected to seek escape from a potential attack (if an avenue of escape is available and practical), before standing your ground and defending yourself with deadly force.

■ Reasons for an inability to retreat or escape can include: The attacker has physical control over you, and you are simply unable to escape; the attacker is already too close, and you have no ability to outrun them; the attacker has a firearm, and it would be impossible to try to "outrun the bullet;" or you are in a location which offers no ability to escape, such as a room where the attacker is blocking the exit.

■ The obligation to retreat never ends. For example, if you are able to wound an attacker such that it opens up an opportunity to escape safely, you must retreat at that point.

What it Usually Doesn't Mean:

■ The "escape" rule doesn't mean that you cannot have been traveling in a forward direction at any point during the timeline (for example, it doesn't bar you from moving toward a person whom you believe has committed, or is about to commit a crime, although it's good *practical* advice to avoid that type of situation), it simply means that at the moment a threat materializes, if you still have an ability to escape the situation, you *should* escape.

■ You are not expected to retreat from a bad situation to a worse one. For example, if your only means of retreat is across a busy road, you are not expected to put yourself in greater danger by retreating.

■ You are not expected to retreat and leave behind a companion in the dangerous situation. That is, if you can outrun the attacker, you are not expected to do so if it means leaving a companion behind.

■ On your way home from work, a dog runs in front of your car on the freeway. You slam on your brakes and are rear ended.

■ Your car is fine, so you continue on until you can pull onto the shoulder, but the other car is out of commission, and pulls over several hundred feet behind you.

■ The other individual jumps out of his car with a machete, and charges your vehicle, screaming that he's going to kill you.

■ You exit your vehicle, and take up a position behind your driver's door. You shout commands continuously for the 40 seconds it takes the other individual to reach you.

■ You shoot the individual as he gets within 20 feet of you.

At this point, you are in immediate risk of death or great bodily harm, but you had plenty of time to drive off (remember that your car was fine in this scenario), leaving the deranged individual behind.

157

THE LEGAL USE OF FORCE | CHAPTER FOUR

HOW WILL THE PROSECUTOR EVALUATE YOUR CASE?

As discussed in Chapter One, when deciding whether or not to file charges against an individual claiming self–defense, the prosecutor is going to care about more than just who was shot and who did the shooting. As outlined in our scenarios, the prosecutor will analyze each time slice of the incident in an attempt to understand exactly what occurred, including whether or not you started the ball rolling or kept it rolling. The prosecutor might also back up to the hours, days, and even years before the incident, in an attempt to understand the entire story. The prosecutor will want to know:

■ Does the timeline include anything that shows you as the aggressor (even if it happened after an initial move by the other individual)? In other words, did you start the ball rolling, or give it a good kick to keep it rolling?

■ Did you know the other individual, and was there any history of bad blood? How far back does the timeline extend?

■ What kind of individual are you? What do your friends, ex-friends, neighbors, and co-workers say about you?

■ What's on your Facebook page, including pictures, philosophy, and behavior? Is there any indication of aggressiveness, a belief in vigilantism, or gang activity?

■ Are you considered a bully or aggressive? Are there any witnesses, prior arrests, or documentation (including anything you've ever written, posted, emailed, blogged, texted, or tweeted) that would substantiate that categorization?

■ Did you pass or fail the "reasonable person" test, including whether or not you used a reasonable level of force based upon the circumstances?

■ Do they believe that you met all four deadly force criteria during *every single moment* of the timeline where you threatened deadly force?

■ Was any alcohol in your blood, and if so, does that affect your "reasonable person" argument?

■ What statements did you make to the police immediately after the incident? (The answer to this question better be nothing.)

■ What did the police uncover during a search of your car or home? (Any search better have been conducted with a warrant, rather than your passive agreement.)

Based upon the answers to those questions, you may not be viewed as the innocent victim. You might be viewed as a hot-headed bully that got the ball rolling, even if the "ball" got rolling months in advance. Here's the reality—in the end, it truly doesn't matter what *really* happened. What matters is what the prosecutor can get 12 people to believe. If your past behavior leads the jury to agree with the prosecutor's version of events, even an incident where you did everything right might result in your conviction, since

If the prosecutor isn't buying your story, he's going to give you a chance to sell it to 12 jurors, who most decidedly will not be your peers. Don't count on any permit holders or lifetime USCCA members to sit on your jury.

If this burglar hasn't yet entered the home, do the deadly force rules outside the home, or inside the home apply? Don't be so sure what the prosecutor will think.

your attacker will have his own version of events which might include, "This crazy dude pulled a gun on me, so I had to pull my knife to defend myself!" Who will the prosecutor and/or jury believe?

Our best advice? Be nice to everyone; be smart about alcohol use; and don't ever say, email, text, tweet or post *anything* that could help a prosecutor's case. To quote Mother Teresa, "Treat people with more kindness than is required." While you can't get Mother Teresa to testify on your behalf, her philosophy might help you in the end.

USING DEADLY FORCE TO DEFEND YOUR HOME

State laws governing the use of deadly force in defense of our homes (or defense of ourselves or our families while in our homes) generally provide a lower threshold when compared to the lawful use of deadly force outside the home. That difference is derived from the belief that "our home is our castle," and laws making that distinction are often referred to as Castle Doctrine laws (which as mentioned in the chapter introduction, are being strengthened in a number of states). While the generally accepted rule for the use of deadly force outside the home is to prevent "death or great/grave bodily harm," most state laws authorize a use of force deadly inside the home when the occupant is attempting to end or prevent a felony in the home. What exactly a "felony" is will vary from state to state, and of course, the prosecutor gets to apply his or her interpretation after the fact. Most states also make a distinction between inside and outside the home when it comes to the requirement to retreat. Outside the home, many states still require the potential victim to retreat if retreat is safe and practical; inside the home, that is generally not a requirement.

When it comes to the applicability of "defense of home" laws versus the general use of force laws, state laws also vary when it comes to defining exactly what the "home" is. Some states will only include the physical structure of your home or apartment, while other states may include detached buildings (such as garages or storage sheds) and others will include any location where you spend the night, such as a hotel, motel, tent, camper, etc. Because of the variety of state laws, and the fact that the "reasonable person" test will usually apply in any defense of home claim, we recommend that you do the following when defending your home:

■ If an intruder is in the home, do *not* attempt to locate him by "clearing rooms." Instead, barricade yourself and your family in a safe location, call 911, and defend that safe location. There is one time and one time *only* that you should even consider advancing through your home to clear a room or rooms, and that's when the bad guy is between you and a loved one. Otherwise you should concentrate your energy on defending your safe zone until the police arrive.

■ If an intruder is outside of your home, in your garage, in your storage shed, or attempting to steal your car, do *not* leave your home in an attempt to stop him. Call 911 and only use force to defend your life or the lives of your family.

Many of today's legal theories originated with Sir Edward Coke (1552—1634), Chief Justice of England from 1613—1616. Coke's "Institutes of the Lawes of England" are in part, the foundation of today's Castle Doctrine, where Coke famously wrote, "an Englishman's home is his castle." Coke's work was also used to establish a defendant's "right to silence," which evolved to become the Fifth Amendment to the U.S. constitution, and the Miranda warning, which reminds us of this right.

WHAT ABOUT USING FORCE TO DEFEND PROPERTY?

While most states' laws allow a use of force to protect property (or to keep it from being stolen) they typically do not allow a use of deadly force. The problem is, if you voluntarily step into a situation with the intent to use force to protect property and the situation escalates to the point where you are forced to use deadly force to protect yourself, the prosecutor could argue that you violated the "innocent party" rule, or, they could argue that you used deadly force to protect the property (which is *not* okay) rather than your life (which *is* okay). Because of that, our recommendation is that you *not use force to protect* property, instead, we recommend that you get to a safe location or *stay* in a safe location, and dial 911.

To illustrate the differences between a "defense of property" and a "defense of person," many instructors use the "shark tank" analogy. The analogy asks us, "What would it take for me to jump into a shark tank? How about if my child fell in?" For most parents, it wouldn't even be a question—they'd jump into the tank in an attempt to rescue their child, even if they knew it could mean their death. The analogy goes on to ask, "Would I jump in to save an expensive watch?" You get the difference? If it isn't worth dying over, then it isn't worth killing over. Dial 911, and stay safe.

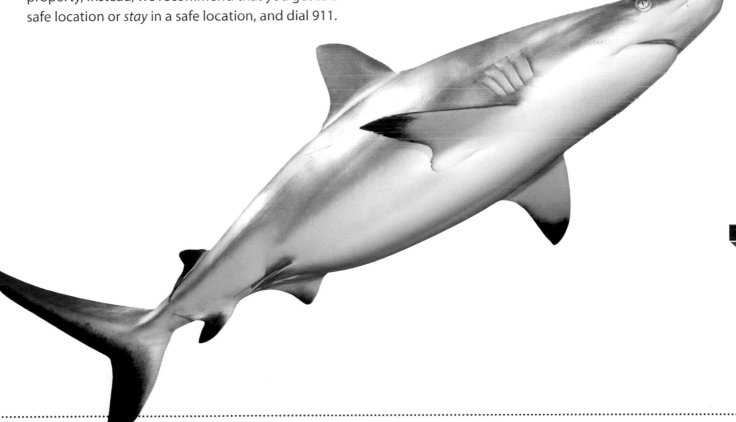

■Although most states' laws allow a use of force to stop property crimes, they typically do not allow deadly force. If it isn't worth dying over, and if it isn't worth going to jail over, then it isn't worth using (or threatening) deadly force. Call 911 and be a good witness instead.

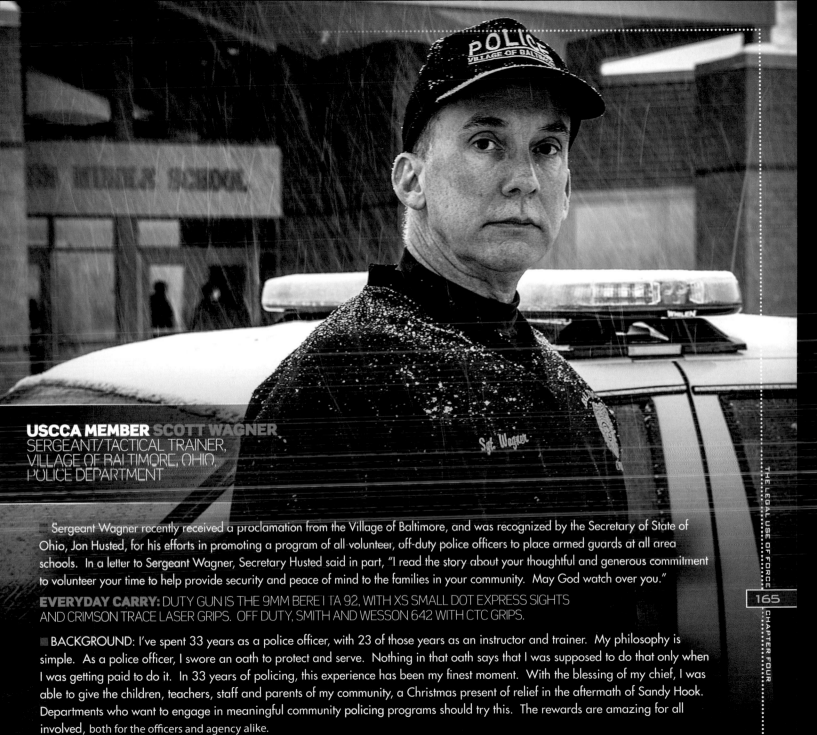

USCCA MEMBER SCOTT WAGNER
SERGEANT/TACTICAL TRAINER,
VILLAGE OF BALTIMORE, OHIO,
POLICE DEPARTMENT

Sergeant Wagner recently received a proclamation from the Village of Baltimore, and was recognized by the Secretary of State of Ohio, Jon Husted, for his efforts in promoting a program of all-volunteer, off-duty police officers to place armed guards at all area schools. In a letter to Sergeant Wagner, Secretary Husted said in part, "I read the story about your thoughtful and generous commitment to volunteer your time to help provide security and peace of mind to the families in your community. May God watch over you."

EVERYDAY CARRY: DUTY GUN IS THE 9MM BERETTA 92, WITH XS SMALL DOT EXPRESS SIGHTS AND CRIMSON TRACE LASER GRIPS. OFF DUTY, SMITH AND WESSON 642 WITH CTC GRIPS.

■ BACKGROUND: I've spent 33 years as a police officer, with 23 of those years as an instructor and trainer. My philosophy is simple. As a police officer, I swore an oath to protect and serve. Nothing in that oath says that I was supposed to do that only when I was getting paid to do it. In 33 years of policing, this experience has been my finest moment. With the blessing of my chief, I was able to give the children, teachers, staff and parents of my community, a Christmas present of relief in the aftermath of Sandy Hook. Departments who want to engage in meaningful community policing programs should try this. The rewards are amazing for all involved, both for the officers and agency alike.

→CHAPTER 5

VIOLENT ENCOUNTERS AND THEIR AFTERMATH

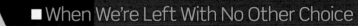

In Chapter Three, we briefly mentioned a number of "automated responses" that typically accompany what is generally referred to as a "critical incident," which is an antiseptic way of referring to a violent attack. We explained that those automated responses would most likely include the motor cortex locking your head and eyes onto the knife or gun in the hands of the attacker; and the automated response of dropping into a crouch, and orienting to face the attacker. In this chapter, we'll not only explain more details around those *physical* responses, we'll also explain a number of *physiological* responses that will most likely occur as well, including tunnel vision, auditory exclusion, and even memory loss or false memories. To do that, we're going to take you on a guided tour of the brain and nervous system, where we'll explain not only *what* responses you'll most likely experience, but we'll explain *why* they happen as well. As you read that section, pay particularly close attention to the "Training Tips" that we've outlined for each topic. These tips are designed to help you embrace each of the physical and physiological responses into your training plan in order to "train the way you'll fight."

Also in this chapter, we'll review what you should do in the opening stages of an attack, including reviewing what your options might be, and the type of language and commands to use (and not to use). We'll also address the very difficult topic of exactly what you'll need to know if you have no other choice but to use deadly force to stop an attack. We'll also explain what you should do in the immediate aftermath of an attack, including what phone calls you should make, how to deal with the police when they arrive at the scene, and what you should and shouldn't say to the police. It's unfortunate, but the reality is that if you've used your firearm in any capacity, however justified you believed it to be, the police are no longer there to serve and protect you. They are there to serve the prosecuting attorney and protect his or her case. For that reason, you'll need to prepare for how to interact with the police after such an incident, including preparing for your arrest. We'll help by explaining exactly what might happen after your arrest, including an explanation of when the police are required to read the famous (or infamous) Miranda warning, reminding you of your right to remain silent. We'll explain what that warning really

means, and we'll also explain what you'll need to do to actually invoke that right (believe it or not, you can't invoke the right to remain silent by simply being silent). It's an unfortunate reality, but once a "critical incident" has ended, the real trouble is just getting started.

THE BRAIN AND CENTRAL NERVOUS SYSTEM

The brain is made up of a variety of interconnected structures, but the ones we'll concentrate on are those involved in sensory input and sensory processing, reasoning and planning, movement, and the brain's "alarm circuits." We'll also take a look at a key component of the nervous system called the sympathetic nervous system. To make it a bit easier to understand, we're going to use everyday descriptive terms (such as "the Switchboard") in addition to using the technical term (such as "the thalamus").

The "Switchboard"

Our senses (things like sight, sound, and touch) provide sensory and emotional input to our brains, which is routed through a structure called the **thalamus**. The thalamus used to be thought of as nothing more than a relay station, simply passing signals from the senses to the sensory cortex. Now, scientists think of the thalamus as more of a "switchboard" within the brain, making determinations about where input is routed, and which information is filtered or blocked. As it receives sensory input, the thalamus routes that input to the cortex (the long route) and the amygdala (the short route). Under periods of extreme stress, scientists believe that the thalamus can block any sensory input that it doesn't consider necessary to the situation.

The "Thinker"

The cortex not only allows us to plan and reason, it also contains sub-structures to interpret sensory input that has been routed from the thalamus. Like the thalamus (the "Switchboard"), the **sensory cortex** will selectively process or ignore input based upon the task at hand. For example, when we're focused on a TV program (visual input) we don't always hear our spouse's request to take out the garbage; or, when we're focused on a radio program in the car (audio input), we might ignore the visual input of a stop sign and blow right by it. When we're under extreme stress, this selective processing and prioritization becomes pronounced.

The "Engineer"

The **motor cortex** receives most of its instructions from the thinking and planning part of our brain, but the amygdala also has a direct connection to the motor cortex for those times when it's necessary for us to do something *right now*, such as freezing, ducking, raising our hands, or crouching.

The "Fire Alarm"

Sitting next to the thalamus is a tiny, almond-shaped structure called the **amygdala**. The amygdala contains most of the brain's alarm circuits designed to react to any imminent threat passed on by

the thalamus. When its alarm circuits are tripped, the amygdala has a direct connection to the motor cortex (that is, it skips the reasoning and planning part of the brain) in order to take *immediate* action (such as making us duck if something is thrown at our heads), and to the hypothalamus, to kick our endocrine system into gear. "Evolved" alarms are contained within the amygdala, such as a fear of large, roaring carnivores, while "learned" alarms are accessed by the hippocampus (the "Scrapbook") such as a fear of snakes with rattles.

The "Scrapbook"

The **hippocampus** provides access to our memories and personal experiences, including any "learned" threats. That recall will include

more than just a visual snapshot of the learned threat, it will also recall information about the context and situation surrounding the object. For example, if an individual had been attacked by a thug wielding a baseball bat, the sight of another individual carrying a baseball bat might fire the alarm circuits if the rest of the context met other stored criteria, such as an aggressive facial expression on the part of the person with the bat. On the other hand, a baseball bat in the hands of a smiling little leaguer most likely would not fire those circuits.

The "Pharmacy"

The sympathetic nervous system involves two additional structures in the brain, namely the **hypothalamus** and the **pituitary gland**, as well as the **adrenal glands**, situated on top of the kidneys. Upon hearing the alarm bells fired by the amygdala, the hypothalamus signals the pituitary gland to release ACTH and endorphins. ACTH alerts the adrenal glands to release adrenaline (also known as epinephrine) into the bloodstream, and endorphins act as a natural pain killer by blocking the body's pain receptors.

UNDERSTANDING FIGHT OR FLIGHT

It's been long known that when under extreme stress (including when under attack) the human body will undergo a series of involuntary changes as part of the "fight or flight" mechanisms built into our systems. Anecdotal evidence from the last five wars plus a number of law enforcement studies, have all confirmed that these effects happen, yet very few delve into *why* they happen or *how often* they happen. Three of the leading researchers in this field, including Dr. Alexis Artwohl, Dr. Bill Lewinski, and Bruce Siddle, have finally begun to answer the "why" and the "how often" side of this question, and the answers are truly astounding.

In her book "Deadly Force Encounters" (written with co-author Loren Christensen) and subsequent research papers, Dr. Alexis Artwohl provides incredible insight through in-depth interviews with 157 police officers involved in deadly force shootings. The many quotations you'll see in this section are from Dr. Artwohl's interviews, and a summary of her findings are shown in the chart to the right, which shows that approximately 80% of the officers interviewed experienced the most well-known physiological effects, including tunnel vision and diminished sounds, and that more than 50% experienced time distortions or memory loss. Most surprising, more than one in five experienced false memories; that is, they remembered something that *never actually happened*. These and other physical and physiological effects have long been attributed to adrenaline or other natural chemicals that flood our bodies during extreme stress, but the "fight or flight" mechanisms that are part of our systems go well beyond a simple chemical dump by our adrenal glands. They exist as a true survival mechanism that is hardwired into our brains, as surely as an electronic fuse will trip when a short occurs. Like any

electrical system, the brain is composed of an incredibly complex set of relays, switches, and multiple paths that signals can travel down. As explained on the opposite page and as shown on the brain schematic on the following pages, "fight or flight" (and everything that cascades from it), all starts with a tiny, almond shaped structure in the brain called the amygdala.

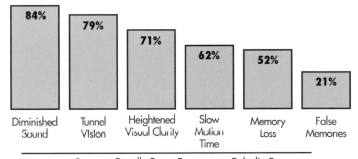

Source: Deadly Force Encounters, Paladin Press
Based on Surveys from 157 Police Officers involved in Deadly Encounters

PHYSIOLOGICAL EFFECTS OF EXTREME STRESS

Effects of the Brain's "Alarm Circuits"
- Reflexive Crouch.
- Hands Elevated to Protect the Face.
- Head Turned and Eyes Locked on Threat.

Effects of Brain's Signals Being Prioritized or Filtered
- Tunnel Vision.
- Heightened Visual Clarity.
- Diminished Sounds.
- Slow Motion Time.
- Memory Loss.
- Memory Distortion or False Memories.
- Inability to Count.

Effects of Adrenaline and Endorphins
- Increase in Strength.
- Heightened Pain Threshold.
- Decrease in Fine Motor Skills.

THE BRAIN'S LONG ROUTE AND SHORT ROUTE

The body's "fight or flight" defenses are coordinated by a variety of interconnected structures in our brain and sympathetic nervous system, including the structures shown below. The amygdala (the "Fire Alarm") is responsible for initiating the body's "fight or flight" defenses whenever it receives sensory input that matches predefined alarm circuits. Sensory input reaches the amygdala from the thalamus (the "Switchboard") along two paths. One path is a direct connection, while the second path is first routed through the sensory cortex (the "Thinker"). The route through the cortex is known as the long route or the higher brain, while the direct connection is known as the short route or the reptilian brain. Although input is passed from the thalamus along both paths, in most cases, the lower brain remains passive, and our

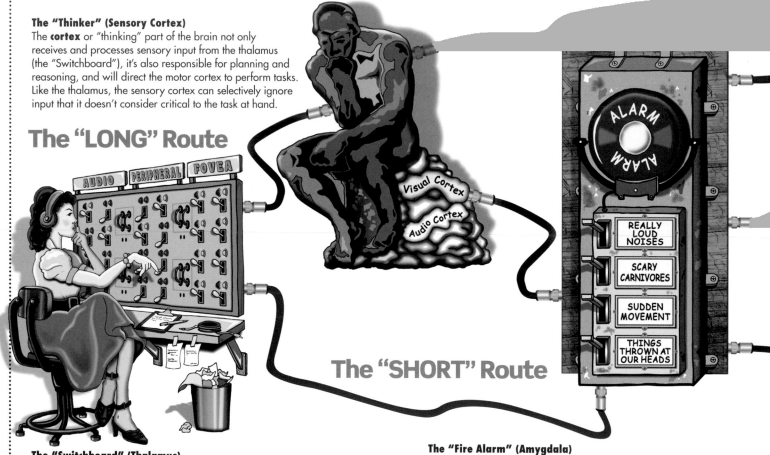

The "Thinker" (Sensory Cortex)
The **cortex** or "thinking" part of the brain not only receives and processes sensory input from the thalamus (the "Switchboard"), it's also responsible for planning and reasoning, and will direct the motor cortex to perform tasks. Like the thalamus, the sensory cortex can selectively ignore input that it doesn't consider critical to the task at hand.

The "LONG" Route

The "SHORT" Route

The "Switchboard" (Thalamus)
The **thalamus** can be thought of as the switchboard of the brain, responsible for routing, blocking, or filtering sensory input. In the illustration above, the thalamus has blocked nearly all audio and visual input other than the high resolution fovea at the center of the retina.

The "Fire Alarm" (Amygdala)
The **amygdala** contains the brain's hardwired alarm circuits which will fire if matching input is received from the thalamus, such as a really loud noise (watch any video of soldiers ducking when a mortar shell goes off, and you just saw the amygdala in action) or when something is thrown at our head.

movement and other activity is driven by our higher brain as it processes and "thinks about" the input that it's receiving. In cases where the information flowing along the paths matches a predefined alarm circuit, the amygdala effectively throws a switch, and within microseconds, it executes a series of tasks that may include signaling the motor cortex (the "Engineer") to duck into a crouch, rotate toward the perceived threat and lock our eyes on that threat; and it might send a message to the hypothalamus (the "Pharmacy") to get adrenaline moving into the system. Much faster than it would take to think through the situation, the short path through our brain has already prepared us for fight or flight, and it might have already saved us from serious injury or death if it froze our motor cortex before we stepped in front of a speeding bus, or ducked our head to protect us from a flying rock.

The "Scrapbook" (Hippocampus)

The **hippocampus** provides access to our memories and experiences, including any "learned" threats and the context surrounding those threats. For example, the hippocampus could access the fact that coiled objects are threats if they're alive and have rattles, but that coiled objects that look like rope are not threats. When matching threat information is identified by the hippocampus, the amygdala will fire its alarm bells.

The "Engineer" (Motor Cortex)

The amygdala has a direct connection to the **motor cortex** for those moments when we need to do something immediately, such as: freezing; raising our hands to protect our head from a flying rock; or ducking into a crouch, orienting toward a threat, and locking our eyes onto that threat.

The "Pharmacy" (Hypothalamus, Pituitary Gland & Adrenal Gland)

Upon hearing the alarm bells fired by the amygdala, the **hypothalamus** signals the **pituitary gland** to release ACTH and endorphins. ACTH alerts the **adrenal glands** to release adrenaline (also known as epinephrine) into the bloodstream, and endorphins act as a natural pain killer by blocking the body's pain receptors.

Training **Tip**

Since the amygdala's direct connection to the motor cortex will force you into a crouch and will orient your body to face the threat head on, then that's the "stance" you should train with. The Isoceles is a natural and neutral stance, matching the body's and mind's natural reactions, allowing you to "train the way you'll fight."

ADRENALINE & ENDORPHINS

As discussed, the amygdala is responsible for *initiating* the body's "fight or flight" defenses, while the sympathetic nervous system is responsible for *sustaining* it through a release of adrenaline. Adrenaline sustains the body's "fight or flight" defenses by increasing blood, oxygen, and glucose to the major muscles including the heart; it increases heart rate and oxygen consumption by the lungs, and it dilates the pupils. Side effects will include a loss of manual dexterity in our extremities (most importantly, our hands) and our hands may shake from the loss of blood and the influx of adrenaline. In addition, the lack of blood on the surface of our skin and the effect of endorphins released by the pituitary gland will provide us with an elevated pain threshold.

This can allow us to fight long after we might have given up from injuries, but it also means that we'll need to immediately check ourselves and loved ones for injuries in the immediate aftermath.

Under Stress
Adrenaline forces a constriction of blood vessels to force blood, oxygen, and glucose to the major muscle groups and away from the skin and extremities to allow us to run faster than we've ever run, or fight harder than we've ever fought.

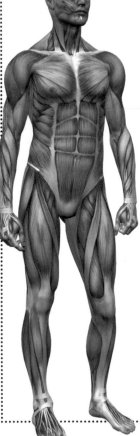

No Stress
When relaxed, the muscles have an equal distribution of blood, oxygen and glucose. The major muscle groups have normal strength and the minor muscle groups have high dexterity.

The manual dexterity that we'll lose under the effects of adrenaline just happens to be the same dexterity required to manipulate holster retention devices, safeties, and slide releases.

Training **Tip**

Learn to manipulate your firearm's controls as though you were missing your fingertips. That means ignoring your slide release, and racking (or releasing) the slide by grasping it between the palm and four fingers of your support hand. If you want a taste of what your hands might actually feel like under the affects of adrenaline and extreme stress, try this: run through our "Slap, Rack, and Roll Drill" in Chapter Seven, after soaking your hands in a sink full of water and ice cubes for a minute or two. The resulting hand shake and lack of feeling will give you a small taste of the real thing.

THE STRUCTURE OF THE EYE

To understand why visual side effects occur, it's necessary to understand the structure of the eye itself. As shown in the diagram below, the human eye can be thought of as being similar to a digital camera. In a camera, the lens focuses the image onto a CCD chip containing millions of light sensitive cells. In the human eye, the lens focuses the image onto the eye's retina which contains more than 100 million photosensitive cells called rods and cones. Rods and cones convert

the exact center of the retina contains a tiny area called the fovea, composed entirely of the higher resolution cones. Interestingly, the area of the visual cortex that's mapped directly to the fovea is disproportionately large when compared to the area mapped to the remainder of the retina. Said another way, not only does the fovea provide a much higher resolution image when compared to the rest of the eye, but the brain also sets aside a much greater amount of power to process that input. Although the entire retina provides as much as

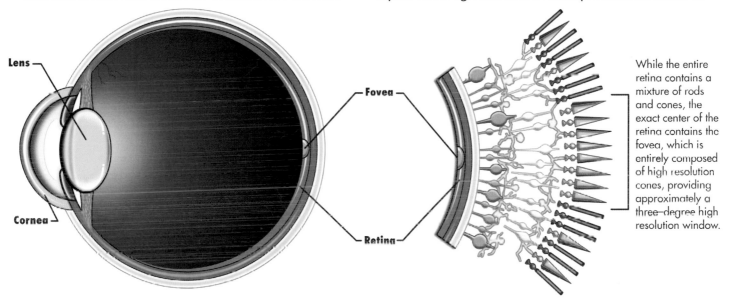

Lens

Cornea

Fovea

Retina

While the entire retina contains a mixture of rods and cones, the exact center of the retina contains the fovea, which is entirely composed of high resolution cones, providing approximately a three-degree high resolution window.

the incoming light into signals which are sent into the visual cortex for processing, via the thalamus (the "Switchboard"). Rods and cones serve different purposes. Rods are designed to operate in low light and they're sensitive to movement, but they see in black and white and are low resolution. Cones provide a much higher resolution image and they see in color, but they are less beneficial in low light. While the majority of the retina has a mixture of rods and cones,

200 degrees of peripheral vision, the higher resolution fovea provides no more than a few degrees of vision. Don't believe it? Try this test—stare at any word on this page and try to identify any other word at least three to four words away. You'll pretty easily see that the word you're focused on looks high resolution, while every other word appears low resolution and is most likely illegible.

TUNNEL VISION AND HEIGHTENED VISUAL ACUITY

So why does "tunnel vision" and heightened visual acuity occur? As shown in our brain schematic, the thalamus acts as the brain's switchboard, not only deciding *where* to route signals, but also *if* it should route a signal at all. Under extreme stress, the thalamus filters out what it considers to be non-critical sensory input, which may include filtering out visual input other than the information from the eye's high resolution fovea. That means that our visual input might be reduced to no more than a few degrees (which equates to about a 12-inch circle at 20 feet) but the input that is processed, is *extremely* high resolution, aiding in our ability to mount a counterattack. In other words, this effect is a survival mechanism built into the brain, and shouldn't be viewed as a negative side effect at all. These effects have been reported from survivors of violent attacks who often couldn't describe their assailant, but who *could* describe their assailant's weapon in great detail, as though they were describing a video shot in 4K rather than a grainy video shot in standard definition.

DISTANCE DISTORTION

Survivors of critical incidents have also reported distance distortion, either believing that their attacker was much closer or much farther away than he actually was. Tunnel vision can cause us to believe that an attacker was farther away than he actually was, since we're losing most of our stereoscopic vision, which is required for depth perception. Heightened visual acuity can lead us to believe the attacker was *closer* than he actually was, since under normal circumstances, we know the difference between how clear and well-focused a person or object is at different distances. Under the effects of extreme stress, when the brain is limiting the visual input to the high resolution area at the center of the retina, a person who is actually at 20 feet may look like he has the same clarity and detail as a person at, say, 10 feet. Our replay of the incident would incorrectly conclude that the person was closer than he actually was.

"I told the SWAT team that the suspect was firing at me from down a long dark hallway about 40 feet long. When I went back to the scene the next day, I was shocked to discover that he had actually been only about 5 feet in front of me in an open room. There was no dark hallway."

Under normal circumstances, the visual cortex is receiving input from the entire retina, which provides up to 200 degrees of vision.

Under extreme stress, the thalamus filters out (or the sensory cortex ignores) visual input from everything but the high resolution fovea, reducing vision to no more than a few degrees, but providing very high resolution images.

Training **Tip**

Take a look through a paper towel tube to get a sense of what the scene will look like with just three degrees of visibility. With that mental picture, train yourself to elevate your firearm up into that three–degree window and physically move your head, rather than just your eyes, when engaging multiple targets.

DIMINISHED SOUND (AUDITORY EXCLUSION)

Selective auditory exclusion happens all the time (just try to get the attention of an eight-year-old when he's watching SpongeBob). This is nothing more than the sensory cortex's prioritization of one signal over another, which also explains why we can hold a conversation in a crowded room full of noise. During non-critical moments, we can easily change our sensory focus by listening to a different conversation or temporarily ignoring audio input while we focus on visual input. This is an everyday function of our sensory cortex—it allows us to selectively process sensory input to accomplish the task at hand. However, once the brain's alarm circuits have been fired, the thalamus (the "Switchboard") appears to literally halt the flow of audio signals to the cortex. This corresponds with interviews from the Artwohl research, where police officers who experienced auditory exclusion *knew* their firearms should be going "bang," they were *listening* for their firearms to go "bang," yet all they heard was a "pop" or no sound at all. Interestingly, while the thalamus appears to halt the flow of audio signals along the "long route," it appears as though the signal flow along the "short route" is uninterrupted. In a study conducted by Bruce and Kevin Siddle

of PPCT Management Systems in 2004, researchers put 49 police officers in an enclosed trailer, and ran the officers through an intense force-on-force drill, where the officers were fired on from three different "attackers." During the 30 second "attack," the researchers sounded an air horn, which in the enclosed space, should have been deafening. During the debriefing, when the officers were asked if they heard the air horn, fully 97% replied that they *never heard it*. The video tape, however, told a different story—39 percent of the officers who said that they never heard the air horn still reacted to it by flinching, or by briefly orienting toward the sound. That indicates that the thalamus-to-amygdala connection remained in place, which allowed the amygdala to continue its automated processes, even though the "thinking" part of the brain was left out of the loop.

■ **How Does Hearing Protection Compare?** Typical ear protection will lower a sound source by approximately 20 to 30 decibels, which means that the "bang" of gunfire might still be as loud as 110 to 120 decibels. Compare that to the reported sound levels from officers in the Artwohl research, where officers reported gunfire sounding like "pops" or no sound at all, and had no recollection of sirens or shouts. That means that the apparent sound reduction was greater than 80 decibels, and as high as 140 decibels.

"If it hadn't been for the recoil, I wouldn't have known my gun was working. Not only didn't I hear the shots but afterward my ears weren't even ringing."

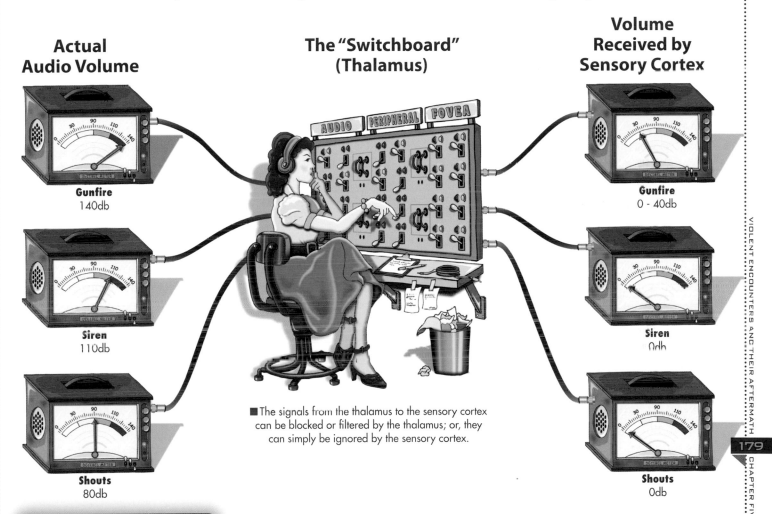

Actual Audio Volume

Gunfire
140db

Siren
110db

Shouts
80db

The "Switchboard" (Thalamus)

AUDIO PERIPHERAL FOVEA

■ The signals from the thalamus to the sensory cortex can be blocked or filtered by the thalamus; or, they can simply be ignored by the sensory cortex.

Volume Received by Sensory Cortex

Gunfire
0 - 40db

Siren
0db

Shouts
0db

Training **Tip**

With a buddy's assistance, try our "Tap and Rack Drill" in Chapter Seven, with live stereo ear pieces inserted under your normal hearing protection. Turn up the volume loud enough so that the combination of music and hearing protection drowns out all other sounds. This will teach you to recognize your firearm's proper operation and failures by feel alone. You'll learn to trust that your firearm actually fired even though you didn't hear the "bang," and you'll learn to identify failures through a lack of recoil, rather than a lack of sound.

SLOW MOTION TIME

Processing the input of sensory information requires processing power, no different than a computer requires processing power to run applications. During non-stressful situations, our sensory cortex must balance the processing of a variety of sensory input, including sound, touch, smell, and about 200 degrees of visual input. Under periods of extreme stress when the thalamus has shut down all sensory input except for the high resolution fovea, we'll suddenly have throughput and processing power to spare. So what does that have to do with the "slow motion effect" reported in the Artwohl research? In part, it's due to the fact that most of our perception of time is based upon the sensory input that we receive. Under extreme stress, the unusually high volume of visual information that's passed to and is processed by our cortex can be interpreted by our conscious self as time slowing down, rather than the "processing" or "throughput" speeding up. To use another computer analogy, let's assume that a computer is running ten applications, including a video processing application that

normally processes one gigabyte of video per second. If the other nine applications were suddenly shut down, the computer might suddenly jump to processing 10 gigabytes per second. If the computer's clock was based upon how many gigabytes were processed, it would now record that ten seconds had passed for each real second, which from the computer's perspective, is the most logical conclusion (rather than concluding that its processing power had somehow magically increased). That's an over simplification, but it paints an easy picture to understand.

Five Seconds at Twice the Volume of Visual Input Can be Interpreted by the Mind as Ten Seconds
During periods of extreme stress when the thalamus is blocking virtually all sensory input other than the high resolution fovea, we'll not only have a much wider stream of high resolution visual input, but we'll suddenly have the processing power to handle it. Continuing the analogy to film, it's like jumping from 24 frames per second to 48 frames per second or more. The result can be like something straight out of "The Matrix," such as the amazing quote from the Artwohl research on the opposite page.

"During a violent shoot-out I looked over, drawn to the sudden mayhem, and was puzzled to see beer cans slowly floating through the air past my face. What was even more puzzling was that they had the word "Federal" printed on the bottom. They turned out to be the shell casings ejected by the officer who was firing next to me."

Five Seconds of Real Time

Although light enters the eye as a continuous stream and not as individual "frames," the analogy to film helps to explain why slow motion time occurs. During normal, non-stressful situations, the cortex will process a balance of sensory information in order to accomplish the task at hand. Visual processing might be comparable to traditional motion picture film at 24 frames per second. That's enough visual input to walk without tripping over our feet, and to catch a ball without getting hit in the face, yet it's slow enough to cause motion blur. For example, empty shell casings flying by our face will appear as a blur.

Training **Tip**

Practice reloads and clearance drills without looking at your firearm. During a critical incident, if your perception is that you're performing these tasks in slow motion, you can rush the task and make mistakes when mistakes can be fatal.

LOSS OF MEMORY

In order to recall a memory, our hippocampus (the "Scrapbook") actually reconstructs it by integrating elements of that memory scattered in various locations of our brain. For example, for us to recall a camping trip from the previous summer, the brain doesn't open a "file" the same way a computer file is opened; instead, the hippocampus reconstructs the memory by recalling separately stored memories connected via pathways of what we did, saw, smelled, tasted, and heard on that trip. Memories are also associative, which means that newer memories are more easily recalled if we can associate them with previously acquired knowledge. For example, if the camping trip reminded us of an earlier trip we'd been on, it would be easier to recall the details of the more recent event. Under extreme stress, we're lacking both of those fundamental "recall" operations. Instead of a variety of elements stored for that memory, we might have only a single element captured (visual) and we most likely have no previous memories to associate it with. In addition, in order to be recalled in the first place, memories must have been transferred to long term memory (also managed by the hippocampus), which required them to be transferred from "sensory memory" (which might last less than a second) to short term or "working" memory (which might last less than a minute), to long term memory. Under extreme stress, the hippocampus may simply discard information that it doesn't consider necessary to survival, never moving the input past sensory or short term memory. The Artwohl research includes multiple incidents where officers blacked out on one or more parts of the incident, including their own actions, such as forgetting phone calls they made, how many rounds they fired, or even whether or not they fired their own gun.

"When I got home after the shooting, my wife told me that I had called her on my cell phone during the pursuit of the violent suspect just prior to the shooting. I have no memory of making that phone call."

Event
Input passed through the thalamus will first reside in "sensory" memory. If it
is passed on, it will next reside in short term or "working" memory.

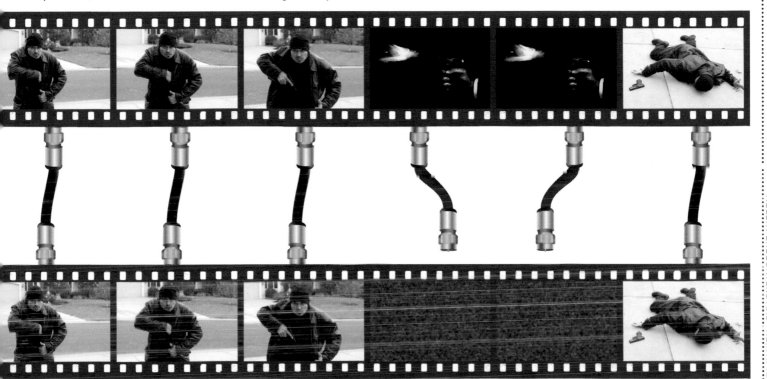

Long Term Memory
Only memories that have been passed to long term memory are available for recall. If the thalamus blocked the input,
or the hippocampus failed to move it to long term memory, it simply will not be there for recall.

Training **Tip**

*Build the aftermath into your mental scenarios to include the phone calls and limited statement to the police
described later in this chapter. In the Artwohl research, more than 50 percent of police officers involved in
critical incidents had memory loss for at least some part of the incident. You must speak with your lawyer
and have him or her review any evidence before you and your lawyer review the incident with the police.*

MEMORY DISTORTION OR FALSE MEMORIES

At any given moment, the information that's within our short term or "working" memory can be anything. It can include sensory input such as what we're looking at or listening to; or it can simply be thoughts or imagination, such as imagining what we'll have for dinner, picturing a loved one, or replaying a tune in our head. When we're in the middle of a critical incident, those "thoughts" might include imagining what it would be like if we or our companion were shot with the attacker's gun; or it could be vivid thoughts of loved ones; or, it could be a tune replaying in our head. Unfortunately, when we're under the extreme stress of an attack, those random thoughts can be transferred to our long term memory as though they actually occurred. Whether or not this is a survival mechanism (for example, the image of a gravely injured loved one might force us to fight even harder) or whether it's simply a "bug," the Artwohl research confirmed that the phenomenon occurred in more than one in five officers interviewed, including the vivid, yet false memory described in the quote below.

Working Memory (or the Subconscious)
Our working memory can include not only input that's been passed on from the thalamus, it can also contain thoughts, fears, and imagination.

"I saw the suspect suddenly point his gun at my partner. As I shot (the suspect), I saw my partner go down in a spray of blood. I ran over to help my partner, and he was standing there unharmed. The suspect never even got off a shot."

Event

Input passed through the thalamus will first reside in "sensory" memory. If it is passed on, it will next reside in short term or "working" memory.

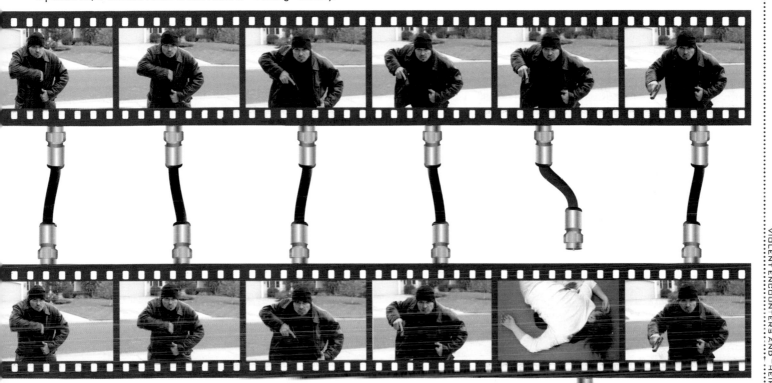

Long Term Memory

Under extreme stress, the hippocampus might not only store actual events into our long term memory, it might also "log" into long term memory images that had resided within our subconscious, as though they had actually occurred.

Training **Tip**

Build the aftermath into your mental scenarios to include the phone calls and limited statement to the police described later in this chapter. In the Artwohl research, nearly one in five police officers involved in critical incidents recalled events that never occurred. You must speak with your lawyer and have him or her review any evidence before you and your lawyer review the incident with the police.

RECOGNIZING A THREAT

Now that we've addressed the physiological reactions that are likely to accompany any violent attack, let's talk about the attack itself. While it's fair to say there is no "typical" attack, it's also fair to say that an attack will not begin with the bad guy 300 feet away, screaming "Give me your wallet!" and waving a knife. Instead, it might occur with an individual angling toward us on the street pretending to talk on his cell phone before he pulls a knife inches away from us; or, stepping out of the shadows when we're already upon him. Because of this, we need to be constantly aware of our surroundings and we must live the color codes of awareness described in Chapter One. We also need to be prepared to shift from Yellow to Orange to Red, without finding ourselves paralyzed by thinking, "this can't be happening" or, "this can't be what I think it is." Once our "mental trigger" has been tripped, we must *immediately* throw our plan into action, which may include engaging the threat. If we do find ourselves facing an immediate threat and there is no possibility of escape, two things should immediately occur. First, we should quickly take a large lateral step to move off the "line of attack." Stepping laterally not only throws off our attacker's advance, it also drops us into a crouched position, preparing us to take up a shooting stance if required. Second, we should forcefully issue commands in a "command voice."

Using lateral movements (moving off the line of attack) while presenting from the holster or when reloading, is an important tactical skill to develop, since it works against the way a human tracks motion, and it will effect your attacker's ability to continue his attack. We know that when something is moving rapidly and it unexpectedly stops, our eyes (which track linear motion in leaps, rather than smoothly tracking the motion) will continue along the path of expected motion. If you have ever shot at a smoothly moving crossing target (a range target designed to move laterally), you probably discovered that it wasn't much more difficult to hit than a stationary target.

"THE LINE"

THE POTENTIAL THREAT

US

On the other hand, if you shot at a crossing target that was moving erratically (stopping and starting unexpectedly or even changing directions), your hit rate was most likely significantly reduced. In fact, if the operator of the target stopped or reversed direction just as you were firing, you probably missed the target entirely.

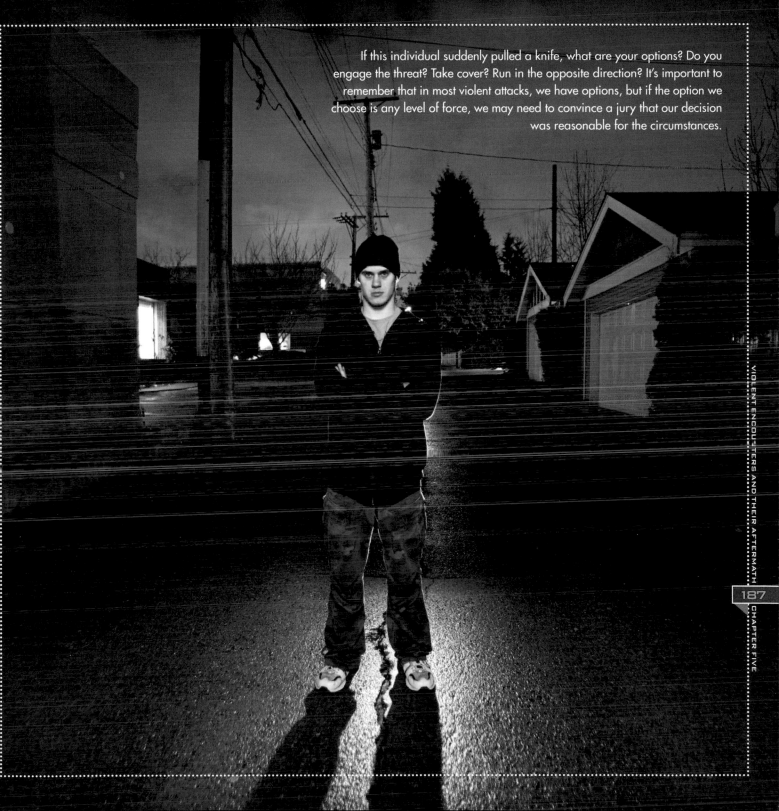

If this individual suddenly pulled a knife, what are your options? Do you engage the threat? Take cover? Run in the opposite direction? It's important to remember that in most violent attacks, we have options, but if the option we choose is any level of force, we may need to convince a jury that our decision was reasonable for the circumstances.

ISSUING COMMANDS & EVALUATING OPTIONS

Issuing commands during a violent encounter does two things. Most importantly, it immediately identifies us as someone who will not be an easy victim, which may cause the attacker to break off his attack. As mentioned in Chapter One, the average criminal is hoping to find an easy victim in "condition white." Imagine his surprise if his potential victim suddenly takes a large lateral step and shouts, "Stay back! Get away from me!" while raising a hand in a stop gesture. Secondly, issuing commands alerts anyone within the immediate vicinity that an attack is underway and that we're the non-aggressor.

When we do issue commands, we need to bark them out in a command voice, deep from the diaphragm. Even the smallest individual can pack a verbal punch when he or she practices commands such as:

"Stay back! Get away from me! Drop your weapon!"

You'll notice that the language we used was non-threatening and identifies us as the victim. Remember that witnesses may repeat everything that you say, so avoid language like this:

"If you come any closer, I'll kill you!"
or, *"I'm going to blow your %*$@ing head off!"*

Our advice is to work these verbal commands into the mental scenarios discussed in Chapter One, as well as into your range or virtual exercises. Training consistently with this method gives us the confidence that commands and movement will be an automated part of our defense in a critical incident.

What Are Our Options?

So we've found ourselves in the middle of a situation that we didn't start and we couldn't avoid. What should our goal be at this point? Besides the obvious answer of survival, our goal should be to do *anything that affects our attacker's ability to commence an attack*. It's important to remember that in most violent attacks, we have options—finding cover, putting barriers between us and the attacker, or choosing a less–than–lethal level of force such as exposing our firearm or even pointing it at the attacker. *Anything* that causes our attacker to break off his attack before it begins is a good thing. Finally, it's important to realize that our decision to use any level of force will be second-guessed by the police, the prosecutor, and possibly a jury. We'll have to meet the "reasonableness" test, and if a prosecutor believes that we used excessive force, we're going to have to try to convince a jury that we're right, and the prosecutor is wrong.

Escape
Even after a violent attack has commenced, if we can escape, we should escape.

Exposing Our Firearm
There are no guarantees, but most violent crimes end if the victim simply exposes a firearm. Most criminals want to leave the scene of the crime with the same number of holes they started with.

Using Cover and Barriers
We should place anything between us and the attacker that can protect us from the attacker's weapon(s) or that can disrupt his attack.

Drawing and/or Using Our Firearm
It's a big jump up on the "Use of Force" continuum, but drawing our firearm immediately indicates to a determined attacker that we're not going to be an easy victim. Forcefully barking out commands such as "Stop!" also gives him a chance to change his mind before it's too late. Remember that just because you've drawn your firearm does not mean that you need to press the trigger but when we have no other choice, we need to be prepared to stop the threat with any force necessary.

WHEN WE'RE LEFT WITH NO OTHER CHOICE

Up to this point in the book, it's fair to say that everything we've discussed has been fairly academic, including the deadly force scenarios that were discussed in Chapter Four. On this page, we're going to need to discuss the most serious topic in the book, namely, shooting at another human being. We truly wish this topic never had to be discussed, but we also wish that criminals didn't murder, rape, assault, and rob. While we'd be the first in line to buy a Star Wars blaster that could be set on stun, we're not lucky enough to have that option. Until that day, if we do find ourselves in a situation that we didn't start and we can't escape from, where all four rules governing the use of deadly force have been met, then we have no choice but to stop the threat with any force necessary.

Where Do We Shoot?

As discussed in Chapter Three on shooting fundamentals, if we must use our firearm, our goal is "defensive accuracy." Defensive accuracy is any round that *significantly affects the attacker's ability to continue his attack*. The illustration to the right is a fair approximation of the human body, internally and externally. Where would you shoot to meet the goal of defensive accuracy? Would you shoot for the arm or shoulder? How about the attacker's hand? If those shots hit, they might affect the attacker's *desire* to continue an attack, but probably not his *ability*. Remember that your attacker will also be under the effects of adrenaline and endorphins, and he'll have a heightened pain threshold. If he's consumed illicit drugs such as Methamphetamine, his pain threshold will be even higher. It's very possible

that he wouldn't even feel a bullet if it passed through one of the areas on the diagram that contains no bone or organs. How about if you missed those small, moving targets? Remember that under the physiological effects that you'll undergo, your accuracy is likely to suffer, and the penalty for a miss can range from lost seconds and one less bullet, to the death of an innocent bystander. Keep in mind that we've moved beyond the academic and we're now talking about what it would take to stop an attacker who is seconds away from (or is already) stabbing you, shooting you, choking you, raping you, or beating you. It's a cold reality, but the fastest, surest, safest way (safest to innocent bystanders, not safest to the attacker) to significantly affect an attacker's ability to continue an attack, is to use the method taught to every police agency in the U.S., which is to aim for the attacker's high-center chest. When that area isn't visible, police are taught to shoot at the "center of exposed mass," which is the center of the largest part of the attacker's body that's visible.

How Long Do We Shoot?

As tempted as you may be to prematurely end your defense to see what effect your bullets have had, it's important to continue your defense until the attack has ended. It won't be like the movies, where one moderately sized bullet throws the bad guy through a plate glass window—odds are, you won't be able to tell where your bullets impact, or even *if* they have impacted. The only information that you'll be receiving will be whether the attack is continuing or whether it's ended. The moment it ends is the moment you *must stop using deadly force.*

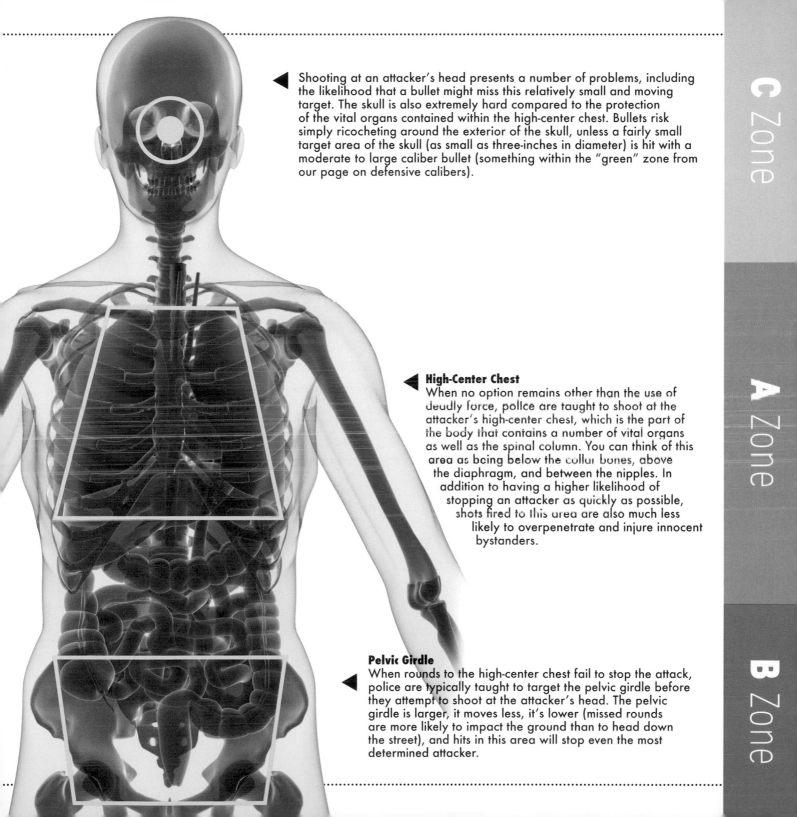

Shooting at an attacker's head presents a number of problems, including the likelihood that a bullet might miss this relatively small and moving target. The skull is also extremely hard compared to the protection of the vital organs contained within the high-center chest. Bullets risk simply ricocheting around the exterior of the skull, unless a fairly small target area of the skull (as small as three-inches in diameter) is hit with a moderate to large caliber bullet (something within the "green" zone from our page on defensive calibers).

High-Center Chest

When no option remains other than the use of deadly force, police are taught to shoot at the attacker's high-center chest, which is the part of the body that contains a number of vital organs as well as the spinal column. You can think of this area as being below the collar bones, above the diaphragm, and between the nipples. In addition to having a higher likelihood of stopping an attacker as quickly as possible, shots fired to this area are also much less likely to overpenetrate and injure innocent bystanders.

Pelvic Girdle

When rounds to the high-center chest fail to stop the attack, police are typically taught to target the pelvic girdle before they attempt to shoot at the attacker's head. The pelvic girdle is larger, it moves less, it's lower (missed rounds are more likely to impact the ground than to head down the street), and hits in this area will stop even the most determined attacker.

C Zone

A Zone

B Zone

AFTER THE THREAT HAS ENDED

Remember that the right to use deadly force ends the moment any one of the rules governing the use of deadly force is no longer true. Some examples of this might include:

■ The attacker has given up or he's run away. If he's run away, let him go. Protect yourself and your loved ones, tend to the wounded, and be a good witness.

■ The attacker has been wounded and can no longer threaten you with death or great bodily harm.

■ An opportunity to retreat safely has suddenly become available, such as after the attacker has been injured or has dropped his weapon.

Any use of force out of anger, retribution, or a misplaced sense of justice is a crime. Once the attack has ended, you can no longer continue to use deadly force, no matter how badly you or another individual might be injured. Picture this horrific scenario—walking through a parking garage, you come upon a rape in progress. You shout a warning and give chase when the attacker flees. You corner him at the end of the parking garage and when he charges you, you shoot and kill him. Your friends and family might call you a "hero," but you may have to hear about it from jail.

■ If your attacker ends the attack, your right to use deadly force ends as well. Regardless of how badly injured you or a loved one may be, or how angry you might feel, any harm that comes to the attacker at this point will be on your head. Come to think of it, any harm that came to your attacker before this point will also be on your head. Don't make the situation worse by continuing to shoot after the attack is over.

After you have determined that the threat has ended, visually scan to the left and the right of the initial threat, while keeping your firearm on target. Then bring your firearm into a high compressed ready position (with your finger OUTSIDE of the trigger guard) and scan the area for other threats. These scans will not only help to identify any other threats, they will also help to break tunnel vision and auditory exclusion (see the box below). Once you've determined that there are no further threats, immediately perform the tasks discussed on the following pages.

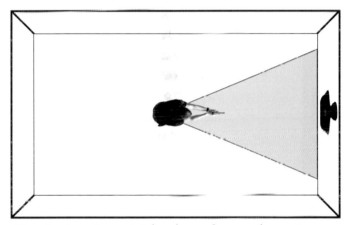

After the threat has ended, break your focus on the previous threat and assess your environment.

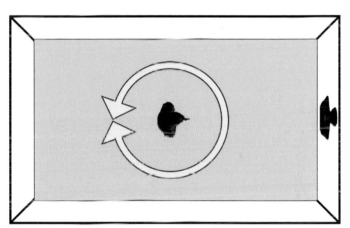

Bring your firearm to a high compressed ready position and perform a 360° scan to ensure there are no other threats.

■ As discussed in the section on the "Physiological Reactions" that typically occur during an attack, you can expect to have tunnel vision and auditory exclusion, which means that you may not see threats beyond the one to your front and you may have diminished hearing. Hunters appreciate auditory exclusion because it means they don't "hear" the shot as it's being fired, but in a defensive situation, auditory exclusion might cause you to ignore a loved one's shouts or the police shouting at you to drop your firearm. Physically moving your head (rather than just moving your eyes) to scan for other threats can break both tunnel vision and auditory exclusion. The brain seems to perceive this scan as a search for new threats and the selective filtering that occurs within the thalamus or sensory cortex is reset to normal.

THE IMMEDIATE AFTERMATH

Once you've confirmed that the immediate threat has ended, you'll need to quickly complete several important tasks. First and foremost, if you believe that you're still in danger, you'll need to immediately retreat to a safe area. Once there, you should closely check yourself and others for any injuries that might be masked by the effects of adrenaline and endorphins, and you should begin emergency first-aid to control any bleeding. Next, you'll need to make several important phone calls, including a call to 911, even if no one (including the attacker) is injured, or even if he's run away. These phone calls are CRITICAL. Even in this stressful moment, you'll need to remember that you've just used a firearm (even if it was just to expose it to end a threat), and you'll need to begin laying the groundwork for your defense in the event that you're charged with a crime. The phone calls to 911 and to your lawyer are the first steps in establishing this.

If you displayed your firearm, but no rounds were fired, make two calls:

1 **Call 911.** Do not let the attacker (or alleged attacker) or witnesses report the incident differently than it happened. This phone call is CRITICAL. Keep the call short and to the point:

A My name is _____ and I need to report (an attack / a possible attack) at (address, intersection, etc.).

B The individual (give a brief description of the attacker) and (ran off / drove off, etc.).

C I do have a permit to carry a firearm, and did expose my firearm to the attacker, but I did not use it.

D I'll contact my attorney and (he or she) will contact you to schedule time to make a statement. Here is my number.

E Be prepared to answer any questions related to the alleged attacker or your contact information, but do NOT answer any questions about your actions. Be prepared to hang up if the questioning gets persistent.

2 **Call your attorney.** If you can't reach your attorney, leave a message and contact information for where and how he or she can reach you.

If rounds were fired, make three calls:

1 **Call 911.** It is your obligation to seek medical attention if someone is injured! Remember that you are being recorded! Keep your 911 call short and to the point:

> **A** My name is _____ and I need to report an attack at (address, intersection, etc.).

> **B** The attacker (ran away / is injured / needs an ambulance).

> **C** I'm wearing _____ and I do have a permit to carry a firearm so let the police know that I'll place my firearm (on the front seat of my car / on my hood / back in my holster) before they arrive.

> **D** I need to (go help my family / watch the attacker / get to a safer place) so I'm going to hang up now.

> **E** Hang up.

2 **Call your attorney.**

3 **Call your family.** Inform them that you've been involved in a defensive situation and instruct them to speak with no one—not the police, not the media, no one! Tell family members to inform the police that they **DO NOT CONSENT TO A SEARCH OF YOUR HOME OR PROPERTY** and that they will answer no questions unless your attorney is present. If you are calling them from jail, do NOT give them any details, as the call may be recorded. Simply tell them where you are and that they should call your attorney.

When the Police Arrive

When the police arrive on the scene, what's your number one goal? Don't get shot. After a violent confrontation where force may have been used, the police will not know exactly what has occurred. They will only know that a firearm has been used and that the armed person remains at the scene. Remember, the police will be nervous, they'll be concerned for their own safety, and their adrenaline will be flowing as well. They will most likely believe that a bad guy has just shot another bad guy, or a bad guy has just shot a good guy.

Because of the perceptions the police will have when they arrive at the scene, here's what you should do:

■ Place your firearm back in its holster or off your body BEFORE the police approach. Where you place it will need to be based upon the current disposition of the attacker. If he's given up and is sitting on the ground in front of you, you'll need to keep ready access to your firearm, so reholstering may be the best idea. If he's run away or is incapacitated, placing the firearm on the hood or top of a car, or on the ground in front of you may be a better idea.

■ Put your hands high in the air as the police approach. Don't even *twitch* if your firearm is back in the holster.

■ Comply with all instructions from the police and keep your hands where they can see them. This is not the time to explain that "you are the good guy."

■ Don't argue, and be prepared to be pushed to the ground, handcuffed, and placed in the back of a squad car.

Digging Yourself a Hole

After a confrontation where a firearm has been used, the police are no longer there to serve and protect you, they are there to serve the prosecutor and protect any case he or she may choose to file. Like they say in the movies, anything you say will be used against you in a court of law. Most police officers carry digital recording devices, which will be rolling the moment they arrive at the scene, and any statement, no matter how innocent (such as "I was mad") can come back to haunt you. Although the police at the scene may legitimately sympathize with you, if the incident results in a trial, the police will be testifying on behalf of the prosecutor, not on your behalf. Finally, it's fair to say that the fatal error of nearly every criminal *and* every responsibly armed citizen involved in an altercation is that they want to talk. In fact, they *love* to talk—to the police, to their family, to the media, and their family even likes to talk to the media. While that may be a natural reaction when you want to shout, "I'm Innocent!" from the rooftops, you must resist that urge during the immediate aftermath of the incident; during intense pressure by the police to make a statement; when walking through a gauntlet of media when leaving jail; or when the media calls the attacker "the victim" and dredges up every questionable incident in your background. You *must* trust your lawyer to get you to the other side intact.

A Four-Part Statement to the Police

There is no upside in speaking with the police without your attorney present, and any statement you make, however true you may believe it to be, is fraught with risk (review our physiological section as a reminder on the distortion that can occur to your memory during an attack). Because of that and other risks, we recommend that you stick with this four-part statement to the police and do NOT go beyond it:

1 I was attacked (by that person / by a person who ran in that direction). Note: If the attacker is no longer present, be very careful about giving a description to the police since you may be suffering from memory loss or false memories, and you may not provide an accurate description.

2 There is the evidence (point out anything that the police may miss or may not realize was used as a weapon).

3 That person / those people were witnesses.

4 I've spoken with / left a message with my attorney and I'm going to wait until (he or she) arrives to give a statement and sign a complaint.

Note: If your mind goes blank, at least remember #4 above and do *not* be embarrassed to read the statement above if you choose to photocopy this page and keep it in your wallet or purse.

You don't have to be a fan of the CSI television shows to know that the police will carefully document everything they find at the scene of the attack. Don't disturb any evidence, and be sure to point out anything to the police that they might miss, such as the attacker's weapon.

THE MIRANDA WARNING

Most Americans are aware that the Fifth Amendment forbids compelling a person to testify against himself or herself in a criminal trial, and any fan of TV police dramas knows about the Miranda warning which reminds suspects of their right to remain silent, but do you know what Miranda *really* means, and when police are required to provide it?

Is it Enough Just to be Silent?

As part of the 1966 "Miranda" decision (Miranda v. Arizona) and subsequent reinterpretations, the Supreme Court has concluded that it is only necessary for police to read the Miranda warning to suspects upon their actual arrest and formal interrogation (Illinois v. Perkins). Prior to the combination of those two events, no warning is required, and most police departments now train their officers to delay the warning until just prior to the suspect's formal interrogation, which gives the suspect plenty of time to say something incriminating. If at any point the suspect does invoke his or her right to remain silent, it officially ends the police's right to a formal interrogation, but it *doesn't* end their right to use any statement that was voluntarily given, before, or after the Miranda warning.

So we know that we have the *right* to remain silent, but it begs the question, what does it take to *invoke* that right? Is it enough to simply remain silent? The answer is no. In 2010, the Supreme Court decided in Berghuis v. Thompkins, that simply remaining silent wasn't the same thing as explicitly *invoking* your right to remain silent with a clear statement. Without that statement, police have the right to continue their formal or informal interrogation for hours, in the hopes that you'll eventually say something to incriminate yourself. Knowing that, after making the four-part statement to the police shown on the previous page, you should state very clearly:

"I want my lawyer present before I answer any questions, and until then, I invoke my right to remain silent."

Keep in mind that even if you've been given your Miranda warning, and even if you've explicitly invoked your right to remain silent, anything that you volunteer (what's called a "spontaneous statement") is admissible in court. In other words, it isn't enough just to invoke your right to remain silent; after that, you'll have to actually *be* silent.

"I want my lawyer present before I answer any questions, and until then, I invoke my right to remain silent."

When Asked if you Consent to a Search

When asked if you consent to a search of your person, your vehicle, or your home, state very clearly:

"I do not consent to a search of my person or my property."

Repeat as often as necessary. Experts have agreed that there is zero upside in agreeing to a search. That said, do not interfere with the police if they choose to go ahead with a search anyway, without your consent. Police will frame their question to you in a way that makes it sound as though it's a foregone conclusion—for example, they won't ask, "Do you give up your rights under the Fourth Amendment of the constitution?" Instead they'll say, "It's okay if we look through your car, right?" Your answer needs to be "No." The problem with consenting to a search isn't just what will happen if the police find something illegal. In the hands of the prosecutor, even legal items can taint a jury. For example, a box of ammunition found in your home or car becomes, "The defendant had enough ammunition to kill 50 people!" That pain pill found under your front seat that was prescribed to you three years ago becomes, "The defendant was found with illegal prescription drugs!" As our friend Marc Berris says, "The laws protecting us from illegal search and seizure are designed to protect the innocent, not the guilty."

When are you Under Arrest?

Unfortunately, it won't be as obvious as when Horatio Cane says, "Take him!" on CSI Miami. When investigating any suspicious activity (which would include the use of a firearm) the police have the right to perform what is referred to as a Terry stop, which allows the police to temporarily detain individuals to request that they identify themselves; to question them about the suspicious activity; and to conduct a limited pat down search for weapons. Whether you've moved from a Terry stop to being under arrest may only be ascertained if you are not allowed to leave. To determine that, after you've made the four-part statement, you'll need to ask, "Can I leave?" If the answer is no, you should assume that you're under arrest.

Advice for your Lawyer

When discussing your case with your lawyer, here are a few extra bits of information that you should pass on. If they don't understand the points below, or are unwilling to complete these tasks, find a new lawyer.

■ Delay any interview with the police for as long as possible, but for at least 48-hours. Refer your lawyer to the International Association of Chiefs of Police (IACP) guidelines shown on the next page, that the police themselves will follow if they are involved in a critical incident.

" I do not consent to a search of my person or my property."

■ Your lawyer should read the physiological section in this book so he or she can understand the distortions that occur during critical incidents. He or she should also review the police interviews by Dr. Alexis Artwohl.

■ Your lawyer and his or her investigator must review the scene of the crime, they must analyze all evidence, and they must conduct their own interviews of all witnesses.

■ Your lawyer may need to seek out expert testimony from professionals who have testified at (and won) multiple self-defense trials.

How are Police Treated when a Shooting Occurs?

Most law enforcement organizations in the U.S. have adopted policies similar to one outlined by the International Association of Chiefs of Police, which provides 20 guidelines for dealing with a police officer who has been involved in a shooting. These guidelines are designed to have the officers avoid a "second injury" by insensitive treatment and to allow the officer to "avoid legal complications."

One of the guidelines states: "If possible, the officer can benefit from some recovery time before detailed interviewing begins. This can range from a few hours to overnight, depending on the emotional state of the officer and the circumstances." It goes on to say, "Officers who have been afforded this opportunity to calm down are likely to provide a more coherent and accurate statement."

If that advice is good enough for the police, it's good enough for us.

In the euphoria of the aftermath, you might think that the situation is a slam dunk in your favor and that you'll be hailed as a hero. We hate to burst your bubble, but it isn't, and you won't. When you run through the mental scenarios in Chapter One, don't forget to include your arrest.

THE FINANCIAL AFTERMATH

In Chapter One, we discussed that the goal of a personal protection plan was not only designed to keep us physically safe, but it was also designed to keep us legally, financially and morally safe as well. While it's easy to understand protecting ourselves and our families *physically*, the legal, financial and emotional aftermath that can occur after a use of force is often forgotten or ignored, until it's too late. While we'd like to think that any defensive use of force on our part would be viewed as a slam dunk in our favor where we'll be hailed as the hero, but reality is far more complicated than that. There are too many stories of individuals who did everything right when it came to a defensive use of force, but still found themselves charged with a crime and facing jail time, the loss of their firearms, and economic ruin. Each year, we hear heart wrenching stories of people just like us who lost their job or even their homes, because of the financial burdens that were associated with defending themselves in court, *after* defending themselves on the street or in their homes. The financial burden for many proves to be too great as "the defendant" must weigh how much justice he or she can afford. Even in cases where the legally armed American did everything right, the individual might find themselves accepting a plea bargain, rather than gambling it all, and running the risk of financial ruin.

How Much will it Cost?

How much will it cost if you're involved in a defensive use of force? Legal experts have concluded that even if you've done everything right, even if no shots were fired, and even if the police on the scene sympathize with you and call you a "hero," you'll still need legal representation right up until the point that the prosecutor publicly states that no charges will be filed against you, and only after any potential lawsuit from the attacker or the attacker's family is thrown out. Until then, you'll need legal support at every point when the police or prosecutor's office has contact with you, including during any formal or informal interviews with police investigators. That legal representation may cost you upward of $10,000, and that's in a case where the police have backed you from the start. If your case has more shades of gray (as most do), you should expect the financial burden to be much higher, as more police investigation occurs, more evidence is gathered, and more interviews are scheduled. If you *are* charged with a crime, you should expect your legal bill to top $100,000 or *more*. And unfortunately, your financial risk doesn't just come from the state, it will also come from your attacker, or his family. In what sound like stories out of *Ripley's Believe it or Not*, the court systems are choked with civil lawsuits, not filed by victims against their attackers, but filed by attackers against their intended victim. Unscrupulous lawyers have recognized for years that simply the threat of a lawsuit will very often cause law abiding Americans to fold, and pay out tens or even hundreds of thousands of dollars, rather than go to court, and risk an even higher settlement.

What about Home Owner's Insurance?

For new gun owners, there is very often the incorrect believe that homeowner's insurance, or general liability insurance will pay legal fees (criminal or civil) in the event that the homeowner is involved in a defensive use of force inside or outside the home. That belief couldn't be further from the truth. Typical home or general

Typical home or general liability insurance is designed to protect you in case of an injury or death caused to another person because of your negligence, not because of a purposeful act. In other words, that type of insurance may protect you if you've done something stupid, dangerous, or negligent, such as leaving the gate to your pool open or having an accidental discharge with your firearm. For purposeful acts (which would include purposefully attempting to stop a home invasion or a violent attack), this insurance wouldn't apply. To state that another way, if you accidentally shot someone in your home (negligence) you might be covered, but if you purposefully shot a home invader, you'd be out of luck.

HOME INSURAN
POLICY

olicy Number: 65-987-62
le: 548-98-987-65   Property

liability insurance is designed to protect you in case of an injury or death caused to another person because of your *negligence,* not because of a purposeful act. In other words, that type of insurance may protect you if you've done something stupid, dangerous, or negligent, such as leaving the gate to your pool open or having an accidental discharge with your firearm. For purposeful acts (which would include purposefully attempting to stop a home invasion or a violent attack), this insurance wouldn't apply. To state that another way, if you accidentally shot someone in your home (negligence) you might be covered, but if you purposefully shot a home invader, you'd be out of luck. So what's the solution?

Self-Defense Insurance

Until recently, there wasn't a lot the legally armed American could do to prepare for the financial aftermath of a lawful, defensive use of force. In fact, too often the potential financial aftermath was dismissed with the phrase, "I'd rather be judged by 12 than carried by six." While we understand the philosophical side of that statement, that is, we agree that it's much better to *have* the right to defend ourselves and our families (and deal with the aftermath) than *not* have that right, and be dead or seriously injured. But the "rather be judged" statement ignores the fact that the actual violent attack or home invasion is just the first of four "injuries" you might face—in other words, if you only concern yourself with protecting yourself from physical injury,

but you don't protect yourself from the legal, financial and emotional aftermath, then your preparation might seem as though it were for nothing. Instead of relying on a tired old cliche, an option now exists to protect against the legal, financial and emotional aftermath, just as a firearm and good training, can protect you from a physical threat.

The United States Concealed Carry Association is now the nation's leading resource for Self-Defense Insurance, designed specifically to protect you from the criminal and civil aftermath that always seems to follow even clear cut self-defense cases. The insurance from the USCCA goes well beyond simply paying for civil and criminal coverage. Here's how it works. If you're involved in a self-defense incident, after calling 911, call the USCCA. The Critical Response Team from the USCCA will connect you with a qualified pro-2nd Amendment lawyer in your area. Your Self-Defense SHIELD will pay for the legal retainer. If you're arrested, you'll receive up-front funding for bail, attorney fees, and upwards of a million dollars or more if you need to defend yourself in civil

USCCA Membership Card
If you are ever involved in a lawful, defensive use of force, the only card that you'll care about in your wallet will be the USCCA Membership card. After a use of force, call 911, and then call us. We've got your back.

Member Name
Membership Level
Membership Number
Member Since Date

www.USCCA.com

■You protect them, and the United States Concealed Carry Association protects you, in the event that you're ever involved in a defensive use of force. Don't survive a violent encounter, only to become financially devastated. A membership with the USCCA is your path to becoming properly educated, trained, *and* insured. To learn more or to become a member today, visit www.USCCA.com.

court. You'll even receive wage compensation for the time you have to spend in court, away from your job. There are no deductibles, no reimbursement fees, and no out of-pocket costs to your family.

Is it Really Necessary?

Like any insurance policy, it's a fair question to ask, "What's the likelihood that I'll actually *need* this insurance?" In other words, is this the type of insurance that can just be skipped? That depends upon whom you ask. To use a simple analogy, most Americans will make it through their lives without ever needing their homeowners policy. But for the millions of Americans whose homes are damaged each year by extreme weather, or for the more than 300,000 families displaced by home fires, their insurance policy is literally a Godsend. For individuals who "bet" the odds, and choose *not* to have a homeowners policy, the result can be financial devastation, or the complete loss of their home. To bring the topic back to self-defense insurance, you can certainly play the odds, and choose *not* to have self-defense insurance, but then you'll have to ask yourself, why are you carrying a firearm at all? Why do you have a firearm at home for self-defense if you're going to play the "odds" that nothing bad ever happens to you or your family? For us, carrying self-defense insurance is done for the same reason that we carry life insurance, or carry a firearm for self-defense. It's the

responsible thing to do. Anything else risks bringing utter ruin onto yourself and your family. At the USCCA, we believe that the responsibly armed American is educated, trained, *and* insured. Does that definition describe you?

More than an Insurance Company

The USCCA is more than just an insurance company, it's a membership organization that also provides some of the best education and training available, through the premier publication, *Concealed Carry Magazine*, through the weekly newsletter *Concealed Carry Report*, and through the thousands of USCCA Firearms Instructors nationwide. The USCCA truly is an organization that educates, trains, *and* insures. To learn more or to become a member today, visit us at www.USCCA.com.

EVERYDAY ENCOUNTERS WITH LAW ENFORCEMENT

Now that we've discussed how to handle contact with law enforcement after a use of force, let's discuss what you should know when it comes to everyday encounters with law enforcement, such as during a traffic stop. The fact, is, with more than 12 million permit holders in the U.S., law enforcement officers are coming into contact with permit holders far more often than even they're aware of (although statistically, permit holders are far less likely than the average citizen to be stopped for traffic violations or driving while intoxicated), but it's a valid subject to discuss since this everyday contact can easily move in the wrong direction if the permit holder and law enforcement officer are not aware of some basic guidelines, including how your state's law might affect your required actions.

State Laws

Each of the state supplements that the USCCA has written for use by our certified instructors contain not only detail on what that particular state's laws have to say about police interactions, but the presentations also include helpful advice on how to handle those interactions to ensure that they are safe, and trouble-free for both the permit holder and the law enforcement officer. We wish there was a single procedure that we could recommend that would work for all states, for all possible scenarios when permit holders interact with law enforcement, but unfortunately, the myriad of state laws makes that almost impossible. To give you a sampling, states such as Florida, Illinois, Iowa, Kansas, Minnesota, New Mexico, South Carolina, Texas, Utah and Wisconsin do not have a "duty to inform," meaning that permit holders are not required to produce their permit or inform the officer that they are carrying a firearm unless the law enforcement officer, acting in an official capacity, requests it. Other states require the permit holder to volunteer the information upon contact with law enforcement, otherwise the permit holder may face charges ranging from a slap on the wrist to a first-degree misdemeanor. Some examples:

Michigan:

An individual licensed to carry a concealed pistol who is stopped by a police officer (a traffic stop or otherwise) while in possession of a firearm must "immediately disclose to the police officer that he or she is carrying a concealed pistol either on their person or in their motor vehicle." Handing your concealed carry license to the law enforcement officer along with your driver's license is *not* considered disclosure in the state of Michigan. You must immediately, and *verbally* disclose to the officer that you are carrying a firearm. In a recent court case, a license holder was found guilty of violating this provision, because he waited *40 seconds* to verbally disclose to a police officer that he was carrying a firearm.

Nebraska:

In Nebraska, the law states that when carrying under a permit, any time you are "officially contacted" by any peace officer or emergency services personnel, you must immediately inform the peace officer or emergency service personnel of the concealed handgun unless physically unable to do so.

Ohio:

If a concealed carry permit holder is stopped for a law enforcement purpose and is carrying a concealed handgun (whether in a motor vehicle or not) the law states that the permit holder "shall promptly" inform the law enforcement officer that he or she is carrying a concealed handgun. If in a vehicle, the licensee "shall remain in the vehicle and keep his hands in plain sight at all times." Violating this section of law is a first-degree misdemeanor.

Oklahoma:

The Oklahoma Self-Defense Act requires permit holders who are carrying a firearm to inform law enforcement officers when the person "first comes into contact" with any law enforcement officer during the course of any arrest, detainment, or routine traffic stop.

Our Advice

Whether you choose to volunteer the fact that you are carrying a firearm or whether you're required to do so by law, the official USCCA training doctrine recommends the following if you are stopped by law enforcement:

1 If possible, retrieve your wallet prior to the officer approaching your window, and place it on the dashboard.

2 Place your hands on the steering wheel. Law enforcement officers like to see hands.

3 Let the officer speak first and then respond with clear, direct language, such as: "I wanted to let you know that I have a concealed carry permit, which is in my wallet, and I am carrying today, in a holster on my right hip. What should I do?"

4 Keep your hands on the steering wheel, listening carefully to the officer's response.

5 If the officer provides any instructions that will require you to move your hands, repeat the officer's instructions before you do so. For example, if the officer asked you to hand him your license, registration and permit, you should leave your hands on the steering wheel, and reply with, "I'm going to take my driver's license, my registration and my permit out of my wallet which is on the dash. Is that okay?"

6 If you weren't able to remove your wallet from your pocket or purse and you must do so, inform the officer about what you are about to do before you do it. For example, you might say, "My wallet is in my back, left pocket. Is it okay if I reach for it?" Get their confirmation before moving your hands from the steering wheel, move slowly, and return your hands to the steering wheel after you've handed over your license, permit and registration.

7 If the officer asks you to step out of your vehicle, or if they suggest that they'd like to temporarily disarm you, do NOT move your hands toward your firearm and instead, allow the officer to direct the disarming. If they are having trouble removing your firearm from the holster (more on this in a bit) or removing your holster from your belt, do NOT move your hands in an attempt to help. They will ask for help if they need it, or they will ask another responding officer for assistance.

Some other advice for permit holders when it comes to everyday contact with law enforcement: Having a permit does not suddenly create a bond between you and law enforcement, it doesn't elevate you to their peer group, and it doesn't lower the officer's guard, simply

Regardless of why you were stopped, if you believe that you'll be subject to a pat down, you should inform law enforcement that you are carrying a firearm BEFORE they find out on their own. Follow their instructions to the letter.

because you have a little plastic card in your wallet. With 26 murdered police officers (so far) in 2016, expect that the firearm on your hip will *elevate* the officer's guard, not *lower* it. In addition, never, never, *never* move your hands without being directed by the law enforcement officer, and if the situation goes south, immediately stop moving your hands, *and* your mouth. Even if you find yourself with a gun pointed at your head and the officer screaming commands at you, do your absolute best to remain calm, and remain *still* until you can understand the officer's commands, and follow them to the letter. If you think the officer is out of line, then file a complaint, which is your right. Being dead is no way to prove that you were in the right, and the law enforcement officer was in the wrong.

Advice for Law Enforcement Officers

On an average traffic stop anywhere in the U.S., the likelihood that the driver will be a convicted felon is about 1 in 12. If you happen to be a law enforcement officer in Florida, it's even worse with about 14 percent of all Florida residents listed as convicted felons. That isn't to imply that all felons who have served their debt to society constitute a clear and present danger to law enforcement officers, but lets at least say that the risk is greater to the law enforcement officer when they come into contact with that class of citizen, rather than another class of citizen, namely, the concealed carry permit holder. With more than 12 million permit holders in the U.S., that means that about 6 percent of all citizens you come into contact with fit into a unique category—by legal requirement in every state, these permit holders will never have been convicted of a felony, they will never have been convicted of a violent misdemeanor, most will never have received a DWI, most will have received state and federal background checks within the last few years, most will have attended legal and firearms safety training, and the vast majority will be huge supporters of law enforcement. You should count permit holders among the good guys. If a driver hands you his concealed carry permit in addition to his driver's license and registration, he is not threatening you, he is simply following the advice from his instructor, or he is following the legal requirement in your state. Your response could be a simple, "Thank you, are you carrying your firearm today?" If the response is, "Yes," you might consider replying the same way *Concealed Carry Magazine* Editor Kevin Michalowski (who is also a police officer) replies. "Thank you for letting me know you have a gun on you. Now, if you don't reach for yours, I won't reach for mine. Please keep your hands where I can see them."

If you do choose to disarm the driver (in most cases, you'd have absolutely no reason to do so), remove the holster from the driver's belt, rather than attempting to remove the firearm from the holster. Remember that negligent discharges only occur during the administrative handling of the firearm. Leave it in the holster, and you eliminate that possibility. Our last bit of advice is to engage the permit holder in some conversation about the topic of legal firearm ownership, such as asking them what they carry, asking them what holster they use, or asking them where they like to shoot. You'll quickly discover that the average permit holder has more in common with you than you might think.

■ **WHY DO YOU CHOOSE TO CARRY A CONCEALED FIREARM?** Personal defense of my family and myself. No one else has a duty and responsibility to protect my family and me. Like an insulating layer while hunting or hiking, I'd rather have it and not need it. I pray often than I will never have to use it.

■ **WHAT DO YOU TELL PEOPLE WHO ARE CONSIDERINGCONCEALED CARRY?** It is a tremendous reponsibility and they should seriously consider it, but I do promote CCW and recommend them having the right attitude and mindset. When we sell a gun, we recommend that the buyer take a CCW class, find a firearm that meets their requirements, rain often with their firearm, and mentally prepare for what could happen. We invite them to attend the USCCA Concealed Carry and Home Defense Fundamentals classes we teach. We also invite them to come to our local defensive handgun competition, for which I am the match director.

CHAPTER 6

GEAR AND GADGETS

- Explaining Holster Retention
- Types of Holsters Including Inside the Waistband, Outside the Waistband, Pocket Holsters, Satchel Holstes, Purse Holsters and More
- Other Gear Including Belts, Tactical Flashlights, Mounted Lights, Night Sights, and Lasers
- Gun Safes and Storage

Walk into any gun shop, and the variety of gear and gadgets available can be a bit overwhelming. Gun vaults, holsters, lights, lasers— where do you start? In this chapter, we'll help to explain each of those pieces of related gear, and we'll talk about the options you should consider when you're ready to go shopping. Some of the gear we'll discuss such as gun vaults, lights, and lasers, will be beneficial regardless of whether you're looking at home defense or if a concealed carry permit is part of your plan. If you *are* considering a concealed carry permit, then your immediate priority will need to be a good holster that not only works for your firearm, but that also works for *you*. Since selecting a holster can be as confusing as selecting a firearm, we're going to start with that topic.

In our section on holsters, we'll start by explaining how holster retention devices work (and which levels of retention work for permit holders, versus what law enforcement might require) as well as explanations of the most common types of holsters, including belt, pancake, paddle, pocket, and others. In our examples, you'll see a number of holsters made with leather and a number made with Kydex, which is a fancy way of saying plastic. Both have advantages—leather can be more comfortable and is usually more kind to your handgun's finish, while Kydex typically has much more of a positive "click" when the firearm is holstered. We have lots of each.

We'll continue the chapter with discussions on other important pieces of equipment, including gear to allow you to operate in low-light or no-light situations. Night sights, tactical flashlights, mounted lights, and mounted lasers have all undergone a dramatic transformation in the last decade, and we'll provide a detailed explanation about what you should consider when selecting these pieces of equipment.

Finally, we'll wrap-up this chapter with a discussion of safe storage devices for your home, including gun vaults designed to hold a single handgun (along with a spare magazine or two), and wall mounted units designed to secure home defense shotguns.

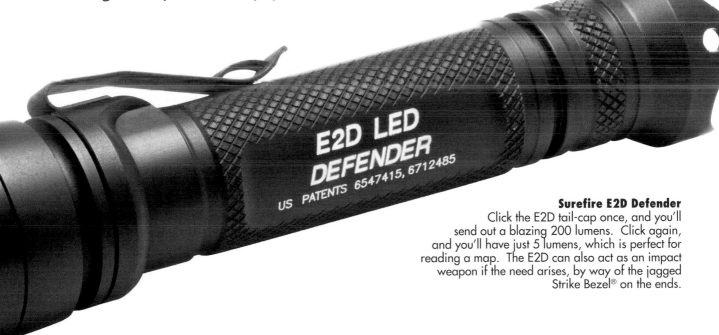

Surefire E2D Defender
Click the E2D tail-cap once, and you'll send out a blazing 200 lumens. Click again, and you'll have just 5 lumens, which is perfect for reading a map. The E2D can also act as an impact weapon if the need arises, by way of the jagged Strike Bezel® on the ends.

LEVELS OF HOLSTER RETENTION

Modern holsters come with a variety of methods and devices to ensure that your handgun remains in the holster until you're ready to use it. The most common retention method that holsters provide is nothing more than a snug fit. Selecting a holster that's molded to your specific firearm make, model, and size usually means that the firearm will remain in place even when you're running, jumping, or bending, but it allows your firearm to be quickly retrieved without an extra step, something you'll appreciate during an attack when your manual dexterity can go to mush. These holsters are typically referred to as "Level Zero" or "Open Top Holsters." For an extra level of retention, a variety of holsters are available with top straps, or some type of release lever, usually activated with either the index finger or with the thumb. These holsters are typically referred to as "Level I" holsters, and can provide an extra level of confidence that your gun will remain in the holster until you need it.

LEVEL ZERO: Firearm Held in Place by Tension only

Retention by Tension
Both leather and plastic Level Zero holsters hold firearms in place by being specifically molded to a particular firearm.

LEVEL I: Firearm Held in Place by Top Strap or Release Lever

Top Strap
Usually unsnapped by pushing the thumb toward the body while drawing.

Release Lever
A release lever is embedded within the holster and is released with either the index or middle finger. A solid "click" should be heard when reholstering.

LEVEL II AND LEVEL III HOLSTERS

Law enforcement officers are often required by their departments to use what are called Level II or Level III holsters, which have multiple retention methods that must be de-activated before the firearm can be drawn from the holster. Our advice is that you leave these holsters to the police. Since police typically carry exposed and have the unfortunate task of getting their hands on bad guys, the extra retention makes sense for them, but not for concealed carry permit holders who normally carry concealed.

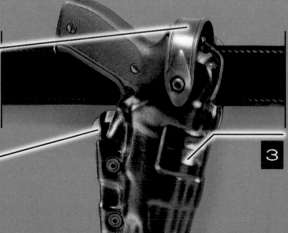

1 **Top Strap**
Usually unsnapped by pushing the thumb toward the body while drawing. Others, such as this Safariland holster, have straps that must be rotated forward before the firearm can be released.

2 **Release Lever**
A release lever is embedded within the holster and is released with either the index or middle finger.

3 **Rocking Release**
Once the top strap is released and the release lever is pushed, the firearm can only be drawn after rocking it back (or forward, depending upon the brand).

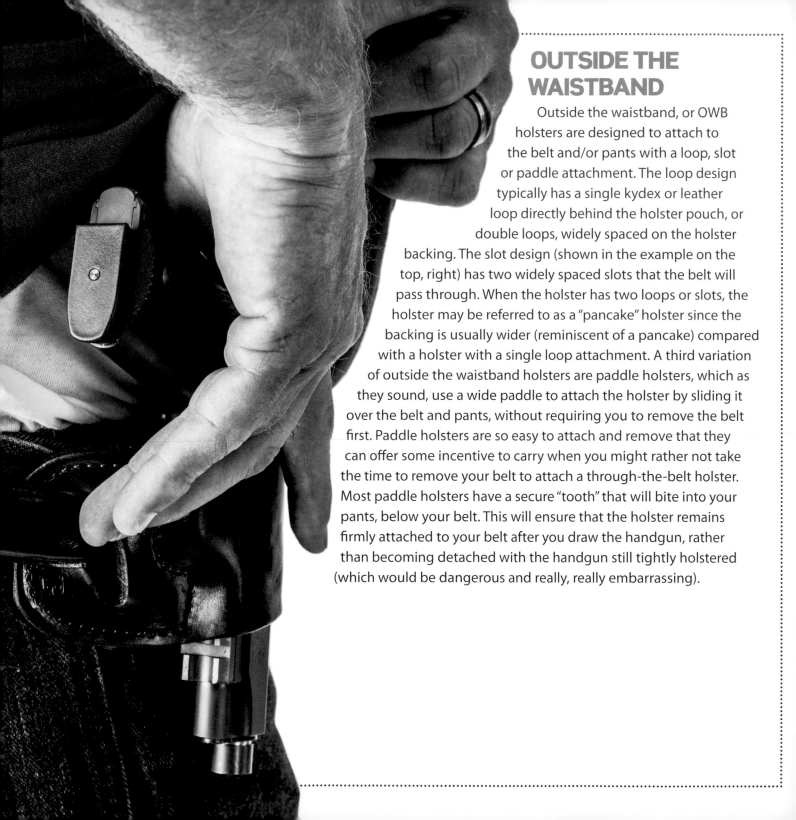

OUTSIDE THE WAISTBAND

Outside the waistband, or OWB holsters are designed to attach to the belt and/or pants with a loop, slot or paddle attachment. The loop design typically has a single kydex or leather loop directly behind the holster pouch, or double loops, widely spaced on the holster backing. The slot design (shown in the example on the top, right) has two widely spaced slots that the belt will pass through. When the holster has two loops or slots, the holster may be referred to as a "pancake" holster since the backing is usually wider (reminiscent of a pancake) compared with a holster with a single loop attachment. A third variation of outside the waistband holsters are paddle holsters, which as they sound, use a wide paddle to attach the holster by sliding it over the belt and pants, without requiring you to remove the belt first. Paddle holsters are so easy to attach and remove that they can offer some incentive to carry when you might rather not take the time to remove your belt to attach a through-the-belt holster. Most paddle holsters have a secure "tooth" that will bite into your pants, below your belt. This will ensure that the holster remains firmly attached to your belt after you draw the handgun, rather than becoming detached with the handgun still tightly holstered (which would be dangerous and really, really embarrassing).

Crossbreed Holsters MiniSlide

The Crossbreed MiniSlide is intended to offer the user a close riding, very concealable Outside the Waistband (OWB) option for small guns such as the Sig238, Ruger LCP and Rohrbaugh R9. Pictured on the left with the new Ruger LCP II.

Alien Gear ShapeShift OWB Paddle Holster

The back view of this ShapeShift outside the waistband holster shows the wide paddle that's used to hold the holster into position, rather than looping the belt through loops or slots. The ShapeShift also allows the user to adjust the cant of the gun in 12-degree increments. By adding the ShapeShift starter kit to your purchase, you can quickly and easily convert the ShapeShift OWB Paddle Holster into an inside the waistband or a traditional outside the waistband holster without the use of tools.

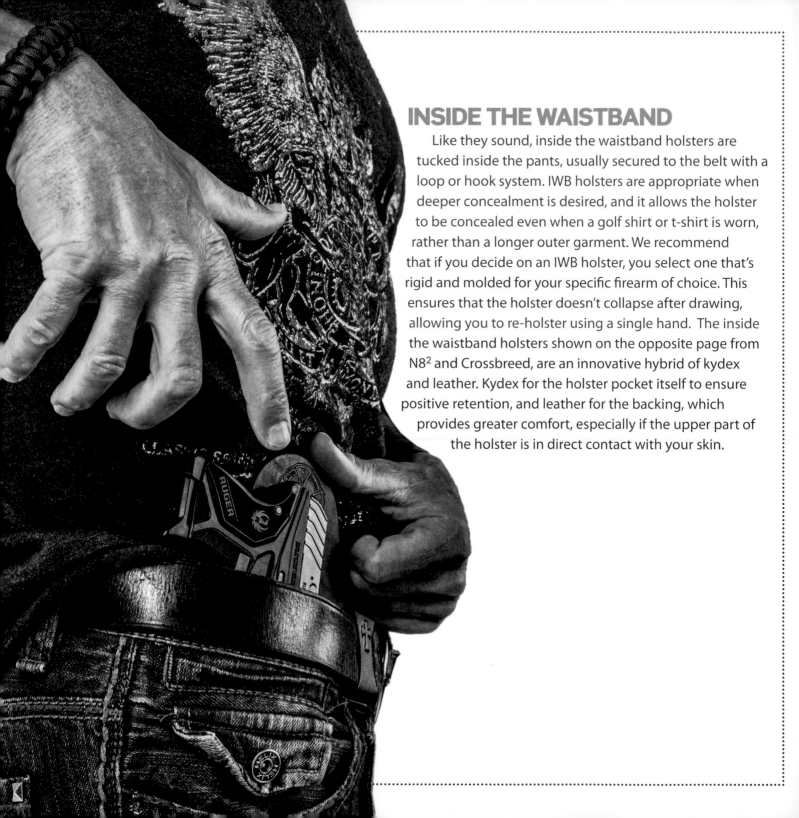

INSIDE THE WAISTBAND

Like they sound, inside the waistband holsters are tucked inside the pants, usually secured to the belt with a loop or hook system. IWB holsters are appropriate when deeper concealment is desired, and it allows the holster to be concealed even when a golf shirt or t-shirt is worn, rather than a longer outer garment. We recommend that if you decide on an IWB holster, you select one that's rigid and molded for your specific firearm of choice. This ensures that the holster doesn't collapse after drawing, allowing you to re-holster using a single hand. The inside the waistband holsters shown on the opposite page from N8[2] and Crossbreed, are an innovative hybrid of kydex and leather. Kydex for the holster pocket itself to ensure positive retention, and leather for the backing, which provides greater comfort, especially if the upper part of the holster is in direct contact with your skin.

N8² Tactical Envoy

The Envoy from N8² (Nate Squared) utilizes a single clip in front, which can be angled for your preferred cant. The relatively small size of the Envoy allows the holster to be positioned inside-the-waistband in multiple locations including the popular "appendix" carry which positions the holster and firearm between the carrier's center line and their hip bone.

Crossbreed Holsters Supertuck

The Supertuck from Crossbreed uses two clips to hold the holster in place, and a wide leather backing to absorb the weight and pressure of the firearm. The Supertuck actually allows the user to tuck their shirt in between the clips and the leather backing, which enables enhanced concealment.

POCKET HOLSTERS

Pocket Pistols are small enough for alternate carry options, including sliding them into a front or back pocket. The holster on the lower left from Crossbreed is designed for the back pocket—the rectangular piece of leather behind the gun faces the outside of the pants, breaking up the outline of the gun, and giving the impression that your back pocket contains nothing more than a wallet. The holster on the lower right from BORAII is designed for the front pocket. At first glance, the holster looks like someone took a full-sized holster and used a precision laser to cut away about three-quarters of it, leaving you with the rest. But the BORAII does exactly what a holster is supposed to do—it snaps tightly and securely over the trigger and trigger guard, and its rectangular paddle holds the firearm in place, upright in the pocket. The BORAII's shape also breaks up the outline of the gun, making it look like you've got a full-sized smart phone in your pocket rather than a pistol. Drawing the gun up and to the rear, the "hook" on the bottom of the holster will catch on the back of your pocket, leaving the holster in your pocket and your gun in your hand, ready to be put into action. The grommet holes in the holster also allow a short lanyard to be attached—looping the other end of the lanyard through a belt loop means that even if the hook doesn't snap the holster off the gun, the holster will be removed when the lanyard reaches its full extension. The minimalistic design of the BORAII also provides another great side benefit. Since the slide is not covered or blocked by the BORAII, it's possible to clear your firearm while leaving the trigger and trigger guard completely covered, for those times that you may be required to disarm and unload. Since the trigger and trigger guard remain covered while performing a clearance procedure, the chances of a negligent discharge are *dramatically* reduced.

Crossbreed Pocket Rocket Holster

BORAII Eagle Pocket Holster

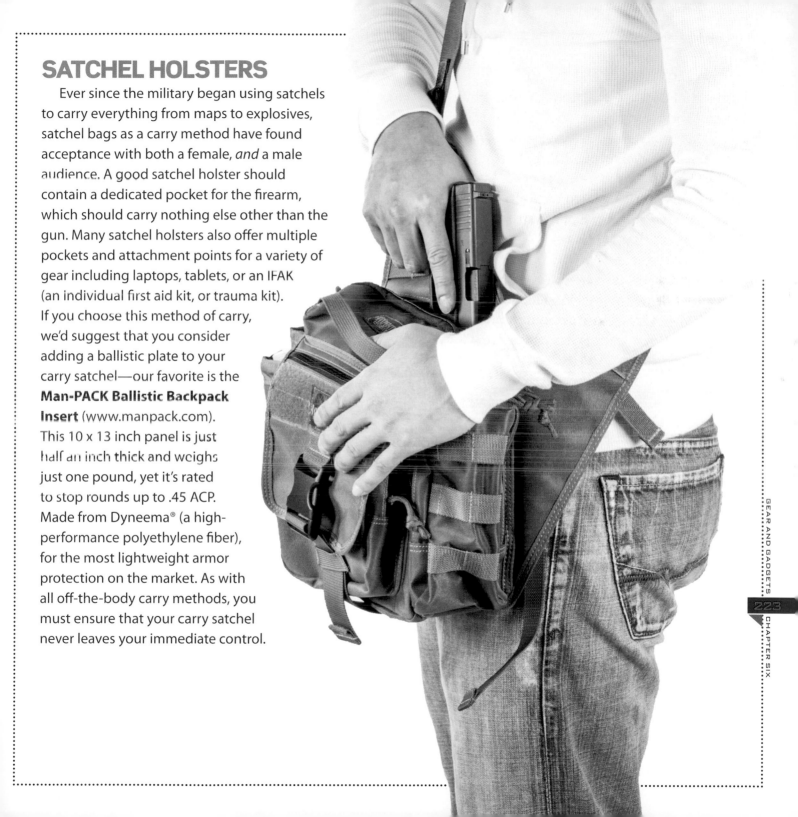

SATCHEL HOLSTERS

Ever since the military began using satchels to carry everything from maps to explosives, satchel bags as a carry method have found acceptance with both a female, *and* a male audience. A good satchel holster should contain a dedicated pocket for the firearm, which should carry nothing else other than the gun. Many satchel holsters also offer multiple pockets and attachment points for a variety of gear including laptops, tablets, or an IFAK (an individual first aid kit, or trauma kit). If you choose this method of carry, we'd suggest that you consider adding a ballistic plate to your carry satchel—our favorite is the **Man-PACK Ballistic Backpack Insert** (www.manpack.com). This 10 x 13 inch panel is just half an inch thick and weighs just one pound, yet it's rated to stop rounds up to .45 ACP. Made from Dyneema® (a high-performance polyethylene fiber), for the most lightweight armor protection on the market. As with all off-the-body carry methods, you must ensure that your carry satchel never leaves your immediate control.

ANKLE HOLSTERS

Ankle holsters don't provide the easiest method to draw from, but they can offer deep concealment when the situation calls for it. Our suggestion is to stick with pocket-sized pistols for ankle carry, otherwise you'll feel like you strapped on an ankle weight. You'll also need to find a range that will allow you to practice drawing from this carry method, which is decidedly more complex than drawing from an inside- or outside-the-waistband holster. Most people would consider this method of carry as one they would use for a back-up gun, rather than for their primary gun.

PURSE HOLSTERS

Like a satchel holster, purse holsters have a dedicated pocket designed to hold a handgun more securely and covertly than simply dropping it into a normal purse. This dedicated pocket however, should carry nothing else besides the handgun. Since a purse is the most likely object to be grabbed during a robbery, you should loop the purse strap around your neck, or consider one with the addition of a thigh strap. It bears repeating—as with all of-the-body carry methods, you must ensure that a purse holster *never* leaves your direct control.

SHOULDER HOLSTERS

Pretty cool if your name is Crocket or Tubbs, but somewhat impractical otherwise. If concealment is desired or required, shoulder holsters will require that an outer garment be worn, and they tend to be more difficult to draw from versus holsters worn on the belt. One exception is for individuals of sizable girth (who are less comfortable with an OWB or IWB holster); another is for individuals who spend most of their time in a vehicle, since a shoulder holster won't be blocked by the seatbelt.

DON'T FORGET THE BELT

Typical dress belts are not nearly stiff enough (and are rarely wide enough) to support the weight of a firearm, however, a number of manufacturers (including Crossbreed, 5.11, Gould & Goodrich, Galco, and Bianchi) offer dress, casual, and tactical versions specifically designed to support the weight of a gun. If fitting to a belt holster, ensure that the width of the belt matches the belt loop slots in the holster. A proper belt can also make a common function a little bit easier and a little bit safer. Using the restroom while holstered presents challenges, so we recommend that you invest in a very rigid belt so that your holstered firearm doesn't drop to the floor, or you can un-holster and put the firearm in your pocket. If your belt is long enough, you can re-fasten your belt with your pants in the lowered position. DO NOT set your firearm on the floor, or hang your firearm on the coat hook on the stall door. That leaves it in a perfect position to be forgotten or grabbed while you're busy doing other things, and it can lead to a negligent discharge, and a lot of embarrassment.

TACTICAL FLASHLIGHTS

When preparing your gear selections for home defense or concealed carry, we'd recommend that you include a tactical flashlight on your short list of things to purchase. The term "tactical flashlight" is more than just marketing—there are major differences between flashlights that should be part of your self–defense line-up, versus what you'd pick up at your local hardware store for $10. Here's what you should look for in a tactical flashlight:

High Output Beam. A minimum brightness should be 60 lumens (the average 2-AA light is about 15 lumens). 60 lumens is bright enough to momentarily blind an attacker even in daylight, while 125 lumens is like staring into the sun. Surefire has lights up to 900 lumens, such as the M3LT-S CombatLight shown below. Personally, we'd rather be Tasered than have one of those hit us in the face.

Lithium Batteries, which have a shelf-life as long as ten years, and have a much higher energy output for their size, versus alkaline batteries. In addition, they aren't affected by cold, so feel free to leave the light in your car, even in the northern states.

Tail-Cap On/Off Switch, rather than a switch on the side. As you'll see in our section on the various flashlight holds in Chapter Seven, a tail-cap on/off switch is critical to getting these holds correct.

We'd also recommend LED lights over traditional tungsten bulbs. You can hammer nails with an LED light without it breaking, while tungsten bulbs can break if the flashlight is dropped or banged on a barrier.

Handheld Lights

A number of manufacturers make handheld flashlights that fit these criteria, including the lights shown here from Surefire and First-Light USA. While it might seem like a simple thing to fire a gun while simultaneously holding a flashlight, it's going to take some practice, so we've provided a number of photos, and a range exercise in Chapter Seven for you to follow.

Surefire M3LT-S Combat Light
The new M3LT-S from Surefire isn't a flashlight you'd use to light up a map on a late night hike unless you want to light it on fire (metaphorically speaking of course). At 900 lumens, the M3LT-S won't just momentarily blind an attacker, it will bring him to his knees.

Surefire 6PX Defender
The new 6PX from Surefire puts out a blinding 200 lumens of power, with a runtime of about two hours. Like the E2D profiled in the chapter introduction, the 6PX also had a strike bezel, which can act as an impact weapon when required.

Surefire Z2S Combat Light
The new Z2S from Surefire puts out 160 lumens, more than enough power to light up a scene or blind an attacker. The Z2S also has rubber rings around the center, which allows you to use the Rogers/Surefire flashlight hold, which we'll explain in Chapter Seven.

First Light Liberator
The Liberator by First-Light, is a unique design that offers a great compromise between handheld and mounted flashlights. The Liberator's handle loops through the support hand and allows a proper grip on the firearm (and also allows magazines to be changed and malfunctions to be cleared without dropping the light). It also allows the user to scan the area independent of the direction that the muzzle is pointed, something not available with mounted lights. The Liberator ST is a blazing 120 lumens and is thumb activated with three switches on the support bar (momentary, strobe, or constant).

Mounted Lights

In addition to selecting a good handheld tactical flashlight, we'd also recommend that you consider a mounted light, whether that light is mounted to your handgun, your home defense shotgun, or your AR-15. When using a mounted light, it's important to remember that when we point the *light*, we're also pointing our *muzzle*, so we need to consider the light part of our firearm system, and not a separate light that should be used to peek into corners. You should consider any mounted light a *secondary* light, not your *primary* light. Three of our favorite mounted lights (or light/laser combos) are from Surefire and Viridian, and are shown below and on the opposite page.

Surefire Forend Mounted Light for Shotguns

Surefire makes replacement forends for Benelli, FN, Mossberg, Remington, and Winchester shotguns. Turning them on or off is done by depressing the momentary pressure pad on the opposite side, or the constant on/off rocker switch shown here.

Surefire X400 Light/Laser for Semi-Automatic Handguns

The Surefire X400 combines an incredibly bright light at 170 lumens with a bright red laser into a single package. With the switch shown at the back, the user can switch between momentary or constant operation for the light only, the laser only, or both simultaneously.

Viridian Universal Subcompact Green Laser + TacLight C5L
Although the Viridian C5L may be best known for mounting on the front of handguns, it is versatile enough to mount to any firearm that has a picatinny rail attachment, including side mounting the C5L on an AR-15. The C5L has ambidextrous buttons which activate the 100 lumen light, and a green laser which is visible in daylight conditions. When real estate is an issue on your AR-15 or handgun, the C5L can be a plus, as it's about half the length of other rail mounted lights, or light/laser combos. When used in combination with a Viridian holster, the C5L will automatically illuminate when drawn from the holster through the use of internal magnets.

LASER SIGHTS

Ask any group of seasoned shooters, and odds are, they might just roll their eyes when you ask about using laser sights on your firearm. In response, you may want to quote a Crimson Trace advertisement: "Don't let your ego obscure your target, because as good as you are with a gun, a laser sight makes you better." Crimson Trace might just have a point. Looking at a summary of shootings by the New York Police Department in 2005, two things jump out. The first is that 72 percent of the reported shootings occurred between dusk and dawn. That high percentage of shootings in low light situations calls into question a training regimen that relies solely on the traditional method of "indexing" on a target by aligning the front and rear sights. The second surprising statistic from the NYPD shootings was that the accuracy of the involved officers was well below what would have been expected, since most officers train frequently with their firearms. To paraphrase Crimson Trace, something is turning these officers from 90 percenters on the range, to 5—50 percenters in the field. Is it because of the extreme stress? Is it the low light? Is it a lack of realism in the officer's training program?

We'll address the last topic in Chapter Seven, but let's hit those first two issues here. As discussed in Chapter Five, we know that our higher brain is going to check out during periods of extreme stress and that automated responses will take over to one degree or another. So if there's a complex way of doing things and a simple way of doing things, we need to pick simple. If there's a method that embraces those natural responses or fights them, we need to embrace them. Let's take sight alignment as an example. A traditional sight plane requires that three objects be aligned—the rear sight, the front sight, and the target. In addition, it fights the mind's natural inclination to focus on the threat, and forces us to change our focus to the front sight.

Kinesthetically aligned shooting takes a massive step in the right direction by reducing the indexes from three down to just one (the target) and it embraces our natural instinct to focus on the target, but the "margin of error" might be greater than we can allow. Unsighted fire also relies on an ability to make the firearm an extension of our arms; that is, we need to know where the firearm is pointing, which requires the arms to be extended as far as possible. When we're unable to use that proper arm extension—for example, when rapidly retreating, when prone, after being knocked over, or with our firearm in a tight retention position (drawn back to our side, rather than extended out straight), the margin of error can be dramatically increased. Like kinesthetically aligned shooting, using a laser simplifies the traditional sight picture from three indexes down to one, and it allows

NYPD Accuracy by Distance

Source: NYPD 2005 Firearms Discharge Report

DISTANCE	SHOTS	HITS	HIT PERCENT
0 – 2 Yards	127	65	51%
3 – 7 Yards	155	68	44%
8 – 15 Yards	205	14	7%
16 – 25 Yards	93	5	5%
Total	580	152	26%

Although most lasers sights on the market are traditional red lasers, Viridian has focused on green lasers, which are considerably more visible than red lasers under a variety of conditions, since the color green is closer to the central spectrum of color visible to the human eye. In particular, in daylight conditions, green lasers can appear as much as fifty times brighter than a red laser. Viridian lasers are rail mounted, and use a custom "draw detection" method to automatically illuminate the laser when the handgun is drawn from a Viridian TacLoc holster.

us to embrace our body's natural reaction to focus on the threat. The edge that a laser provides is that it allows us to become indexed on the target much more rapidly, and with a much smaller margin of error. While there's no such thing as laser guided bullets, it's fair to say that if we've followed just two of the building blocks of shooting fundamentals (a solid grip and proper trigger press) our margin of error can be dramatically reduced, even when shooting from those awkward positions described earlier. A laser also allows us to combine indexing strategies. For example, if we've trained using the kinesthetic shooting method, then we've already trained ourselves to elevate the firearm into our sight plane. We can then transition from unsighted fire, to focusing on the red dot, to focusing on the front sight.

Why Train with Anything Else?

It's possible to draw the conclusion that since the physiological reactions that we'll experience will very likely force us to look at the threat rather than the sights anyway, why train with anything but a laser? There are several reasons. First, like all technologies, lasers can fail and batteries can run out. Second, there are environments that are inhospitable to lasers, such as bright light situations, situations where the attacker is wearing a red shirt, or a situation where more than one defender is using a laser on the same threat (that is, how do you know which laser dot is yours?) Combining training and technology is a better way to use the laser as a tool, without becoming dependent.

Our advice is that if you do chose to add a laser aiming device to your firearm, be careful not to train using it as your primary means of aiming. Doing so usually results in the shooter moving the gun out of their line of sight in order to see the dot, which will result in poor kinesthetics, and it will reduce your ability to withstand the firearm's recoil.

Combining Training and Technology

When used properly, lasers can actually help us to become more proficient at unsighted fire *and* sighted fire. It can even help us to improve our trigger control. Here's how:

Unsighted fire. Using a side mounted laser (such as the one from Crimson Trace shown on the opposite page) start from a low ready or high ready position, with your index finger blocking the laser. Fully extend your arms (elevating the firearm up into your sight plane) and point at the center of the target. Once indexed on the target, move your finger to identify where the firearm's barrel is actually pointing. This method will help you identify when your arms are too high, too low, etc., and, it can help you determine if your pistol's natural point of aim is right for *you*. Repeating this drill dozens of times per day will begin to build in the proper pathways into the cerebellum, all without a shot being fired.

Sight Alignment. For new shooters who are having difficulty grasping the idea of sight alignment, the use of a laser can help them understand exactly what it means to align the front sight, rear sight, and target. Using a handgun with a laser which has been calibrated to align with the sights at a target 21 feet away, start from a low ready, and then extend your arms, bringing the firearm up into your sight plane. Concentrate on the position of the laser dot, and slowly move your focus to the front sight. Place the laser dot on top of the front sight, and then slowly adjust the firearm until the front sight is centered between the rear sight. Many new shooters will have an "Ah ha!" moment using this simple technique.

Trigger Control. During a traditional dry firing exercise, pay close attention to what happens to the laser dot prior to and immediately after the hammer/striker falls. If the dot dances up, down, or off the target, you should revisit the topics on proper grip and trigger press. Check out Chapter Seven for an additional laser based exercise.

GUN SAFES AND STORAGE

We're going to end this chapter with the subject of firearm safety, and in this case, we're talking about the safe storage of firearms. It is FEDERAL LAW that loaded firearms may not be accessible to minors (that is, anyone under the age of 18 years old). Even without this law, it's the obligation of every responsibly armed American to keep firearms out of the hands of minors, or individuals who are not legally allowed to possess firearms. Any good gun shop or sporting goods store will have multiple options for firearms storage, including options for completely enclosing a loaded handgun, or completely enclosing the trigger and trigger guard on a loaded shotgun, including each of the options we'll be reviewing in this section.

We'll add that occasionally, we'll hear from students who have said something to the effect of, "I trust my kids around firearms, so there's no reason to lock up my guns at home." While that statement might be true,

(and we'd admit that we trust our own kids around firearms), it isn't just your kids that you have to worry about. It's your kid's friends, and their friends, and anyone else who shouldn't be getting their hands on your firearms, including any potential burglar. Just like a personal protection plan is designed to keep you physically safe, legally safe, financially safe, and morally safe, we'd suggest that a gun safe isn't just designed to keep your guns physically safe, it's also designed to keep YOU legally, financially, and morally safe as well. Don't be the guy who makes the national news because your gun was used in a horrible crime.

Gunvault SpeedVault

For securing a handgun at home or at the office, the new Speedvault from Gunvault is at the top of our list. Unlike traditional handgun vaults, the Speedvault is designed to drop open in a perfect position to get a proper grip on the handgun, for those times when you need access to your handgun right now. The Speedvault is available in either a biometric model or with a more traditional keypad as shown here. Both versions come with back-up cylinder lock.

Shotlock Solo-Vault

The Solo-Vault from Shotlock are wall mountable units, with options sized for any handgun and just about any long gun size you can think of including AR-15s and almost any style of shotgun including pump, semi-auto, side-by-side, over-under, and most shotguns with pistol grips. The vaults are designed to completely enclose the shotgun or rifle's trigger guard, something not available with other wall mounted units. Opened by pushing the proper sequence of the five push-buttons, the Solo-Vault is designed to keep your firearm out of the hands of unauthorized individuals, but allows quick access when you need your shotgun *right now*.

Gun Bunker GS-1

When the need arises to secure your firearm while on the road, locking the gun in your glove box or center console may be asking for trouble since those are the first two places that a thief will look if he's broken into your car. Most glove boxes and center consoles can be broken open in less then three seconds, with nothing more than a screwdriver. Instead, a secure gun vault can be added to your vehicle hidden under your seat, and locked securely to your vehicle's frame using the heavy duty steel cable included with the vault. The GS-1 is tough as nails, and can be opened quickly with its keyed entry.

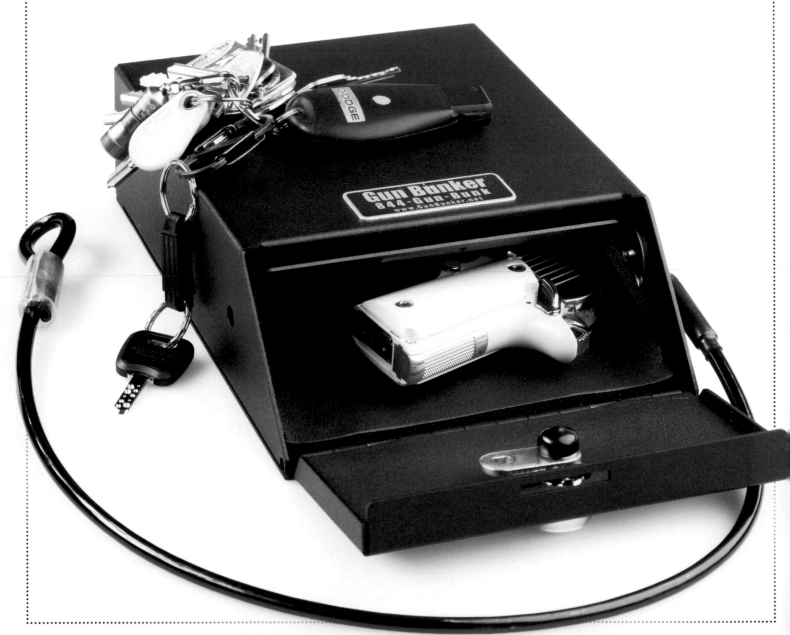

USCCA MEMBER LEE MICHAELS,
OPERATIONS MANAGER, SALEM COMMUNICATIONS,
TWIN CITIES MARKET.

Lee Michaels has been a long time supporter of the USCCA and Armed American Radio. AM1280 The Patriot was one of the first major radio stations to carry Armed American Radio, and Lee's story is featured in the book, "Lessons from an Un-Armed America" by Mark Walters and Rob Pincus.

EVERYDAY CARRY: SMITH & WESSON M&P40, IN A CROSSBREED SUPERTUCK.

BACKGROUND: In late 2004, I was robbed and carjacked at gunpoint as I stepped out of my garage, just steps from my house. In my case, I had used good situational awareness, but I still found myself staring down the barrel of a gun. With only $20 in my pocket, my two assailants forced me to get back into my car, telling me that I was going to drive to the bank to withdraw more cash. At that point, I changed my mindset, and decided that in order to survive, I wasn't going anywhere with them. When I saw an opening, I took it—when the gun wielding thug tried to squeeze in between the garage wall and the passenger side of my car, I started the car and rocketed out of the garage. The thug in the garage was knocked down, and the thug in the backseat decided that the situation had suddenly turned against him, and he jumped out of my moving car after taking a few swings at me. After living through that experience, I made the decision that I would never end up in a situation like that again, completely defenseless. In addition to getting my concealed carry permit, I also trained at Sealed Mindset, with retired Navy SEAL Larry Yatch.

→CHAPTER 7

BASIC AND ADVANCED SKILLS

- Muscle Memory Revisited
- Properly and Safely Conducting Dry Fire Exercises
- Self-Led and Instructor-Led Range Exercises from Beginner to Expert
- Drawing from the Holster
- Flashlight Hold Options
- Getting your Spouse Involved
- Raising Kids around Guns
- What's Next?

In Chapter Three, we introduced you to the building blocks of defensive shooting fundamentals. Of course, it's fair to say that simply reading about those skills from *any* book won't do a thing for you; it's repeated and consistent practice that will build those skills into your neural pathways. The variety of exercises in this chapter are designed to help you gain the competence and consistency that we mentioned in the introduction to Chapter Three. Once you've developed competence and consistency with the basics, the next major challenge is to advance your accuracy and speed, which will constantly be in balance. Many of the exercises in this chapter will work toward speed, others toward accuracy, and some will work toward a balance of both, including three of our personal favorites called the "SEB Drill," the "Colored Number Drill," and the "Push Your Limit Drill." While most of these exercises can be accomplished through self-led training, others require the guidance of an instructor or the assistance of a friend.

Speaking of building those neural pathways, we've started this chapter by revisiting the topic of "muscle memory," where we'll discuss some of the key items that should be a part of your training regimen, including dry firing, fundamental drills, speed and accuracy drills, and even virtual training. We'll also introduce you to the concepts of drawing from the holster, low light shooting techniques, and the use of lasers, but keep in mind that this chapter is an *introduction* to these topics. If you'd like to dramatically increase your skill sets in speed and accuracy, drawing from the holster, low light shooting, and other advanced techniques, you'll need to spend the time and money to attend one of the advanced shooting schools. On that note, we should mention something else that can't be taught solely through visits to the range, and that's the "stress inoculation" that's a major goal of programs that provide reality-based training (RBT) through force-on-force scenarios, including the use of Simunition® rounds and virtual simulations. Police departments which have undergone extensive reality-based training have seen their accuracy in critical incidents surpass 90%, including the California Highway Patrol, the Toledo Police Department, and the Salt Lake City Police Department. Despite those impressive statistics, none of us can say with absolute certainty what will occur if we become involved in a critical incident. What we *can* say with certainty is that ongoing training will help us to survive an incident when compared to someone with little or no training. Ongoing training on the fundamentals, the speed and accuracy drills, and up to and including reality-based training, are the best methods of moving toward becoming a 90-percenter rather than a 10-percenter when it counts.

Finally, as we mentioned in Chapter One, when you run the drills in this chapter, don't just *shoot*. During each drill, you'll need to create a hypothetical problem requiring a solution. Your solution should include the checklist items on page 43, including evaluating your options, determining the requirements for speed versus accuracy, and what to do in the aftermath.

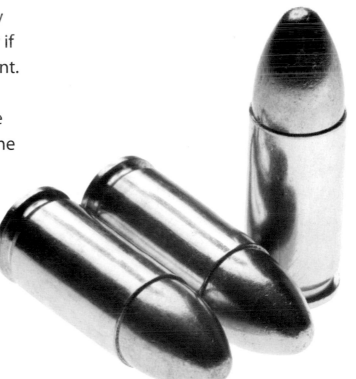

"MUSCLE MEMORY" REVISITED

In Chapter Three, we explained that "muscle memory" was actually a process that takes place in the brain's memory center (the cerebellum), and occurs when a skill or movement was practiced repeatedly. This repetition results in modified pathways in the cerebellum, which stores and links individual movements, similar to how individual still frames are stored and linked on a spool of film. You'll recall that the more a skill or movement is repeated, the stronger the pathways linking the individual steps becomes, and the result can be near automatic playback of the stored memory of movements. In Chapter Three we focused on how repetition could be used to build neural pathways to store the fundamentals of proper grip, stance, trigger control, and aligning our muzzle to the target, but the truth is, we also need to think about building those pathways for everything else that might be involved in a violent attack, including balancing speed and accuracy; reloading and clearing malfunctions under stress; movement; seeking cover; searching for other threats to our front, sides, and rear, etc. In order to build all of the skills (not to mention the neural pathways) that might be required to survive a violent encounter, we're going to suggest that you include at least four things in your training regimen, and that you train frequently with each of them. They include: dry firing, fundamental drills, speed and accuracy drills, and virtual simulations. Virtual *what*? Don't worry, we'll explain it all in this chapter.

Dry Firing

Dry firing is one of the most effective exercises that we can use away from the range because it allows us to build the pathways in our brains to consistently follow the four Universal Safety Rules. It also gives us an opportunity to practice the building blocks of safe and accurate shooting, including those outlined in Chapter Three, without spending hundreds of dollars in ammunition. Dry firing itself is not inherently dangerous, but it can become dangerous if performed in a manner that ignores the Universal Safety Rules, or when done without a specific set of steps from beginning to end.

Dry firing by its nature may sound as though it is a direct violation of the "rules" but in fact, it's the opposite—it allows us to live within the Universal Rules, and to make those rules instinctual in our lives. Let's take the rules one at a time.

Treat all guns as though they are always loaded and always perform a clearance check every time you pick one up!

When dry firing, we treat our firearm (which we've cleared) with exactly the same respect as one that we've just loaded—we don't treat it as though it's a dummy blue or red gun.

Never point your gun at anything that you are not willing to destroy! As we described in Chapter Two, our firearm needs to point somewhere, and when we dry fire, we ensure that it is ONLY pointed at something that can serve as a bullet stop and will not damage property or lives (pets included) if a round were fired.

Keep your finger OFF the trigger and outside the trigger guard until you are on target and have made the decision to shoot!

Dry firing is one of the most effective drills that can be run to instinctively drill this rule into our brain. We never, never, *never* put our finger in the trigger guard until we have aligned the barrel on our dry fire backstop, and have made the decision to press the trigger. Performing this exercise thousands of times while dry firing will make it instinctive on the range or during a defensive use of force.

Always be sure of your target and beyond!

On the range we're usually aware that there is an earthen or concrete backstop that can serve as an effective bullet stop. At home we need to be confident that our dry fire target can also stop a live bullet, otherwise we CANNOT perform dry firing at home. Effective backstops include cinderblock or concrete walls, but those run the risk of a ricochet if they were struck by a bullet. Commercial bullet blocks made with steel backing and bullet absorbing rubber are available from Law Enforcement Target Inc., Bullet Bunker, and Action Target, but these solutions can run from $80 to several thousand dollars. Simpler (and less expensive) homemade options include a box of paper reams, or a bucket of sand or dirt.

Too often a dry firing exercise begins without planning. Dry firing requires *more* planning than going to the range because it involves the removal of ALL ammunition from our dry firing area and it involves *triple* checking that our firearm has been cleared. We find it best if we perform our dry firing exercise with three distinct stages—prior to, during, and after the exercise.

Before Dry Firing Begins

1 Remove ALL live ammunition and magazines (empty or loaded!) from your dry firing room. Better yet, pick a room which never has ammunition or magazines in it in the first place.

2 Establish a "bench rest" in front of your dry fire shooting position, just like you'd have on the shooting range. This can be as simple as a TV tray, but it should be at waist level.

3 Prepare your backstop and attach an actual target to the backstop. Never perform dry firing by just picking a spot on the wall, even if the wall itself can serve as an effective backstop!

Dry Firing Procedures

1 Clear your firearm in a room OTHER than the one you're using for your dry firing exercises. Take the round that was ejected from the chamber, plus the magazine, and lock it in your gun safe. Case the firearm with the slide / cylinder open and carry it into your dry firing room. Just as you'd do on the range, uncase your firearm and place it on the benchrest, muzzle down range.

2 Pick up the firearm and perform THREE clearance checks as described in Chapter Two.

3 Only now can you perform dry firing. If firing a true double action, you can remain on target and dry fire as many "rounds" as you'd like. When dry firing a single action or striker fired semi-auto (which requires a racking of the slide between dry fire "shots") maintain good muzzle control when you bring the firearm off target to rack the slide, and take your finger OUT of the trigger guard.

After Dry Firing Ends

1 As on the range, perform a clearance procedure and case your firearm. Return it to its proper place. Do NOT reload the firearm at this point.

2 Remove the target from your backstop.

3 After a reasonable amount of time has passed, you can reload your firearm in preparation to reholster.

The "Dime" Test

When dry firing a semi-automatic, we occasionally add an extra factor to our exercises which helps to eliminate any "flinch" and works to ensure a proper grip

and smooth trigger press. The "dime" test performs the dry firing exercise as described but has the shooter balance a dime on the top of the semi-auto's front sight. During dry firing, the shooter should focus on a solid grip and smooth trigger press so that the dime doesn't "dance" or fall off. When you can consistently do this test without losing the dime, you're ready for the range.

Fundamental Drills

This chapter includes a number of drills meant to reinforce the fundamentals, and "warm-up" the neural pathways that you've already been building. Regardless of how confident you are on the range, we'd suggest that you always start your range exercises with drills such as the "Shoot Small, Miss Small" or the "Ten-to-the-One" drills explained in detail in this chapter.

Speed and Accuracy Drills

Once you've warmed up your neural pathways, you're ready to run through one of the "speed and accuracy" drills such as the "SEB," "Colored Number," or "Push Your Limit" drills, also outlined in this chapter. During these drills, if you find yourself "missing fast," take the time to step back to one of the basic drills, or even back to dry firing. Too often we'll see people on the range trying out a complex drill, yet it's apparent that they haven't mastered a smooth trigger press or sight alignment (when they're attempting a high degree of precision). Remember our friend the retired Navy SEAL. After one-and-a-half *million* rounds, he *still* begins every range exercise with dry firing and the basics.

■ While dry firing and drawing from the holster with a cleared firearm are great methods to keep those neural pathways strong, there's nothing like a trip to the range to work on the fundamentals, and the speed and accuracy drills outlined in this chapter. The range can also be a classroom, as demonstrated in this photo (taken with a remote camera).

270 and 360 Degree Ranges

While dry firing, the fundamental drills, and the speed and accuracy drills can build an incredible skill set in shooters who are willing to dedicate the time, we're still lacking a couple of fundamental training elements when we conduct those exercises on a typical indoor or outdoor range. The problem is twofold: first, while we might run a *mental* exercise in our heads about a paper target actually being a bad guy, the paper target isn't actually shooting back or charging us with a knife. Second, our targets on a typical range are usually restricted to a narrow window of 5—10 degrees to our front. That shortcoming can build the wrong "muscle memory" when it comes to situational awareness. In other words, when shooters *know* that the only targets they'll need to engage are to their front (regardless of whether or not they're practicing a "scan" after the shots are fired), they'll build that narrow focus into their neural pathways which can result in self-inflicted tunnel vision during an actual violent attack. So how do we condition ourselves for threats that are actually shooting back, and for threats that can come from all sides? We've got a couple options, and both involve moving beyond the traditional range, and stepping up to live fire or virtual ranges configured in 270 or 360 degrees, literally surrounding the shooter.

Virtual training, or training using laser modified guns and projected images, used to be limited to grainy videos on small screens, and "guns" that didn't come close to simulating the real thing. That's all changed. Multiple virtual ranges now exist across the country, which use simulated firearms, high-definition video, and wrap-around screens that literally immerse you in the action. This immersion environment forces shooters to maintain up to a 360-degree awareness of their surroundings, engaging threats to the front, sides, and even the rear. And of course, unlike traditional paper targets, the "simulated" threats can shoot back, so it's possible to *lose* during a scenario, just as it is in real life. Multiple decision points typically exist within these virtual scenarios, allowing a variety of outcomes based upon the shooter's decisions.

For a live fire version of this immersion environment, advanced defensive shooting schools now offer 270 degree and 360 degree live fire ranges, which literally put the shooter in the center of the range, with targets possible on all sides. These special ranges have tall berms surrounding the range on all sides for outdoor ranges, or they use a special, rubberized coating on the walls and ceiling for indoor ranges which can absorb bullet impacts. During shooting exercises, an instructor will move with the student (with no other students or instructors on the range) and the student will engage targets as they see them, or the instructor may call out specific targets or threats. Very often, these range exercises will involve "shoot/no-shoot" decisions, or shots that require shooting around barriers or even around virtual "hostages."

One shortcoming of typical range drills is that shooters may build the wrong "muscle memory" when it comes to situational awareness. In other words, when shooters know that the only targets they'll need to engage are to their front (regardless of whether or not they're practicing a "scan" after the shots are fired), they'll build that knowledge into their neural pathways, which can result in self-inflicted "tunnel vision" during an actual violent attack. Virtual ranges and specialized life-fire ranges now offer students an immersion environment in 270 or 360 degrees. Nothing comes closer to an actual critical incident, than training in these environments.

Skill Level

BEGINNER

Instructor-Led

Target: Official USPSA / IPSC Target

THE "TEN-TO-THE-ONE" DRILL

Description: We learned this drill from instructor Lou Ann Hamblin at the 2011 IALEFI Master Instructor Development Course in Cortland, New York. The drill is designed to allow shooters to gain a perfect understanding of exactly where their trigger's "break point" is, and to apply a smooth trigger press from start to finish. Starting from a shooting stance, the shooter will slowly press the trigger while their assistant counts down from ten to one. When the assistant reaches "one," the student should have reached the trigger's break point, and the gun should fire—not before, and not after. After warming up, the assistant will speed up the drill with the commands, "Ten-to-the-five, four, three, two, one!"

Goal: Many shooters begin their trigger press smoothly, and then "jerk" the trigger in the final stages of the trigger press, which will cause the shot to pull in the direction of the shooting hand. This exercise is designed to force an intense concentration on learning exactly where a pistol's break point is, and to keep the trigger press slow and smooth from the trigger's rest position to the break point where the pistol will fire, without jerking the trigger.

Distance: 21 Feet

Things That a Coach Can Watch For: Listen for shots before or after the assistant reaches a count of one.

Alternatives: Occasionally reverse the count, so that the shooter must release pressure on the trigger, such as "Ten-to-the-five, four, three, two, three, four, five, four, three, two, one!"

THE "SHOOT SMALL/ MISS SMALL" DRILL

Description: The "Shoot Small/Miss Small" drill is one of our favorites, that we first learned from our friends at Bill's Gun Shop & Range in Robbinsdale, MN. Starting from the low or high ready position, the shooter will fire a single round at the back of a USPSA / IPSC target (or any piece of cardboard) then fire strings of two to five rounds at the hole she just made.

Goal: This exercise is designed to force an intense concentration on accuracy by making the "target" no larger than a bullet hole. Many shooters will allow their degree of "slop" to be dictated by how large their target is, so the "Shoot Small/Miss Small" drill is designed to force extra attention on precision.

Distance: 7—14 Feet

Things That a Coach Can Watch For: Watch for the shooter attempting to use the same speed she uses for much larger target areas or for relying only on sight shooting to be extra precise. With plenty of practice (and these distances), the average shooter can become very accurate using point/instinctive shooting, even with a target as small as 22/100ths of an inch.

Skill Level

BEGINNER

Self-Led

Target: Back of an Official USPSA / IPSC Target

DRAWING FROM THE HOLSTER

A safe draw from the holster is done in five steps, all while abiding by the Universal Safety Rules, including keeping your finger out of the trigger guard until you are on target and have made the decision to shoot; and, ensuring that the muzzle doesn't point at anything you're not willing to destroy, including your own hand or leg.

If you're just starting out, we'd recommend that you begin by performing each of the five steps as discrete steps as demonstrated in the photos to the right, before picking up the pace. Performing these steps repeatedly and smoothly will slowly build those steps into your neural pathways, and after thousands of repetitions, your draw should feel as though it's a single, fluid step.

1 **GRIP** the handgun properly and firmly (with the shooting hand high on the backstrap and the trigger finger straight alongside the side of the holster).

2 **LIFT & PULL** the handgun straight up and out of the holster with your elbow held high, close to the body and pointed backward.

3 **ROTATE** the handgun up and out to face the target (by moving your elbow down to your waist) without sweeping your support hand.

4 **MEET & MOVE** the support hand to the shooting hand at approximately the center of your body and complete a two-handed grip for support.

5 **EXTEND & DRIVE** your arms and the gun straight out towards the target with good sight alignment and sight picture.

While many of the advanced drills in this chapter require the assistance of a coach, even the fundamentals require some assistance and coaching to perfect, such as taking up a proper grip.

THE "SEB" DRILL

Description: The SEB drill is one of our favorites, as it forces a great balance of speed and accuracy. Starting from the holster, or from the low or high ready position, the shooter will fire on command of an assistant. The assistant will vary the commands between calls of "Up!" and one of the numbers (such as "Two!") On a call of "Up" the shooter will fire at the large square in the high center of the silhouette, and on the command of a number, the shooter will fire at the appropriately-numbered shape surrounding the large silhouette. The assistant can choose to call more commands of "Up" or more commands of the numbered shapes, in order to vary the shooter's need to balance speed with accuracy.

Goal: This exercise will force the shooter to vary his balance of speed and accuracy on the same target and within the same exercise.

Distance: 7—14 Feet

Things That a Coach Can Watch For: Watch for the shooter attempting to shoot the smaller, numbered targets with the same speed that he uses to shoot the larger square in the silhouette. If he is consistently missing the smaller targets, he'll need to slow those shots down. On the other hand, if he's shooting with a consistent speed for the large and small targets and consistently hitting each target, he can afford to speed up his shots on the larger square.

Skill Level

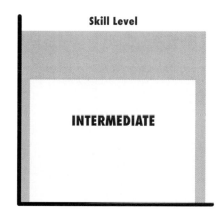

INTERMEDIATE

Instructor-Led

Target: SEB Training Target

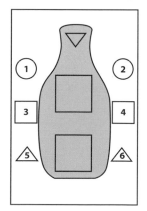

Skill Level

INTERMEDIATE

Instructor-Led

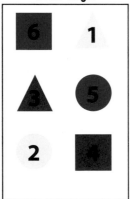

Target: Law Enforcement Target Co.'s DT-2C Target

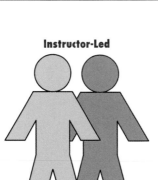

THE "COLORED NUMBERS" DRILL

Description: Starting from the holster, or from the low or high ready position, the shooter will fire on command of an assistant. At stage one, the assistant will call four of the six colored numbers, an equal number of times. The distance to the target will then be doubled and stage two will be fired with the assistant calling the two remaining colored targets.

Goal: This exercise allows the shooter to understand how distance affects his "personal balance of speed and precision." The shooter's goal should be to maintain 100% defensive accuracy with no shots off the colored numbers.

Distance:
Stage One: 6—8 Feet
Stage Two: 12—16 Feet

Things That a Coach Can Watch For: As with all exercises, watch for "fast misses," indicating that the shooter needs to slow down; or overly tight groups, indicating that the shooter can speed up.

THE "PUSH YOUR LIMIT" DRILL

Description: The "Push Your Limit" drill is used to force students to shoot at a progressively faster pace until they eventually move beyond their own personal balance of speed and accuracy.

Stage One: The shooter will fire five rounds at target #1 (the circle in the upper left hand corner) on a count of "one-one-thousand, two-one-thousand," etc., up to "five-one-thousand." This will require a shot fired approximately every second.

Stage Two: Same exercise as above, into target #2 (the circle in the upper right hand corner) on a count of "one and two and three and four and five." This will require a shot fired approximately every half-second.

Stage Three: Same exercise as above, into target #3 (the square in the middle left) on a count of "1, 2, 3, 4, 5" as fast as the shooter can count. This will require all five shots to be fired in approximately one second.

Goal: The first string of fire allows the shooter to concentrate on trigger press and reset separately. The second string of fire will force the shooter to bring the two parts of the process together. The third string of fire forces the shooter to push herself to the limits of her ability. It's important to maintain the appropriate pace throughout the drill's strings, instead of relying on your perception of how long it should take to get defensively accurate hits.

Description: 5—7 Feet. If the shooter was able to keep all 15 shots on the targets, the distance can be increased 3—4 feet and repeated.

Things That a Coach Can Watch For: Watch for misses, especially on the slower paced rounds, which indicate that the shooter should return to the "SEB" or "Colored Numbers" drills.

Skill Level

INTERMEDIATE

Self-Led

Target: SEB Training Target

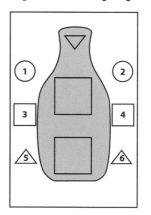

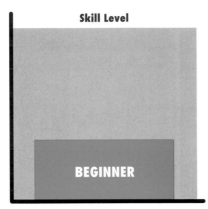

Skill Level

BEGINNER

Instructor-Led

Target: Official USPSA / IPSC Target

THE "TAP AND RACK" DRILL

Description: Another favorite from Bill's Gun Shop & Range. The "Tap and Rack" drill is designed to give the shooter opportunities to clear malfunctions while engaged in the exercise and to determine if he is prone to flinching in anticipation of the recoil. To conduct the exercise, an assistant will load the shooter's magazine with a mixture of live rounds and dummy rounds. When ready, the shooter will fire a full magazine.

Goal: This exercise allows the shooter to build appropriate neural pathways ("muscle memory") to quickly clear malfunctions. The shooter's goal should be to safely clear the dummy round while maintaining his eyes and muzzle on the target.

Distance: 21 Feet

Things That a Coach Can Watch For: Watch for the shooter to maintain his muzzle downrange when clearing the dummy round (which will require him to turn his body slightly, not the muzzle of the gun) and watch to see if he maintains his eyes on the target. Also watch for any flinch when the shooter pressed the trigger on the dummy round.

Alternatives:

■ The assistant can also load the magazine into the firearm, which would allow him to have the top round be a dummy round.

■ Place two or more dummy rounds in sequence.

■ To simulate the effects of adrenaline on the hands, run this drill after holding your hands in icy water. In the northern states, an alternative is to leave your steel firearm in your car overnight on a freezing winter night, and shoot the next day on an outdoor range with no gloves. It's not fun.

■ To simulate the effects of auditory exclusion, run this drill using the technique described in our "Auditory Exclusion" section in Chapter Five.

■ An advanced version of this drill combines the dummy round exercise with either the "SEB" drill or the "Colored Number" drill.

FLASHLIGHT HOLDS

The flashlight holds described in this section offer a variety of methods for using a tactical flashlight to first illuminate a room or area to search for a threat, and then rapidly bring the muzzle in alignment with the light to engage the threat. All three holds have pros and cons, but it's fair to say that any handheld flashlight hold causes the fundamentals to suffer, and that these holds should be practiced frequently. Note that you can practice these holds on the range in full light to become comfortable with them, but we suggest that you invest in at least one session under true low light conditions.

FBI Hold

The FBI flashlight hold allows the light to be positioned in a variety of locations and momentarily flashed to check out your surroundings. Positions might include placing the light high and outside the body, above the head, or under the firearm. The theory with this hold is that if the light acts as a "bullet magnet," the changing light locations would confuse the bad guy about where you actually are. Drawbacks of this hold include the difficulty of lining up the light beam with exactly where you need to shoot. It also forces you to shoot one-handed, which is rarely as accurate as a two-handed hold.

Harries

Like the FBI hold, the Harries still requires shooting one-handed, but the back-of-hand to back-of-hand pressure can steady your shooting hand. Make sure that you feel solid pressure between the backs of your hands, and are not simply resting the strong hand on the wrist of the support hand (picture holding a piece of paper firmly in place between your two backs-of-hands). Also, when setting up this hold ensure that you do NOT pass the muzzle of your firearm over your support hand.

Surefire/Rogers

Also described as a "cigar" hold, because it holds the flashlight between your index and middle finger. Best used with a light that has rubber rings around it to allow you to pull the flashlight tightly into your palm, which will activate a light with an end-cap activation switch. This hold keeps the light beam fairly aligned with the muzzle of the pistol, but with small motions of your palm, it allows you to move the light around. This flashlight grip comes the closest to allowing you to maintain all basic fundamentals, although it doesn't allow as solid a grip as you'd get with a mounted light and it still throws in the extra variable of activating the light.

THE "LIGHTS OUT" DRILL

Skill Level

ADVANCED

Description: The "Lights Out" drill is designed to give the shooter opportunities to gain experience with the different flashlight holds and/or a mounted light. We recommend that these drills be learned first in a full light environment before transitioning to a low light environment.

Goal: The goal of this drill is to safely gain experience with the different flashlight holds. There is no time limit specified which will allow the shooter to ensure she is performing each hold properly.

Distance: With two targets one yard apart at seven yards, start with the firearm and flashlight on the benchrest. On command, fire two rounds at each target. Shooter MUST NOT fire until the flashlight beam has lit-up the target. Repeat three times.

Instructor-Led

Stage #1, FBI Flashlight Hold—Lighted Conditions
Stage #2, Harries Flashlight Hold—Lighted Conditions
Stage #3, Surefire/Rogers Flashlight Hold—Lighted Conditions
Stage #4, Mounted Light—Lighted Conditions
(Note that firearm MUST be cleared prior to attaching mounted light)
Stages #5 to #8, Repeat the exercises above in low-light conditions. This portion of the exercise MUST be instructor-led until the student has proven proficiency in low light shooting situations.

Target: Official USPSA / IPSC Target

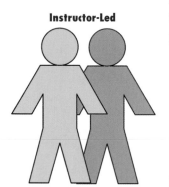

Things That a Coach Can Watch For: Watch to ensure that the shooter doesn't cross her hand in front of the muzzle when setting up the Harries hold, and watch for her ability to place the light beam on target with all three flashlight holds. The FBI hold and Surefire/Rogers hold in particular can take time to master properly aligning the muzzle and beam of light.

Alternatives: An advanced version of this drill combines the "Lights Out" drill with the "SEB" drill, the "Colored Number" drill, or the "Tap and Rack" drill. When performing the "Tap and Rack" drill, ensure that the shooter has the flashlight's lanyard looped around her wrist so that the light can be "dropped" while performing the clearance procedure.

THE "LASER" DRILL

Description: The "Laser" drill is a scored exercise designed to allow the shooter to compare and contrast point/sight shooting to shooting with a laser.

Goal: The goal of this drill is to push the balance of speed and accuracy on all three stages. The "Comstock" scoring (which creates a composite score between time and accuracy) should give the shooter a good indication of how a laser might fit into his overall training and self–defense program.

Stage #1, Dry Firing

One target at seven yards, start with firearm on benchrest, dry fire five "rounds." Repeat three times. Focus on a solid grip and good trigger control. Instructor should watch for a "dancing" laser just prior to or after the trigger press. No score

Stage #2, Left Target, with Laser OFF, From the Holster

Two targets one yard apart at seven yards, start with firearm holstered, on command fire five rounds at LEFT target. Repeat three times. Scored Comstock (Score/Time)

Stage #3, Right Target, with Laser ON, From the Holster

Two targets one yard apart at seven yards, start with firearm holstered, on command fire five rounds at RIGHT target. Repeat three times. Scored Comstock (Score/Time)

Things That a Coach Can Watch For: On stage one, watch for the laser "dancing" just prior to or just after the trigger press, which can indicate a grip or trigger control problem. On stage three, watch for the shooter falling back on sighted fire. It may take several runs through stage three before the shooter learns to trust the laser and begins picking up his speed.

Alternatives: An advanced version of this drill combines the "Laser" drill with either the "SEB" drill or the "Colored Number" drill.

Skill Level

INTERMEDIATE

Instructor-Led

Target: Official USPSA / IPSC Target

MAKING THIS A CO-ED SPORT

We're tempted to pretend that there is an equal need for wives to get their husbands comfortable with firearms, but let's face it—firearms ownership has been a boy's club for more years than we can count. The great news though is that during the last decade there has been a dramatic shift in ownership and attitudes of women when it comes to guns. In part, that's due to firearm manufacturers recognizing that they were leaving out a major demographic in the products they developed and the marketing programs they ran, but in a larger sense, firearm attitudes have shifted among women at the same pace as other gender shifts in the job market and the military. Women are also realizing that they're very often their family's "first responder" when it comes to other emergency needs (from scraped knees to broken bones to the smoke detector going off in the middle of the night), and that attitude extends to what to do if the unimaginable occurs. Women also carry an unfair burden when it comes to violent crime. With more than 90 thousand rapes occurring in the U.S. in 2015, women are getting the fact that when seconds count and the police are minutes away, they'll need to depend upon themselves to end a violent attack *before* it's too late. For you guys, we have four recommendations if you'd like to assist your significant other in becoming more comfortable with the idea of using a firearm for personal and home protection:

■ Buy your wife a copy of the USCCA book, *Women's Handgun and Self-Defense Fundamentals* by Beth Alcazar. Beth's book is written for women, and takes the approach that self-defense (and defense of family) is a personal responsibility that very often falls on the shoulders of the women of the house. Beth's book also discusses shooting fundamentals, carry methods, and other topics strictly from a woman's perspective.

■ Have your wife enroll in a women's only gun course, through the "Well Armed Woman" which as it sounds, is an organization dedicated to women learning the art of personal protection. While most guys who attend gun classes don't fit the stereotype that some people would have you believe, the "women only" approach guarantees that fact.

■ Schedule time with your spouse at the local gun range, but schedule it for a non-peak time. Avoid choosing a lane next to shooters with large caliber guns, and be smart about what caliber guns you start *any* new shooter on. Nothing will take the joy out of shooting faster than starting new shooters (female *or* male) on a large caliber gun before they've worked their way up to it. One of our favorite training pistols is the .22 caliber Walther P22. It's small-framed, so smaller hands will have no problem getting a proper grip, and the recoil and "bang" are almost nonexistent. Most new shooters, even if they've bought into the negative stereotypes about guns, have a dramatic attitude change after their first trip to the range. They'll quickly realize that not only is shooting relatively easy, it's also *fun*.

■ Keep the discussion on any gun-related topic to things that matter to you both, such as your joint responsibility to protect your children, and the fun you can have at the range. Just because *you* enjoy spending hours a day on gun forums debating the meaning of the Second Amendment, and fighting the "Glock versus 1911" war, doesn't mean that your spouse will like it. Come to think of it, if she finds out that you're spending hours a day on gun forums, she won't like *that* either.

From biathlons to trap leagues, and from the USPSA to the Bianchi Cup, hundreds of options exist for women to become actively engaged in shooting sports. The USCCA and other training organizations also offer specific classes set aside for women only, such as the USCCA's *Women's Handgun and Self-Defense Fundamentals.*

"Freedom is never more than one generation away from extinction. We didn't pass it to our children in the bloodstream. It must be fought for, protected, and handed on for them to do the same, or one day we will spend our sunset years telling our children and our children's children what it was once like in the United States where men were free."
Ronald Reagan

RAISING KIDS AROUND GUNS

When it comes to kids and guns, you have two choices: Ignorance or education. But here's the reality— if you take the ignorance approach, your kids will get their firearms "education" from movies, video games, or from their friends. While we're not advocating that you take your four-year-old out shooting, we *are* advocating that you answer your children's questions about your firearms, and allow them to interact at a level that's safe for their age group. Regardless of how old your child is, you'll need to begin his or her education with an understanding of basic firearms safety. Here are a few safety tips that our family and extended family have used for kids of various age groups:

2—6 years old:

■ Introduce your children to knowing what they should do if they find a firearm left unattended at your home or any other home: They should leave It alone, leave the room, and find an adult. This isn't a "one and done" kind of education. Every single time you handle a firearm in front of your child, or any time the topic of firearms comes up, quiz them on this rule.

■ As silly as it might sound, teaching your child to maintain "muzzle control" on his toy dart gun and to keep his finger out of the trigger guard until he's "on target" and is ready to shoot, will build that rule into his neural pathways, which will serve him for the rest of his life. At this age, a child's brain is twice as active as an adult's, and most of the brain's connections are being made. Anything they learn at this age stands a good chance of becoming hard-wired behavior.

7—12 years old:

■ Depending upon your child's maturity and his or her ability to grasp all four Universal Safety Rules, as well as his or her *physical* ability to handle a firearm safely, this age group is ready to shoot a BB gun (or a .22 caliber rifle when they're at the upper end of this age group) under your close supervision. Make these sessions about abiding by the Universal Safety Rules and enjoyment, rather than treating it as a scored event. Personally, we'll ask our sons to recite the universal rules for us before we begin the "Shoot Small/Miss Small" drill (which is not scored) shown in this chapter.

■ Regardless of how many times you have to say, "watch your muzzle" or, "take your finger out of the trigger guard," *keep* saying it. You own the responsibility for drilling these rules into your child's brain. They'll return the favor by doing the same with your grandkids.

■ At the first hint of fatigue, or enjoyment turning into boredom, end the session for the day. Praise your child's accuracy, but even more so, praise them for the great job they did in adhering to the Universal Safety Rules, and review any time they failed to follow them.

13+ years old:

■ Teenagers who have demonstrated maturity and rock solid safety when using a BB gun and .22 rifle, may be ready to step up to learning how to operate a handgun. With their shorter barrels, handguns can sometimes reintroduce muzzle control problems, so watch closely to ensure that all safety rules are being maintained.

So how will you know if your lessons are sinking in? In our house, we had a good indication on the success of our lessons when our youngest son (who was four at the time) told one of his friends, "Watch your muzzle!" as they were running around the house shooting their dart guns at everything in sight. Remember, as with all things in life, your children will learn more by watching what you *do*, rather than listening to what you *say*. Be a good teacher.

SO WHAT'S NEXT?

After finishing this book, we'll bet that your next question is, "So what's next?" We'll leave you with a few suggestions.

Take a Class

While many skills can be self-taught, the benefits of instructor led training for new shooters can't be overstated. As mentioned in Chapter Three, practice makes *permanent*, so beginning your shooting experience with a skilled, experienced, and patient instructor can lead to a lifetime of enjoyment and success on and off the range, rather than a lifetime of bad habits. To find a list of USCCA Certified Instructors who teach the USCCA course, *Concealed Carry and Home Defense Fundamentals* or other courses, visit www.USCCAInstructors.com.

Train at Home

If you're not quite ready to take a live class but would still like to learn more about these important topics, you now have the option of taking the full USCCA Course, *Concealed Carry and Home Defense Fundamentals*, from the comfort of your own home. With an introduction and seven lessons paralleling the chapters of this book, *Concealed Carry and Home Defense Fundamentals eLearning* contains five hours of video instruction by author Michael Martin, with Michael acting as the online student's very own, personal instructor. But unlike a traditional class, our online course allows the student to take the course based upon his or her own schedule and preferred pace, and the student can rewind any portion of the course as many times as he or she would like. The course also contains dozens of interactive widgets which allow the student to explore a variety of topics in more detail, and at the end of each lesson, the student's knowledge is tested with a highly interactive quiz. To learn more, visit www.USCCA.com or call 877-677-1919.

Concealed Carry and Home Defense Fundamentals eLearning
USCCA online training opens up this important education to the millions of Americans who are unable to fit a concealed carry class into their hectic schedules, or who haven't taken a class because of the "fear of embarrassment" that they imagine can occur in a traditional classroom.

■Author Michael Martin, on the range with two concealed carry students. While many skills can be self-taught, the benefits of instructor led training for new shooters can't be overstated. As mentioned in Chapter Three, practice makes permanent, so beginning your shooting experience with a skilled, experienced, and patient instructor can lead to a lifetime of enjoyment and success on and off the range, rather than a lifetime of bad habits.

Go Mobile with the iPad Edition

If you're one of the millions of Americans who consider your iPad indispensable, you can now take an interactive edition of this book wherever you go. Available for download through the iBooks app, the iPad edition of *Concealed Carry and Home Defense Fundamentals* contains the same interactive widgets and quizzes contained in our online course, as well as more than 25 video tutorials including author Michael Martin explaining many important legal topics, and demonstrating a number of basic and advanced shooting fundamentals.

Join an Organization

While the Second Amendment has seen a great deal of forward progress in the last couple decades, that wouldn't have happened without the efforts of the millions of members of organizations such as the National Shooting Sports Foundation, and the United States Concealed Carry Association. If you're not already a member, sign-up *today*. If you're a law enforcement officer who's looking for a new level of training, we can't recommend highly enough a decision to join the International Association of Law Enforcement Firearms Instructors (IALEFI). This organization is dedicated to making law enforcement firearms instructors more effective at training their students, and it succeeds wildly through the Master Instructor Development course.

Conclusion

We hope that you've found the information in this book useful, and we hope that you can put it to good use. Have fun at the range, shoot straight, and stay safe! In closing, remember that *you* are your family's first responder. Take that responsibility seriously, and use this right *wisely*.

The iPad Edition of Concealed Carry and Home Defense Fundamentals
Available through the iBooks app, the iPad edition of *Concealed Carry and Home Defense Fundamentals* is filled with more than 25 video tutorials, 40 interactive widgets, nine interactive quizzes, and hundreds of high resolution photos and photo galleries.

USCCA MEMBER
CARRIE LIGHTFOOT
FOUNDER AND OWNER OF
THE WELL ARMED WOMAN, LLC.

■ WHEN CARRIE LIGHTFOOT BECAME INTERESTED IN PURCHASING AND CARRYING GUNS, she was frustrated with the lack of resources available, specifically for women. Determined to change that, she launched *The Well Armed Woman* in 2012. Currently comprising 353 chapters, 913 leaders, and more than 10,500 members, this growing organization is a powerful resource for woman gun owners, sharing the ins and outs of armed self-defense, gun ownership, gun safety, shooting skills, and products.

"We, as women, have grown in confidence and in numbers," Carrie stated. "We're speaking up, and companies are paying attention. There has been a really huge shift in the industry. When I started, there wasn't really anything for women—it was all over the place. There was no community or one source for information, and resources were few and far between, and very scattered. What a difference a few years have made. The whole idea about women and guns is not taboo or unusual anymore. It's now a mainstream conversation!"

With Carrie at the helm and a host of amazing members and leaders offering classes, meetings, and events, *The Well Armed Woman* offers a perfect option to get started with firearms and/or to improve upon shooting skills and knowledge. And Carrie, who is a proud USCCA member and a Certified USCCA Training Counselor, hopes that both *The Well Armed Woman* and the USCCA will be organizations that women will turn to for all their firearms needs.